H50 319 936 5

Please renew/return this item by the last date shown.

So that your telephone call is charged at local rate, please call the numbers as set out below:

	From Area codes 01923 or 0208:	From the rest of Herts:
Renewals:	01923 471373	01438 737373
Enquiries:	01923 471333	01438 737333
Minicom:	01923 471599	01438 737599

L32b

Dr Wilhelm Fürtwangler rehearsing the Berlin Philharmonic Orchestra in the Musikhalle for their concert on 26 April 1952

(*Alexander McKee*)

THIS IS THE BRITISH FORCES NETWORK

The Story of Forces Broadcasting in Germany

Alan Grace

Foreword by General Sir Brian Kenny GCB, CBE

ALAN SUTTON PUBLISHING LIMITED

in association with Services Sound and Vision Corporation

First published in the United Kingdom in 1996
Alan Sutton Publishing Limited · Phoenix Mill · Far Thrupp · Stroud · Gloucestershire
in association with Services Sound and Vision Corporation

British Library Cataloguing in Publication Data

A catalogue record for this book is available from the British Library.

ISBN 0-7509-1105-0

For June and all members, both past and present, of BFN/BFBS Germany

Endpapers
Front: Lt Tom Dean setting up for a recording of the pipers at the 51st Highland Games at
Verden in 1945
Back: SSVC in the Gulf, 1991

Typeset in 11/13 Bembo.
Typesetting and origination by
Alan Sutton Publishing Limited
Printed in Great Britain by
Butler & Tanner, Frome, Somerset.

Contents

Foreword

General Sir Brian Kenny GCB,CBE

Having spent 20 years of my military service with the British Army of the Rhine, I am delighted to write a short foreword to this history of BFN/BFBS Germany.

I first became aware of the importance of Forces Broadcasting when I was posted to Germany in 1955. At that time, the highlight of the week for many National Servicemen in my Regiment was Bill Crozier's '1800 Club', but for the families 'Two Way Family Favourites' was their favourite programme.

During the subsequent years I was able to see at first hand the development of BFBS, with the opening of their satellite studios in Berlin and Herford, and their response to the separation of military families caused by the troubles in Northern Ireland. The first time I heard Gloria Hunniford was when she became the regular presenter of 'Ulster Calling'.

In 1975, after many years of battling with the Treasury and the MoD, BFBS was finally able to launch its television service in Celle. The impact of BFBS TV on families' morale was dramatic, and did an enormous amount to help all those living in Germany to feel part of the BAOR family, and to keep them well informed about what was going on. For example, during the first Christmas of BFBS TV, the incidence of drink driving was reduced to almost zero! It also enabled families in Germany to follow the many activities carried out in BAOR. As commander of 1 British Corps, and subsequently as Commander-in-Chief of BAOR from 1985 to 1989, I became very accustomed to meeting the BFBS reporters, both radio and TV, covering the stories that made up service life in BAOR. At Christmas time I even managed to do an outside broadcast to wish everyone a Happy Christmas and New Year.

During the Falklands War, and later during the Gulf War, BFBS Germany provided an essential link between the men at the front line and the families left behind in Germany, a situation that has been repeated for the men and women in Bosnia, with BFBS's 'Calling the Balkans'.

BFBS Germany has survived 'Options for Change' and the drawdown, and, despite staff cuts, has not only managed to maintain its standards but has actually increased its output.

During the many years I have served in BAOR, I have watched BFN/BFBS grow and develop. Life for the serviceman and his family in Germany would not be the same without Forces Broadcasting.

The garden view of BFBS Germany's Broadcasting House, 61 Parkstrasse, Cologne. It was under the patio that an unexploded bomb was discovered in 1993 when the building was demolished

(*Charlie Decker*)

Acknowledgements

The idea for this book grew out of a chance remark made by Peter McDonagh, SSVC's director of broadcasting, at my retirement party. 'Why don't you write a book about BFN and forces broadcasting in Germany?'

Although I had started my career with BFN Cologne in 1956, most of my broadcasting life had been spent in other parts of the Forces broadcasting world. The first problem arose when I discovered that most of the records from the BFN Hamburg days had either been lost or destroyed in a subsequent clear-out. When in 1989 BFBS moved to Herford, history repeated itself. Luckily Trevor Hill, Douglas Brown, Denis Shaw, Gordon Savage, John Harrison and Pat Pachebat had kept a fine selection of memorabilia which I was able to add to the late Alexander McKee's archives.

I am particularly indebted to Jane Carmichael, the Keeper of Photographic Records at the Imperial War Museum and Chris Horrocks of *Soldier* magazine for allowing me to use their photographs. The recollections, comments and help of members of Forces Broadcasting have been vital in the writing of this book, and I wish to thank them all:

Axel Alexander, Mike Allen, Richard Astbury, Peter Attrill, Michael Baguley, Nick Bailey, Norman Bailey, Ron Balaam, Ralph Barker, Richard Barnes, Fred Bassett, Raymond Baxter, Alan Bedford, Jon Bennett, Bernd Beyer, Eric Blake, Bob Boyle, Heidi Brauer, Steve Britton, John Bussell, Tom Chalmers, Paul Chapman, Ron Chown, Alan Clough, Mike Colcutt, Tony Cook, Douglas Cooper, John Crabtree, Tom Crossett, Joan Crozier, Frank Daunton, Nigel Davenport, Barry Davies, David Davis, Tony Davis, Charlie Decker, Ralph Dellor, Bernard Denn, Kay Donnelly, Aidan Donovan, Don Durbridge, Patrick Eade, Don East, Bob Egby, Lady Evans, Tony Fawcett, Ian Fenner, Keith Fordyce, James Gibb, Dan Gilbert, Nigel Gilles, Ted Greenfield, John Grey, Ilse Griffiths, Tim Gudgin, Simon Guettier, Liz Halsall (née Shaw), Bryan

Hamilton, David Hamilton, John Harris, John Harrison, Sir John and Lady Harvey-Jones, Thomas Hausmann, Herbert Hawelleck, Jack Hayward, Christopher Headington, John Hedges, Bryan Hodgson, Sir Trevor Holdsworth, Paul Hollingdale, Peter Holwill, Michelle Horn, Petrie Hosken, Chris Howland, Roger Hudson, Bob Humphries, Fred Hunt, Richard Hutchinson, John Jacobs, Stuart James, Bob Jones, Derek Jones, Richard Jones, Sandi Jones, Lilo Karacz, Sarah Kennedy, Cathy Kingsbury, David Lamb, Colin Livingstone, Charly Lowndes, Patrick Lunt, Jim Luxton, Peter McDonagh, Alastair McDougall, Jock McCandlish, Ilse McKee, D.B. McNeill, Glen Mansell, John Mayo, John Mead, Jutta Meier, Robin Merrill, Jean Metcalfe, Gunter Meyer-Goldenstadt, Cliff Michelmore, Alan Miller, Karl Miller, Vivian Milroy, Don Moss, Torsten Muske, Steve Mylles, Ted Nash, Robert Neill, Dick Norton, Gunnar Oldag, Rob Olver, Tony Orsten, Pat Pachebat, Ron Penny, Leslie Perowne, Geoff Pexton, Alan Phillips, Nan Pomeroy, Alan Protheroe, Gordon Randall, Dave Raven, Keith Rawlings, Vernon Rees, Baz Reilly, Pam Rhodes, Katie Roy, John Rudler-Doyle, Colin Rugg, Chris Russell, John Russell, Gordon Savage, Vaughan Savidge, Tom Scanlan, Ken Scarrott, Brian Scott, Dennis Scuse, Denis Shaw, Jack Sheard, Tom Singleton, Gerald Sinstadt, Keith Skues, Padre Alec Smith, Norman Spires, Tom Stephenson, Joachim Szymanski, Philip Towell, Michael Townley, Marc Tyley, Sir William Utting, Tommy Vance, Eddie Vickers, Stephen Withers, Ian Woolf, Stanley Wyllie, Margaret Yates, Caroline Young, David Young, Oliver Zoellner.

A very special thank you to: Douglas Brown for his research into the BLA units and his subsequent help in putting together this book. Nicol Raymond – the Queen of Commas, Colons and Capital Letters – and my wife June, who between them contributed phrases and support when my brain had switched itself off. Finally, Trevor Hill, who explained so much about the early days of BFN and 'Family Favourites'.

Prologue

There are many misconceptions as to why young servicemen apply for announcing posts at BFN. The most usual is the romance of radio or the lure of fame, or the prospect of being a golden voice.

First, there is no romance in radio – for the announcer has no name, and he will spend *his* time telling *you* the time and identifying the station. In the beginning he will be scared to death of the microphone, then after a few days, he will realize that he is on air and be thrilled to bits, but shortly afterwards the boredom factor will set in.

There is nothing miraculous or exceptional in knowing that his voice is coming out of the radio. The wonder lies in the fantastic machinery and the engineers who make it possible.

With regards to fame – well, if you meet an announcer outside BFN you may well be deceived into thinking that he is somewhat above St Peter and slightly below God, whereas back at BFN he is regarded as being slightly better than the cleaners, but below the typists. Ideally, an announcer should possess a university education, speak four languages and be a master of elocution as well as the proud possessor of a golden voice.

The BBC pay large sums of money for those qualities but BFN announcers only get their normal service pay, usually in the rank of private. For two shillings and sixpence a day, you are not going to get Stuart Hibbard!

The announcer will not get away from the Army or rise late just because he is at BFN. He will do duty shifts just like a sentry, and once or twice a week he will get up at 4.00 a.m. to open the station and wake up the rest of the Forces. He will be expected to go on parade and keep his uniform free from modifications and to work seven days a week without complaint and certainly no overtime. Above all else, he will be expected to cover up the mistakes of others while making none himself.

Alexander McKee, 1948

Leading Aircraftman Geraint Evans and Capt Tony Foreman outside the BFN studios

(Lady Evans)

CHAPTER ONE

The Road to Hamburg and Bless 'Em All Radio

Except ye utter by the tongue words easy to be understood,
how shall it be known what is spoken?
For ye shall speak into the air.

First epistle of St Paul to the Corinthians   14:9

(A notice displayed in a studio of the Forces Broadcasting
Station attached to the Eighth Army)

The Château des Cretes in Algiers was once a Turkish pirate's harem. Now it was home to the British Forces Experimental Radio Service in North Africa. Its tiled floors and hand-painted ceilings were covered with army blankets to provide a form of sound-proofing, and the equipment had been acquired by a mixture of begging, borrowing and misappropriation. The transmitter was a German model captured in Tunisia and had to be de-sanded before it would work. It was then installed in a pigeon loft at El Bair, the highest point in the city.

Finding staff was to prove more difficult. No soldier under the age of thirty could be considered, but by bending King's Regulations the three men sent out from London by Army Welfare, Lt-Col Gale Pedrick-Harvey, Maj Philip Slessor and Maj Emlyn Griffiths, found enough men to run the Algiers station. They came from those who had been found medically unfit or were recovering from their wounds. The would-be broadcasters brought a variety of regional accents to the new station.

BFES Algiers opened on 1 January 1944, with Philip Slessor making the opening announcement: 'This is the British Forces Experimental Station Algiers and the time is half-past six'. This was followed by the BFES signature tune 'Lilli Marlene', the song of the Eighth Army. However, it was pointed out by headquarters that as the Germans used the same melody it could lead to confusion, so the new station changed to 'Rule Britannia'.

Although the men in North Africa were in favour of their station, the Central Mediterranean Force's Welfare Fund had no extra funding for broadcasting to continue, but the broadcasters pressed on regardless. In March 1944 four mobile

Capt Leo Bennett introducing a programme from the British Forces Experimental Station, Algiers, 1 January 1944. With him is Capt Malcolm Luker who begged, borrowed and adapted various items of equipment   *(IWM NA 10540)*

radio transmitters, complete with trailer generators, arrived from Cairo. The only problem was – the keys had gone missing; so Norman Spires, recently arrived from the British Forces Broadcasting Unit in Iceland, and three colleagues 'wired' the engines and prayed they did not stall on the way to the studios.

Next two mobile units consisting of three vehicles to house the studio, gramophone library, office and transmitter were assembled. Later that month they left for Italy, and Forces Broadcasting was on its way to the war in Europe.

The two mobile stations, B3 and B4, split on arrival in Italy. B4, looked on by the Eighth Army as its own, travelled east towards the Adriatic coast. Meanwhile B3 drove to Campobasso, a small hill-top town in the Apennine mountains, and set up in the garden of the Monastery of Santa Maria. In Philip Slessor's report to Gale Pedrick-Harvey he wrote: 'The Brigadier showed some concern as to whether our presence might be disturbing the devotional activities of the monks. I was able to inform him that on the previous night, the Father Superior had invited our troops to help themselves from a large bottle of wine, which he had produced from beneath his habit. He gave them to understand that he must hurry away and hide the bottle among the full ones in the monastery cellar as apparently he had not consulted his flock before uncorking it.'

Life was spartan in Campobasso with Norman Spires sharing a monastic cell with his technical sergeant. The duty monk, on his way to ring the bells for Prime, would wake up the duty announcer whose live continuity went out with the accompaniment of the bells. After discussions with the abbot – he being loath to suspend the calls to prayer – the station decided to ignore the bells in the background on the basis that our enemy knew all about Campobasso. B3 could claim to be the only station in the world to have broadcast 'In a Monastery Garden' from a monastery garden.

The first static Army Broadcasting station was opened in Bari and straight away the new service was experiencing a lack of essential items. Gale Pedrick-Harvey sent the following note to his admin. officer: 'Check if Station Controller may buy a clock and if so can we reimburse him? It is absurd to have to rely on an erratic wrist-watch. Even the Station Controller Bari, until he was given a good watch, had to train a pair of binoculars on a not specially reliable clock three hundred yards away from his station.'

In the Central Mediterranean Force, the station commanders were their own masters and developed the art of playing off local authority against GHQ. In practice, there were virtually no restrictions as to who would be allowed to broadcast. Some station commanders invited useful 'local people' to put on their own record shows, including Lt-Gen Sir Richard McCreery, the Eighth Army Commander, who broadcast several half-hour record recitals on B4 – but incognito.

When the battle for Cassino was over B3 headed for Rome and then moved to Pozzo and Jesi. Later, as the battle moved eastward, B4 travelled to Riccione. By now this mobile studio had acquired the name of GLADYS. As Norman Bailey, one of the B4 team, remarked in later years, 'You have to understand that at the time the mobile studio was our main focal point; soldiers tended to humanize equipment and Gladys seemed a dependable and affectionate name.'

B4's record library was limited, although the chief signal officer had given permission for all broadcasting material to be moved between stations by the Army Despatch Service. However, the German version of 'Lilli Marlene' and much of the Glenn Miller repertoire were unobtainable. Nevertheless, GLADYS had a way of getting her hands on the most up-to-date American music.

Her main rival, Axis Sally (the German propaganda station), would broadcast the very latest music from the States and intersperse it with propaganda messages; B4 would record the whole output editing out her messages and rebroadcasting the music. After demanding that B4 ceased its radio piracy, Axis

B3 on the road in Italy

(*Norman Spires*)

Sally took her revenge by sending in three Focke-Wulf bombers. They machine-gunned and bombed the surrounding countryside, but they missed GLADYS.

Although B4 was a mobile station, it received up to 200 letters a week, as well as phone calls for its various programmes. At one time there was a Canadian announcer attached to Gladys to broadcast to the Canadian troops who were then in the neighbourhood. He remained, churning out Canadian programmes and requests for the troops who, by then, were en route for the landings in the South of France. D.B. McNeill, one of the engineers of the Army Broadcasting Service visiting B4 at the time, found that the broadcasters were fed up with having to spend time broadcasting to non-existent listeners; it never dawned on them at the time that they were part of a deception programme.

The exploits of B3 and B4 were noted by the D-Day planners and decisions were made to capitalize on the experience gained in Italy when designing the field broadcast units that would work with the Forces during the invasion of Europe.

At this time L/Cpl Vivian Milroy RAOC was enjoying service life as a member of the London District Theatre Unit, an unofficial organization that had been dreamt up to give London district its own tame ENSA-type unit. For the members of the unit it was the perfect posting. Those who lived in London were able to stay in their own homes. The headquarters was just off Park Lane and pay parade was on a Friday, when usually two or three taxis drew up and discharged a very unmilitary-looking bunch of soldiers.

However, as D-Day approached, there was no place for unattached soldiers and the unit was disbanded. The members were given the chance to join the Army Film Unit, the Army Broadcasting Unit or return to their own regiments. Vivian opted for broadcasting and, together with a dozen or so would-be broadcasters drawn from a mixed bag of regiments, was sent to the BBC to learn the art of silently dropping needles on 78 rpm discs and how to cue long-playing records. Later on others would go to the Army Broadcasting studios in Eaton Square. Here passers-by, usually pretty girls, were buttonholed by trainee service broadcasters clutching a microphone on a long lead and asked to say a few words. The results were recorded in the studio, but never broadcast.

Signalman Douglas Brown was serving with 9 Armoured Division Signals installing and maintaining Tannoy systems at 'Overlord' assembly camps. After D-Day he was seconded to the Army Film studios at Wembley assisting in the making of Army Signals training films. Following an advanced teleprinter maintenance course at Dollis Hill, he was posted to a Signals transit camp near Lewes from where groups were assembled to reinforce the units already in France. Instead of crossing the Channel, he and a dozen others were sent to the Ordnance Road barracks at St John's Wood in London. On arrival they discovered the barracks knew nothing about the men from the Signals. Several days later a Capt Shepherd arrived at the barracks asking for No. 1 Field Broadcasting Unit. After a check with the office, he discovered that Douglas Brown and his colleagues were the technical nucleus of No. 1 FBU. Now all they had to do was to find some equipment.

After a week or so, Vivian and the would-be broadcasters were introduced to the mobile studios and, together with the mobile transmitters and generators, set off for Highgate for a test outside broadcast (OB), the only practice session they had before they left for Europe.

By October 1944, the merging of the broadcasters and the engineers had begun in earnest and by early November they were mobilized. Then came the news that No. 1 FBU was to be inspected by the Adjutant-General. The officer-in-charge of the new unit was Maj John McMillan of the 2nd South Wales Borderers, who had worked for Radio Luxembourg before the war. He remembered his sixty-four would-be broadcasters as a 'collection of misfits'. Several months later one of those misfits wrote a poem about No. 1 FBU called 'C'est effroyant mais c'est pourtant la guerre.'

Next to the mobile studio was the record library and office. Here, Cpls Norman Bailey and George Sallows get out the records for B4's evening request show 'MAYLI' (Music As You Like It)

(IWM NA 19737)

> . . . Neath dreadful threat of cancelled passes,
> They blancoed belts and polished brasses,
> Trousers were pressed and badges placed
> Upon best blouses with frantic haste,
> Until, when all had been corrected,
> On Clapham Common they were inspected
> several times. . . .

Afterwards, the men were addressed by a senior officer with the Adjutant-General's party. 'Now that we are fighting on the continent, you men are going to be the nucleus of a new Army Broadcasting Unit. The value of a broadcasting service by the troops for the troops was recognized some time ago, when Army Broadcasting Units were formed in North Africa, Italy and the Middle East, to fill the gap which existed between the BBC and what the troops required in the way of local entertainment and humour. On the continent, our advancing forces are drawing away from the reception area of the BBC. Also, enemy propaganda stations are cleverly relaying the AEFP, that's the Allied Expeditionary Forces Programme, and inserting their own news and propaganda. Our troops are picking this up on their sets, and you men with mobile stations will counteract this and at the same time, fill the gap, now that the BBC can no longer be picked up clearly in the areas over there. Well, the broadcasters will stay here for training while the REME complement are assembling transmitters and equipping studio trucks for four mobile stations. You will then assemble all together at the London District Assembly Centre sometime in November, when you will be known as No. 1 Field Broadcasting Unit.'

As the teams practised, Lt-Col David Niven, Director of Troop Broadcasting SHAEF visited the front line. His report was brutally frank: 'Signal strength very bad east of line Bruges–Brussels–Rheims. In Holland only station heard was Radio Arnheim (the German propaganda station). Men along whole front line not well equipped with good sets, consequently tuning to any station coming in with good signal and music. Nationality of station no consequence, any talks in English with the exception of news immediately switched off. BBC Home Service much better than Allied Expeditionary Forces Programme. British badly off for sets.'

As a result, John McMillan was given two days to finalize the mobilization plans for No. 1 FBU. On 1 December No. 1 FBU was divided into four mobile stations consisting of one studio vehicle, two generators and one 1kw transmitter, plus four 96 ft steel masts. They were known as BLA 1, 2, 3, 4, and twenty-four hours later, they moved to Tilbury to embark on LST 408 for Europe. It was a very rough journey with the LST making several attempts to disembark. Finally, after criss-crossing the Channel, on 7 December sixty-four very weary and seasick members of No. 1 FBU landed at Ostend and made their way to Quatre Bras near Brussels.

The importance of the new unit could be judged by the endorsement in the pay-books of the members of No. 1 Field Broadcasting Unit: 'The holder of this AB64 part 1 has been highly trained for employment with a specialist unit. In the event of his becoming a casualty he should not at a later date be used as a normal reinforcement to a unit of his own Corps, but instructions for his disposal should be obtained from Army Welfare Services (Broadcasting), Rear HQ, 21 Army Group.'

The BLAs were billeted in a convent at Stockell, just outside Brussels. Gradually, the battered troops recovered their equilibrium and even tested out the purchasing power of the army-issue cigarettes and chocolate in the local dance-hall. Vivian Milroy, who was driving one of the 30 cwt trucks, had cunningly filled the built-in tool compartments with coffee beans, which were to prove invaluable as their journeys progressed. By now, Vivian Milroy was part of BLA 2 and Douglas Brown had joined BLA 3, commanded by a Canadian, Captain Bob Kesten.

On 16 December BLA 2 started test transmissions and three days later, the first list of banned records was published by John McMillan: 'Ladies in the Forces', 'She'll Never Be the Same Again', 'Mr Jones' and 'Lilli Marlene'. A station identification was agreed: 'You're listening to Station BLA 2 operating in the field by the British Liberation Army Units', and this was followed by a whistled phrase of 'Bless 'Em All'.

As 1944 drew to a close Signalman Ken Scarrott, who had been with 50th Division, found he was being posted to No. 1 Field Broadcasting Unit. When he discovered they needed eight instrument mechanics, he wanted to know why they needed so many, and what the life-expectancy was of the men of No. 1 FBU. On 1 January 1945, he almost got the answers when the Luftwaffe flew directly overhead on their way to attack a nearby aerodrome. 'How they missed the BLA vehicles, all neatly line up, we'll never know.'

The BLAs split up, with Vivian Milroy and BLA 2 moving into the north of the area: 'We were trundling along towards our next rendezvous and suddenly realized all the traffic was going against us, including tanks. At the same time we noticed a certain amount of shell fire and fighter plane activity. When we stopped a vehicle and asked what was happening, we were told the Germans had broken through in the Ardennes, so we turned very quickly and followed the tanks.'

Douglas Brown and Ken Scarrott moved off with BLA 3 on 1 January to Spoordonck where they were to stay for the next three months. The men of the BLAs were supposed to carry out guard duties but Capt Bob Kesten, the OC of BLA 3, had recruited several Dutchmen led by Raoul Dekker to do this for them. Ken Scarrott recalls, 'They wore battledress uniforms with orange flashes and took over all the guard duties. In fact, I'm sure they had our rifles but we fed and watered them and they seemed very happy.' BLA 1 was still in Asch and BLA 4 had moved to Willebreek.

The number of personnel with each BLA unit was sixteen, but each member was expected to have a thorough knowledge of the equipment and the ability to pull his weight, especially during a move. Like the servicing of the equipment, this had to be carried out after closedown. As Douglas Brown recalled, 'When we moved, we had to have as much equipment as possible packed before midnight and we had to ensure that we were "on air" in the new location for the station opening the next day.'

Their arrival had not gone unnoticed by 'Hans the Peace Philosopher' whose insidious broadcasts from Radio Arnheim were designed to undermine the confidence of the Allied troops. He started his broadcast: 'Hello Tommy, Hello Yanks, I have been presented with three little baby brothers. That's it – triplets.

These brand new mobile broadcasting stations have been set up behind the Allied Armies in Holland to re-broadcast Allied programmes to you. Now you can't say that I am not a peace-loving fellow. Then why have your British authorities cause to be angry with me and install these transmitters to counteract my programmes? Be honest we have done nothing but work for peace. Our programmes are aimed at creating understanding. I have a good mind to withdraw my outstretched hand.'

Life in the BLAs varied from the fairly uncomfortable to the spartan except for BLA 3 which, attached to the 1st Canadian Army, was clothed and provisioned by both the British and the Canadians – a ploy of its Canadian OC! For the rest the cooking was rudimentary and, like most soldiers, they learned to live off the land with chickens and eggs the most frequent additions to the rations. The BLAs opened up at 6 every morning with their station identification followed by the news from the Allied Expeditionary Forces Programme. This was repeated every hour, with local news, if they had any, and record programmes built from their own mobile libraries which had about 400 discs available for use, a great improvement on the original 55 used by BFES Algiers.

Sgt Jack Sheard of the REME, after five years in the United Kingdom, found himself at No. 54 Reinforcement Holding Unit in Bruges where he soon fell foul of the unit's elderly RSM. Jack was charged with 'failing to produce a fire-picquet for changing, failing to turn out the guard for the visit of a Brigadier and allowing a deserter to escape'. He was exonerated by his CO and asked if he would like to join No. 1 FBU at Malines! He started work by helping Jack Dickinson adapt speech frequency equipment for an outside recording unit. 'Our first attempt on 15 February to record a concert in Brussels was, according to John McMillan, not up to standard, and so it was back to the drawing board.' Although good progress was being made, John McMillan kept everyone on their toes with a stream of orders. 'To save our American Allies any form of embarrassment, the BLAs will not play either the Confederate or the Union songs "Marching through Georgia" or "John Brown's Body". However, it was now all right to play "Lilli Marlene".' Harmony with the Allies was very important, and the BLAs closed each evening with a blend of the 'Stars and Stripes', 'O Canada' and 'God Save the King'.

Vivian Milroy's most enduring memory of the winter of 1944–5 was the biting cold, but as he had had the foresight to take his ice-skates with him, he was able to keep warm for a while by skating on the frozen Wilhelmina Canal near Eindhoven.

Still more orders came from HQ 1 Field Broadcasting Unit: 'There will be no mention of food or drink on the BLAs. The stations will ensure that they do not give away their locations and under no circumstances will commercial items be mentioned by the BLAs', although it was all right to talk about Blanco!

By March 1945 BLA 3 had moved on to Kleve. Ken Scarrott recalls driving the transmitter on to some high ground, and having parked the vehicle and erected the aerial he had time to look around with some of his colleagues, including Alec Storey. They found they were sharing their site with several dead German soldiers, a reminder that the war was not very far away. After Kleve it was on to Haren, then Meppen and finally Apen, a small farming village north-west of Oldenburg.

On 1 April Radio Werewolf began broadcasting. Created by Goebbels, it was intended to rally the Germans to suicidal resistance with the slogan '*Besser tot als rot*' (better dead than red). Douglas Brown recalls while in Meppen where BLA 3 was sited, on 8 May 1945 when the war ended, they had a silent and quite frightening audience made up of German sailors from Emden. Their presence gave his colleagues cause for concern, especially at night, but luckily the sailors did not respond to the Radio Werewolf broadcast.

The BLAs were travelling through a wasted country. Many of the buildings had been destroyed and the Allied Armies were the only legal authority. As Vivian Milroy spoke reasonable German, he was often called upon as an arbitrator. On one occasion, a group of disgruntled Polish slave labourers complained that the farmer for whom they had been working had stopped feeding them. Vivian confronted the farmer, demanded to see his store-room and found eight or nine sides of bacon. He made the farmer cut one down and give it to the Poles and threatened him with the military police if he ever kept the men on short rations again.

Alexander McKee, who was later to become a member of the BFN Features and Drama Department, wrote a poem which summed up the feelings of many of the soldiers who were advancing into Germany:

> O spires and steeples strange to me,
> Ye crowned the corn of Normandy;
> Ye stood like statues on the plain,
> And drowsed beside the winding Seine;
> Like minarets in gothic guise,
> Ye touched the sighing Flemish skies;
> And sheer above the frozen grass,
> Ye rose along the sullen Maas.
>
> But in the spring I stood beside
> A German church where God had died.

By mid-April, the BLAs were deployed across the Rhine, and BLA 2 headed for the north coast and Norderney. There they had the use of a powerful German transmitter. In place of their single 96 ft aerial and the small mobile transmitter with just enough room for two engineers, there was a futuristic control room with fluorescent displays and six 100 ft aerials, spread over an area equal to two football pitches. When the station was switched off at night, it took ten minutes for the current to drain down before it was safe for the maintenance men to go on the field.

At the beginning of May, John McMillan and the Field Broadcasting Unit's headquarters were in Liebenau, just over 40 miles south-west of Hamburg. It was here that Lt-Col Eric Maschwitz, of the Welfare Branch of 21 Army Group, joined McMillan to plan for the acquisition of a permanent base for Forces Broadcasting and a powerful transmitter. As Hamburg was to be their final destination, they began by examining street maps of the city. On 3 May units of XII Corps had occupied the Hanseatic city and a day later John and Eric set off for Hamburg to locate the Musikhalle.

Although Hamburg had suffered 70 per cent damage from the Allied bombing raids, when they arrived they found the building was undamaged. After several minutes banging on the doors, they managed to rouse a terrified caretaker who had been hiding in the boiler-room. A quick inspection showed them that the building would be ideal for the studios and headquarters of the British Forces Network. To secure the tenancy of the Musikhalle, they wrote out a pencilled note 'Requisitioned for Army Broadcasting' and signed it 'Bernard L. Montgomery'.

Having secured a 'Broadcasting House' their next objective was to acquire a transmitter powerful enough to cover the whole of the British Zone. The ideal station was at Norden, said to be the most modern in Europe and already in use by BLA 2. A small detachment from No. 1 FBU HQ drove through the remnants of the defeated German army and arrived at the site. The German staff were ordered to rearrange the aerial array to give less coverage to the north and west and more to the south and east, which they did with remarkable speed, and the station remained on air carrying BLA 2's signal until the Musikhalle was ready to broadcast.

Jack Sheard recalls with a certain amount of satisfaction seeing the powerful transmitter which had once broadcast 'Germany Calling' to Britain, now controlled from a BLA studio vehicle via a cable through a window. Next John persuaded the German Post Office engineers to link the transmitter with the Musikhalle. In the meantime, soldiers from the Royal Signals, REME and the Royal Engineers started to convert the Musikhalle into a broadcasting complex.

While all this was going on, the BLAs had celebrated VE-Day with 24-hour broadcasting and a few celebrations. On 10 May, only 48 hours after the German surrender, the station identification, 'The British Forces Network', was heard for the first time. None of this had official approval, but in the chaos of the days that followed the capitulation, nobody was going to stop the BLA broadcasters.

Soon the BLAs would be on the move to Hamburg to assist in the conversion of the Musikhalle into broadcasting studios. While they installed equipment and wired up the various studios and control room, German workmen were helping with their building, carpentry and painting skills. On 29 May, after 132 days the BLAs' signature tune, 'Bless 'Em All', was discontinued. Though not as haunting a melody as 'Lilli Marlene', it had played its part in raising the Allied Forces' morale.

John McMillan decided that the listeners should be kept informed about the progress of BFN, and on 2 June he made the following announcement: 'Next Tuesday, 5 June, a radio service known as the British Forces Network will come on air for the first time. This service will be operated in Germany entirely by members of the armed forces, but programme contributions will come from the BBC, the Canadian Broadcasting Corporation, the Overseas Recording Broadcasting Service and the American Forces Network in order that the finest programmes from all the English-speaking broadcasting organizations can be used to build up the best possible radio service. In addition, there will later be included entertainment and sporting programmes from our own resources.'

However, John McMillan had 'jumped the gun', and the service still retained the name of BLA 1. The title British Forces Network had been reserved for the official opening in July but the Musikhalle was officially referred to as British Forces Network House. That day, 5 June 1945, was the occasion when the Allied Proclamation that officially ceded all governmental control to the four powers came into effect. This control explicitly included all forms of telecommunications and broadcasting, which meant that anything the Allies did could be considered legal. This was probably the reason for the choice of that date to begin the regular BLA transmissions from the Musikhalle.

The need to get the Musikhalle on air as quickly as possible meant that servicemen with particular skills were sought from the Forces in and around Hamburg. Sapper Bob Humphries was with VIII Corps Engineers waiting for the final onslaught on Hamburg when it declared itself an 'Open City'. While other units pushed on towards the Baltic, Bob's unit moved into the city. The next thing he heard was a request for soldiers who had any form of technical skills to report to the Musikhalle. 'I found myself at the Musikhalle, checking the electrics and keeping my fingers crossed when I saw the ersatz wire and cable the Germans had developed. It was terribly crumbly insulation around aluminium conductors encased in flimsy aluminium sheathing. Obviously it worked, as the building had not gone up in flames!'

When Sgt Gordon Crier suggested that Bob should join BFN, his CO was outraged. 'Army Broadcasting is not soldiering,' he declared, and so Bob was posted to the Far East and arrived in time to celebrate VJ-Day. On 21 July *Soldier* magazine informed its readers that the AEFP was going. 'Criticized by its American audience because it sounded too British and by its British audience

The officers of the British Liberation Army Mobile Broadcasting Units, 5 June 1945. Left to right: Capt Burgess, Lt Dean, Capt Shepherd, Maj John McMillan (OC No. 1 Forces Broadcasting Unit), Capt Rogers, Capt Kesten, Capt Evans and Capt Stanley   (*Crown Copyright/MoD*)

because it sounded too American, the AEF programme of the BBC closes on 28 July, having done a hard job well. Its task – set by the Supreme Commander – was not only to provide the best entertainment programmes from American, Canadian and British sources, but to give the fighting men the broad view of the battle – an invaluable stimulus to those engaged in bitter, almost static, warfare when others were exploiting a breakthrough. Well done, AEFP – and sorry to see you go. The BBC programme to replace the AEFP as a parent service on 29 July in the British Zone will be the BBC programme "B", largely light items. Although designated for the home audience it will contain many features of equal interest to occupation troops. On 29 July it is hoped another station, the AWS British Forces Network in Germany, will provide a seventeen-hour a day service for the occupation zone – with the help of re-broadcasts of BBC programmes, special army-produced transcriptions, gramophone record shows and broadcasts from the new Hamburg studios. The task is being keenly tackled by the army's own broadcasting men. One headache to be overcome is the often indifferent reception of BBC stations for re-broadcast purposes – especially at night. Good luck BFN. We look to you!'

CHAPTER TWO

The Musikhalle –
the Early Days

The war-time army left a legacy to the peace-time army.
It was called – Forces Broadcasting.

Richard Elley – Soldier *magazine 1947*

On 2 May 1945, Gauleiter Karl Kaufmann broadcast to the people of Hamburg: '*Morgen kommen die Englander. Es wird keinen Kampf geben.*'

The next day the Bürgermeister, Carl Krogmann, handed over the government of the Hanseatic city of Hamburg. The entire eastern section of the outer city, a large part of the inner city and the dock area were derelict. As many as 255,000 dwellings had been destroyed – more than the number ruined in the whole of the United Kingdom – and 55,000 people had perished. This once proud city presented an aspect of utter disaster, with thousands of acres reduced to rubble as a result of the air raids. The worst of these had happened in late July 1943, after which a pall of smoke and dust hung over the city and prevented the sun breaking through for ten days. Small wonder that this period has gone down in Hamburg's history as *die Katastrophe*. It was against this chaotic background that BFN had to aim for an initial transmission timed for 0700 hours on Sunday 29 July, because the Allied Expeditionary Forces Programme was due to end at midnight the day before.

When the Allied Forces occupied Germany after the war, they needed labour. At BFN many Germans were taken on as typists, clerks, drivers, library assistants, engineers and cleaners. Many of the technicians were German too, and like their colleagues felt they were fortunate to have work.

Gunnar Oldag was fifteen years old when the war ended. He can still recall the raids on Hamburg. In his diary he wrote: 'Our bunker jumped and juddered. Our home is in ruins, what we dig out is moved to the next undamaged house and stored in the staircase. Three days later we move again, and again. A few personal things are left.' On the morning of 3 May he wrote: 'Everybody has to stay at home. Windows have to be kept closed. Looking out of the windows can be misunderstood as a hostile act. Hamburg is as quiet as a tomb. We are afraid. What will happen? Propaganda made us believe that all British people are cruel and the RAF hardened this point. Lorries with British soldiers turn into our street and drive on. The soldiers huddle on their seats, rifles on their laps. My mother says: "They look afraid, don't they?"'

Gunnar's father was a prisoner of war, his home was in ruins and he had to earn some money to keep his family going, so he went to the Musikhalle and introduced himself to Capt Burgess of BFN. 'He tested my English and then in German checked on my political background.' Gunnar explained that he had had no option but to join the Hitler Youth, 'But once the war was over, I threw my armband into a sewer'. His clothing was threadbare but after he found an abandoned RAF battledress jacket and a pair of denim trousers, he reported for work and started in the BFN orderly room on 13 June 1945. He quickly acquired the nickname 'Oscar' and learned to operate the Gestetner, deliver messages to the various departments and every afternoon collect tea and cakes from the NAAFI for the orderly room staff. He soon discovered that one of the major perks in the Musikhalle was emptying ashtrays. 'Twice a day I had to clear all the ashtrays in the offices and I found that if you recycled the cigarette ends, you could end up with the finest Virginia tobacco. Cigarettes were the "golden keys" to everything, especially when a single cigarette could be sold for five Reichsmarks.'

The ruins of Hamburg, 1945   (*Alexander McKee*)

In the days that followed the surrender, the British had plenty of the necessities of life (200 cigarettes and a ration of soap and chocolate per soldier per week). Although the British claimed not to know of the existence of a black market, in Hamburg they were the chief suppliers! Their surplus could be exchanged for jewellery, cameras, fur coats or sold for marks which could be exchanged for pounds. The official exchange rate at the time was 40 marks to the pound. Vivian Milroy remembers buying four gold teeth for 50 marks and having a local jeweller turn them into a ring for his wife.

The British in Hamburg lived in a world apart from their German staff. All the best buildings still undamaged had been requisitioned for messes, clubs, barracks and offices. John McMillan was living in a beautiful house that belonged to a Hamburg banker. The bedrooms appeared to have been designed to house Madame Pompadour, and two superb concert grand pianos came with the house. Ever a resourceful man, he had recruited a first-class chef and waiter who before the war had worked in New York. Eric Maschwitz recalled later that the brigadier in charge of Army Welfare was to remark, after a superb meal, 'Don't you think this fellow McMillan's going a bit too far?'

Although one could speak to the Germans working in the Musikhalle, the non-fraternization laws were still in force, and announcements to this effect were still being broadcast several weeks after the opening of the station. Maj Fred Bassett, who became the CO of No. 2 FBU in 1946, remembers working on a twice-weekly record show for NWDR with a German co-presenter. Because of the fraternization policy, he could not speak to her except on matters concerning their programme.

Ken Scarrott and Douglas Brown had now arrived at the Musikhalle and started work on continuity studio C. Ken recalls, 'We commandeered all sorts of sound-proofing including some awful fibre-glass which took us weeks to get out of our skins.' At the same time, Sergeant Geoff Pexton was 'lent' by the REME-based workshops in Hamburg to help with the conversion of the Musikhalle into a studio complex: 'On the first day I was shown to an enormous pile of boxes and cables in the foyer and told to start installing the equipment in the new studios.' After many months of indifferent accommodation, much of it under canvas in Belgium and Holland during the winter of 1944–5, working at BFN was 'like a holiday'.

While the engineers were working on the studio conversions, the programme staff, drawn from the BLAs, started to work on programme schedules, with fierce competition between the various departments for the prime slots.

Once the studios had been finished Geoff was charged with looking after the sound-recording facilities. There were three 78 rpm disc recorders, made by Telefunken, with a rather baffling design feature to the uninitiated. They cut only from the centre outwards, but the result looked like any normal disc. Confusion could – and did – reign once the discs were passed on for playback elsewhere! There were also a number of Magnetophon tape machines all commandeered from German studios. The main challenge in operating these was to avoid dropping the middle out of the spool of tape, since about half a mile of tape was wound on to a central boss with no backing plate. If you dropped it, you had to re-wind by hand!

All the tape used at BFN had been reclaimed from various German sources, and at one stage Geoff visited German military bases in and around Hamburg with a view to acquiring spare machines, spare parts and tapes. In the end there were so many tapes it was impossible to listen to them all before using them. By sheer good luck, one of the tapes that was monitored was Lord Haw Haw's last drunken broadcast on 3 April (a copy of which is now in the BFBS Archive). Once news of the discovery had leaked out, the tape was removed by Military Intelligence. Nothing more was heard about it until the spring of 1948, when Lt Jack Hayward, BFN's technical officer, received around a hundred tapes with the instruction: 'These recordings are to be destroyed.' The BFN engineering staff, being possessed of an inquisitive nature, played some of the tapes. Most seemed to be speeches made at political rallies, but then they came across the Lord Haw Haw tape. Unaware of its earlier appearance at BFN, they made three 78 rpm acetate disc copies, one of which was sent to the BBC by Jack Hayward. The others quietly disappeared. (Years later it was realized that the tape sent by Jack was approximately three minutes longer than the one found by Geoff. Were there two tapes? Who edited the 1946 tape and why? Perhaps we will never know.) The rest of the tapes were wiped, using an electrical coil made up in the workshops. Looking back, Jack has often wondered how many other historic recordings were wiped as a result of that order.

Meanwhile back in the Musikhalle, the broadcasters had requested an echo chamber. After experimenting with drums and tubes, Ken Scarrott and Douglas Brown discovered a downstairs toilet with tiled walls. 'It was ideal – but we had one problem. What happened if someone used the toilet for its real purpose when we had set it up for a play or feature?' Tony Friese-Green, who later became a producer for BBC Radio 3, often used it to practise his violin.

In the meantime the Royal Signals, REME and Royal Engineers were working non-stop to repair hundreds of miles of broadcasting cables. A powerful German transmitter was moved from the Danish border to a site north of Cologne, and plans were laid for low power transmitters in Hanover, Herford and Berlin. In exactly forty-six days and nights, the task was completed with just four minutes to spare. At 7 a.m. on 29 July Sgt Gordon Crier announced, 'This is the British Forces Network in Germany', followed by the news and then the first edition of 'Sunrise Serenade'.

To Vivian Milroy fell the honour of introducing the first 'live' programme at 8 p.m. that same evening. 'This is the British Forces Network . . . in a few moments you will hear an All Services Variety Concert, our first big programme from the new BFN Studios. This is, in its small way, a red-letter day for Army Welfare in

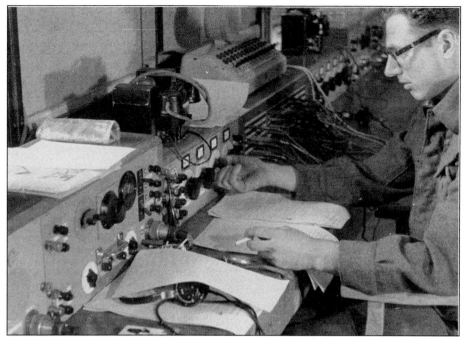

Ken Scarrott on duty in the control room of BFN Hamburg on the opening day – 29 July 1945
(*Ken Scarrott*)

the BLA and here to introduce the programme is the Director of Army Welfare Services 21st Army Group – Brigadier Ware.' The brigadier started by congratulating the AEF Programme which had done so much to lift service morale. 'You came to know well the announcements – This is Station BLA 2, BLA 3, or BLA 4, and to many of you it must have been a comforting sound being a refreshing relief from difficult conditions. . . .This is your service, and we want, so far as it is in our power to do so, to give you the programmes you like.'

The following day John McMillan wrote to all members of the new BFN: 'We have launched the British Forces Network on the day we planned without a hitch of any sort. On all sides people are congratulating us on what we have done. I think in fact it is a big achievement to which everyone – drivers, cooks, broadcasters, clerks, technicians, etc. – has equally contributed in hard work and long hours. Now I propose to do something for ourselves. During August, all personnel (except some of the officers who landed in December) will go on leave. A proper system of rest days for all personnel must be organized and there must be a good canteen at Broadcasting House.' John was aware that many of the men who had travelled across Europe with the BLAs would soon be demobilized, so he set in motion a system for finding their replacements. Notices were sent to all units informing them of BFN's requirements. 'To men who are interested in radio, BFN invites you to write for an audition. Demobilizations have created vacancies on our staff and if you have the necessary qualifications, you stand a very good chance of getting in now, provided you apply at once. Essential qualities are a sound educational standard, good voice, clear diction, intelligence, initiative and a capacity for work. Knowledge of music is also an advantage. There is no point applying if you have less than six months' service to run. If you are interested write immediately to The Station Director, BFN, BAOR 3.'

One of the first to respond was Tpr Bob Boyle of the Inns of Court Regiment and the Royal Dragoons, who had battled his way across Northern Europe from Normandy to Denmark. After the rigours of war came the problems of peace with a series of exhausting parties as the Danes celebrated their freedom with their liberators. Feeling in need of a rest, Bob, having seen the routine order, decided to apply for an announcing post with BFN in Hamburg. Apparently 3,000 young servicemen applied, but only a small percentage was called forward for the audition at the Musikhalle. The chairman of the selection board was John McMillan, and the audition consisted of selecting six records from a pile of 78s and introducing them. Only two candidates were successful, Bob and Driver Peter King RASC.

Another recruit to BFN was LAC John Jacobs who had been with the 84 Group Welfare show *Liberty Run* when it played in Hamburg. As the audience reaction had been so good, the players were invited to BFN to take part in a variety show. Flt Lt Bill McLurg, of BFN's Variety Department, was so taken with the young impressionist that he invited him to join BFN with the promise that he would soon be promoted to corporal. However, the only vacant slot in the establishment was for a corporal horse-riding instructor and, as John Jacobs recalls, the nearest he had been to a horse was riding a donkey on Margate sands. However, he accepted the offer.

Having at first met with all-round approval it didn't take long for the letters of criticism to appear in *Soldier* magazine. On 18 August LAC Pilsbury wrote: 'Why, oh why did the AEFP have to go? I and the rest of the lads in the billet have just sampled today's British Forces Network, and in our opinion, there is no comparision. Our silent radio bears tribute to the AEFP.' Others were more concerned with accents. Major Sykes wrote: 'We get more than our quota of North American accents on films, not to mention AFN. Surely it is not too much to ask for an announcer on the BFN who speaks the King's English without an American, Canadian or – for that matter – a Cockney or Glaswegian accent? If it is popularly supposed that one must talk with an American accent to be slick or snappy, then the sooner we *British* explode that theory, the better.'

The Army Welfare Service's spokesman was quick to reply: 'It would appear necessary to correct what is clearly a misunderstanding. The Canadian voices on BFN are there for the specific purpose of bringing the voice of home to the Canadian Occupation Forces which are part of the BFN audience. American voices are heard in American transcriptions which bring to Rhine Army listeners the best American radio entertainment. The occasional local accent to be detected in BFN announcers is not considered sufficiently strong to offend. Indeed, the warmth of a local accent is considered by many to bring a refreshing note to the world of radio voices where the King's English or what is popularly interpreted as the King's English is cultivated to the degree where the sense of the words spoken is obscured by the local virtuosity of the reader.' However, most letters either to the station or to *Soldier* magazine were complimentary.

No programme schedules of the early days of BFN have survived, but on 7 October 1945 the first *BFN Bulletin* was published. It was distributed along with *Soldier* magazine in the form of a pull-out supplement and covered two weeks of programming. The early morning Sunday programme 'Sunrise Serenade' was joined during the week by 'Milkman's Matinee', billed in the *BFN Bulletin* as 'Fifty minutes of pint-sized rhythms delivered by Canadian L/Cpl George Lunn (late of BLA 3) and Driver Peter King'. Another presenter of this popular programme was L/Cpl Bill Kemp, another very talented Canadian, who decided he should be promoted and informed John McMillan of this fact. When his suggestion was turned down, Kemp decided to go on strike and refused to turn up for his early show. Determined not to give way, John McMillan presented the show, and then informed Kemp he no longer had a future with BFN and sent him back to his unit.

Other members of the BLAs were now well established on BFN. Roy Bradford (BLA 2) introduced the mid-morning show 'Random Records', Vivian Milroy 'Poets' Corner' and 'Words and Music' and Johnny Brandon presided over the '1600 Club', the top request programme of the day. Listeners to BFN could hear the BBC Light Programme relays 'ITMA', 'Appointment with Fear' and 'Desert Island Discs'.

Johnny, considered by many to be BFN's most gifted presenter, was chairing the weekly quiz programme which came live from the studios in Hamburg. When he asked the teams 'Where would you expect to find a list of the clergy?', he was met with blank looks. He repeated the question and then 'off mike' said 'Whatever you do, don't say the *News of the World.*' This remark so incensed the chief padre he demanded Brandon should be disciplined. With reluctance, John Humphreys suspended him for a month. However, Johnny made good use of his free time by listening to the AFRS comedy records and writing down all their jokes. They would stand him in good stead when he went to America in his 'life after BFN'.

BFN PROGRAMMES

18 NOVEMBER *to* **24** NOVEMBER

ISSUE NO. 4

BRITISH FORCES NETWORK IN GERMANY • ARMY WELFARE SERVICES RHINE ARMY

SUNDAY

November 18

06.55 NETWORK OPENING

07.00 NEWS

07.10 SUNRISE SERENADE
Bright and Breezy
listening for a Sunday
morning

07.55 DAILY PRAYER

08.00 POT POURRI
Record Variety

08.55 PROGRAMME
PARADE

09.00 NEWS

09.10 WEATHER FORECAST
FOR THE BRITISH
ZONE

09.11 REPEAT OF LAST
NIGHT'S CANADIAN
NEWS

09.15 MUSIC TIME

09.45 HOUR OF CHARM
An American pro-
gramme of Morning
melody

10.15 MORNING SERVICE
From the BFN Studios

10.45 B B C SCOTTISH
VARIETY ORCHESTRA
Conductor
Kemlo Stephen

11.15 FAMILY FAVOURITES
Exchange programme
of requests for families
at home and forces in
Germany. (Programme
produced in co-ope-
ration with the B B C)

12.15 AS THE COMMEN-
TATOR SAW IT
A highlight from yester-
day's sport

12.30 MELODY HOUR

13.00 DOWNBEAT
Featuring a big name
American Band

13.30 NEWS

13.40 GREGOR AT THE
ORGAN
(By arrangement with
the North West Ger-
man Radio Network)

14.00 SUNDAY SERENADE
Ronnie Munro and his
Orchestra

14.45 TRANSATLANTIC
QUIZ
America v Britain, a
contest to find who
knows most about the
other's country

15.15 ORCHESTRAL
CONCERT

15.55 ASSOCIATION
FOOTBALL
COMBINED SERVICES
GERMANY
v SCOTTISH F.A.
(A commentary on the
last fifteen minutes of
play)

16.15 AMERICAN ALBUM
OF FAMILIAR MUSIC

16.45 GYPSY TRAIL

17.00 MUSIC FOR SUNDAY

17.30 BRASS BAND

18.00 NEWS

18.05 HOME NEWS FROM
BRITAIN

18.10 THE ORGANOLIANS

18.30 MELODY WARD
WAGGON
A programme of hos-
pital requests

19.00 DO YOU REMEMBER

19.30 SUNDAY SERVICE

20.00 SERENADE FOR
STRINGS

20.15 BANDWAGGON

20.30 THE ARMY RADIO
ORCHESTRA
Conducted by R. S. M.
George Melachrino
with guest artistes

21.00 NEWS

21.10 WEATHER FORE-
CAST FOR THE
BRITISH ZONE

21.11 SUMMARY OF
TOMORROW'S
PROGRAMMES

21.15 FOUR HANDS, TWO
PIANO'S
Sjt. Reginald Brigden
& Gnr Stan Blackmore

21.30 THEATRELAND
Songs and News from
the Shows presented
by Sjt. Alan Clarke

22.00 SUNDAY HALF HOUR
Community hymn
singing

22.30 POETS CORNER
Verse written or
chosen by the Forces
edited by L/Cpl. Vivian
Milroy

22.45 SUPPER CLUB

23.00 NEWS

23.10 TALKING WITH YOU

23.15 THE TWILIGHT HOUR
A programme of
melody introduced and
played by Sandy
Macpherson

23.45 AT EASE

24.00 CLOSE DOWN

MONDAY

November 19

06.55 NETWORK OPENING

07.00 NEWS

07.10 MILKMAN'S MATINEE
45 minutes of melody
and madness delivered
by L/Cpl. Bill Kemp

07.55 DAILY PRAYER

08.00 NEWS

08.10 WEATHER FORECAST
FOR THE BRITISH
ZONE

08.11 SONG PARADE

08.25 MUSIC WITH A LILT

08.55 PROGRAMME PARADE

09.00 RETURN ENGAGE-
MENT
The Army Radio
Orchestra

09.30 RANDOM RECORDS
Sjt. Roy Bradford's
morning selection

10.00 RHYTHM & ROMANCE

10.15 MORNING MELODIES
Direct from London

10.45 KEYBOARD
CAVALCADE

NEWS BULLETINS

Weekdays: 07.00
08.00
13.30
18.00
21.00
23.00

Sundays: 07.00
09.00
13.30
18.00
21.00
23.00

Weather forecast for the
British zone read after:
08.00
21.00

Wavelengths: 455 *m.* (658 kcs.), **274** *m.* (1095 kcs.)

(Add one hour to all above times for listening in Berlin)

BFN Bulletin, No. 4, 18 November 1945

Vivian Milroy, one of the original BLA members now in charge of 'Poets' Corner' (*Vivian Milroy*)

As autumn turned to winter, BFN began to experience power failures. Trains bringing coal from the Ruhr never arrived with a full load. Everytime a train stopped in a siding during its journey northwards, it was looted by the local populace. As a result, the local power supply was erratic. So BFN arranged for a large generator to be set up to ensure a constant power supply. The only snag was that with no self-starter, this generator was a 'beast' to start. Ken Scarrott recalls, 'We had to get several lads to pull on ropes while we knocked the valves; when it didn't work, the lads fell over like a pack of cards.' So advice was sought. 'We found a veteran in the local REME workshops and in exchange for a mention on the new request show "Family Favourites", he agreed to help. He took a long piece of wire, coated one end with "scrim", dipped it in the diesel, lifted up the air filter on the generator and then set fire to the scrim.' The result was one very large bang and the generator sprang into life. If, during the bitter weather, it was allowed to stop, the generator could only be started after hours of work as the fuel would freeze in the pipelines.

Although the Musikhalle now had a reliable power supply, it was not centrally heated. Many of the staff had paraffin heaters in their offices, and when the fuel ran out they discovered liquid insecticide worked just as well, although it played havoc with their throats. The cold was so intense that many worked in their greatcoats over whatever else they could put on. The same situation applied to their accommodation. John Grey, who was a regular broadcaster with BFN, worked for the Control Commission in Hamburg. He found playing chess by the light of a candle in a freezing bedroom was a novelty that soon wore off. 'As for going to bed, I dressed for it by putting on more clothes than I wore in the office and using my greatcoat as an extra eiderdown.'

In November the BBC and BFN extended their joint productions beyond 'Family Favourites'. On Saturday 24 November listeners to 'In Town Tonight' heard this rather patriotic introduction: 'We stop the roar of London's traffic to bring to the microphone some of the interesting people who are "In Town Tonight", and we take you over to BFN Hamburg to hear from the men of the victorious British Army of the Rhine telling you about their experiences. The programme is introduced by Flt Lt Roy Rich in London and Sgt Alan Clarke in Hamburg.' Later that same evening, Roy Plomley's 'Desert Island Discs' came live from the island of Norderney in the North Sea. The castaway was Able Seaman Henry Wheeler and the engineer was Jack Sheard. Norderney in November could hardly be described as an idyllic desert island!

BFN had two OB units that produced on average eight outside broadcasts a week. A typical weekend for Ron Chown, who had been a BBC engineer before being called up, was a 'live' sports commentary on a Saturday afternoon, a dance band recording in the evening, followed by one or sometimes two church services on a Sunday. The OB van contained one tape recorder, two disc recorders (using glass discs), one OBA 8, a four-channel mixer and four microphones (one ribbon and three moving coil). 'There was nothing we were not prepared to do. When we recorded a band, we would listen to the sound and place the mikes in the right spot. If we had to use all four, then there was nothing left for applause or announcements, so often we would record the extras after the show and cut them in later.'

On 14 December 1945 Field Marshal Montgomery recorded his Christmas message to the troops from a Combined Services carol concert. Apparently, he had been given a script, took one look at it and muttering 'Rubbish', threw it away. He then delivered an excellent spontaneous Christmas message.

The new year, 1946, ushered in changes at BFN. John McMillan, Alan Clarke, Gordon Crier and Jack Sheard returned to the UK and their replacements, Fred Bassett, the new CO, Trevor Hill, Derek Jones, Cliff Michelmore, Raymond Baxter and Alastair McDougall would soon make their mark. Trevor recalls that John was adamant about what he wanted for BFN: 'We're not just another relay station. We are here to make programmes and in the year ahead I want to see features, drama, and light entertainment, and if not of the standards of our current Music Department under Captain Trevor Harvey, then at least that is the goal to aim for.' John encouraged his staff to push back the boundaries of broadcasting. For features and drama, there would be no money in the kitty to pay copyright fees, so they would have to write their own material.

Field Marshal Montgomery broadcasting his Christmas message to the British and Canadian forces in Germany, 14 December 1945. In the background is Capt Trevor Harvey who has just led the audience in the carol singing   (*IWM BU 1193*)

BFN's programme schedules had become more varied. Forces educational broadcasts were now a regular feature: 'German from Scratch' (Bill and Jock of the Rhine Army try to get a working knowledge of the language) and 'French for the Forces'. Series aimed at men and women going on demob were 'Job in Hand' and 'No Previous Experience Necessary', which examined catering, teaching, forestry and the police force. The comedy mix was still the same, with the Abbott and Costello and Charlie McCarthy shows from America still proving very popular.

Other changes had taken place with the new station opening. Now the announcer began each day's broadcasting with 'Good morning everybody, this is —— of the British Army signing on the British Forces Network in Germany – a radio service operated by the Army Welfare Services Rhine Army, for the Occupation Troops'.

On the first anniversary of VE-Day a very senior officer came to BFN to broadcast a message to the forces. After the broadcast the VIP along with the officers of BFN went to the Atlantic Hotel for supper. Gunnar Oldag remembers the visit: 'I was in the orderly room when the telephone rang, I picked it up and found myself talking to the VIP. "I put my teeth on the table in the studio and I forgot to pick them up. As I cannot eat without them, could you check and see if they are still there?" I checked and reported back that I had found them. "Excellent", said the VIP, "I will send my driver round to collect them – do you smoke?" Minutes later the driver appeared, collected the teeth and gave me five two ounce tins of tobacco – I think that night everyone was happy.'

The imagination of the newcomers was allowed to run riot when BFN was asked to write a series of 'Safety First' announcements. The results, including a terrifying crash effect, positively reeked of Hollywood. Reactions to these announcements came quickly. A senior officer with HQ 30 Corps District sent the following:

> A Driver whose age group was 33 C
> Got immediate release when his car hit a tree.
> 'Twould have paid him, I think, to have gone a bit slower –
> His release group from Hell is five million and fower.

BFN were finally convinced that the campaign had been a resounding success when the following testimonial arrived from the men of the REME, LAD, attached to 13 (HAC) Regiment RHA: 'We wish to protest. Since these announcements have been on the air, our Scammell has had very little recovery work to do. The night duty crews are complaining that their sleep is never disturbed, the telephone orderlies that the telephone never rings. You are putting us out of work.'

On 11 May 1946 the BFN Dance Orchestra made its debut. Its leader, Juan Llossas, had been spotted playing in a local club and had been recruited by BFN. His twenty-seven piece orchestra specialized in the tango and the rumba. He was a flamboyant character who loved to be seen in the company of beautiful women. He was known for his gold bracelets, gold rings and gold teeth, and a splendid Opel limousine whose horn was tuned to play the opening bars of his signature tune 'Tango Bolero'.

John McMillan, who had set up No. 1 FBU and BFN Hamburg, was due to return to the United Kingdom. Maj Fred Bassett heard about the proposed move on the military grapevine and with his previous experience at All India Radio decided to lobby for the position. He was successful and after a ten-day handover became the new Commanding Officer of BFN Hamburg. He was very impressed with the pool of talent he had inherited among the young servicemen. They were Geraint Evans, Barney Colehan, Geoffrey Webb, Ray Lakeland and Trevor Harvey, who while others read newspapers at breakfast, preferred to study musical scores instead. When Alan Clarke went back to the BBC, Fred turned to his first love of sports broadcasting. He recalls a cricket match in Hamburg when the Rhine Army played the MCC captained by Gubby Allen. Fred's co-commentator was Flt Lt Cliff Michelmore, who was making his debut on radio.

In October 1946, the first families began arriving in Germany, including Fred's wife Mary. As he recalls, she was 'labelled and under escort'. Mary, who broadcast under the name of Mary Marshall, presented a regular hospital request programme called 'For You in Blue' and a cookery programme. However, after two shows it was dropped; apparently she said on air that if she had any rations over, she gave them to the German staff – thereby encouraging other service wives to do the same. While this was happening unofficially, BFN should not broadcast such radical ideas!

By now Gunnar Oldag was back at school in the mornings and worked in the orderly room in the afternoons. He recalls that he was assisted with his homework by other members of the orderly room. On 1 October the loudspeakers in BFN relayed the decisions of the War Crimes Tribunal in Nuremburg: 'The orderly room went very quiet as the decisions were read out – condemned to death by hanging.'

Fred Bassett left BFN at Christmas 1946, but BFN had not heard the last of him. On Boxing Day 1946, he broadcast a commentary for the BBC on the match between Brentford and Sheffield United, which was carried by BFN. As Fred admitted later, he was told he was not up to BBC standard. However, the BBC must have had second thoughts; on 28 May 1947 he was asked to make a 'live' broadcast while doing a parachute jump. The event was carried by BFN under the heading 'Parachute Drop – sensations of a parachutist while jumping from an aeroplane. Maj F. Bassett will broadcast during the actual jump.' With him was Wynford Vaughan-Thomas, who remained in the aircraft, and Stewart Macpherson, who was on the ground to meet him. Fred was replaced as Station Director BFN by John Humphreys from the BBC.

Although BFN was now in civilian hands, the peculiar status of 2 FBU irritated the army and from time to time they made efforts to regularize things. On one occasion, a spick and span CSM was posted in to instil some discipline into the troops. He was a regular soldier, and tough. Scandalized by the informal dress of some of the team, he issued an order: 'All BFN staff working in Broadcasting House will in future wear army issue boots.' Next morning, Bob Boyle arrived to introduce 'Canteen Break' correctly dressed. The programme was broadcast from Studio B which had a wooden floor and was large enough for the weekly dance to be held there in comfort. As each piece of music ended, there was the sound of approaching thunder as Bob marched the full length of the floor, doing a smart 'about turn' as he reached the microphone before announcing the next item! The order to wear boots was hastily rescinded but Bob remembered the CSM's instruction brought about a sudden and mysterious influx of requests for Peter Dawson to sing 'Boots, Boots, Marching Up and Down again'! Of course, none of the staff could account for its amazing popularity!

Undaunted, the new CSM now insisted on having an inspection every morning before the staff started work. As they were drawn from a variety of units in the Army and Royal Air Force, he must have surveyed the motley crew with quiet desperation. The roll call didn't help! By the time he'd accounted for those who had been on late duty the night before and were still in bed, and those who had already gone to BFN for the early programmes, the driver of the duty bus was complaining that he was now running late. Slowly the members of BFN began to knock some 'broadcasting standards' into the CSM. But he never came to terms with BFN's German tailor, who removed field-service pockets from army issue trousers and re-faced battledress jackets so that the lapels could no longer be buttoned up.

The second civilian to arrive at BFN was Raymond Baxter, who had made his Forces Broadcasting debut in Cairo reading the NAAFI news. After he had been demobbed he heard through a contact at the BBC that there was a vacancy at BFN, and he joined in late 1946. Like so many others, he could recall that bitter winter of 1946–7 with people dying in the streets from hunger. The heavy falls of snow and the flooding in the UK meant that transport movements became more difficult. The food supply to the services was affected and their diet consisted mainly of M & V (meat and veg.), dehydrated potato, apple and egg. The cigarette ration was reduced to 40 a week. However, conditions for the local population were a great deal worse. Although the German ration level was set at a daily intake of 1,500 calories, in practice it seldom rose above 1,000. Raymond's wife, Sylvia, would find food to give the German children and he can still remember the little boys clicking their heels and the little girls curtseying as they received their gifts.

As a former fighter pilot Raymond had seen a great deal of war, but he still found the ruins of Hamburg a dreadful shock. In the winter months, a wisp of smoke would appear in this barren landscape, a sign that life still existed. In order to assist the civilian population, the army embarked upon 'Operation Woodpecker' – the felling of trees around the Uelzen and Celle areas so that some of the timber could be brought by tram into the cold and starving city. But as Trevor Hill recalls, 'What good was green timber to homes without any heat, never mind light?' The rest were turned into pit props and sent to the coal mines in the UK as part of the reparations programme.

Raymond's role was deputy station director and production manager. He insisted that the standards 'on air' should be as good as the BBC in every respect. He soon became involved in 'Poets' Corner', which had been started in 1945 by Vivian Milroy. It still had a good audience response, judging by the number of letters Raymond received, and he ensured that whenever leading figures from the world of

Raymond Baxter, BFN Hamburg's production manager   (*Alexander McKee*)

theatre came to Hamburg, they were invited to take part. Marius Goring, Dame Peggy Ashcroft, Sir Ralph Richardson and Sir Frederick Ashton read poems, both well known and those submitted by servicemen. Raymond was responsible for Pte Derek Jones becoming a broadcaster. Following a chance meeting in the BBC's Broadcasting House with Alan Clarke, who had just left BFN, Derek was posted to Hamburg. Alan was getting ready to present the UK end of 'Family Favourites' when Derek, who was on a weekend pass, called in to see some of his former engineering colleagues. He still remembers Alan's remark, 'BFN is looking for chaps like you.' Derek applied to join and quickly got a posting to BFN Hamburg.

Although he had trained as an engineer working on the Allied Expeditionary Forces Programme alongside Franklyn Englemann, Jean Metcalfe and Ronnie Waldman in the British contingent at the BBC, Derek was to make his name in Germany as a versatile announcer. Shortly after arriving in the Musikhalle, he was asked by Raymond if he could do an American voice for his jazz programme. Recalling the Americans who had worked with him on the AEFP shows, he passed the test and was soon doing continuity, news reading and record presentation.

Denis Shaw joined BFN's Engineering Department simply by making a phone call. At the time he was working in the BBC's London Control Room and during a link-up with Hamburg, he asked how he could join BFN. 'My call-up date was getting close, and BFN sounded an ideal posting. They told me to contact them once I had received my army number, and they would do the rest.' After basic training Denis was posted to the Army Broadcast Depot in Eaton Square and arrived in Hamburg in December 1946. One of his non-broadcasting duties was to operate a portable 16 mm film projector, which was set up in Studio B. One Friday afternoon, the entire German staff were summoned and had to watch the British film of the Belsen concentration camp with a German commentary: 'They arrived, watched and left in total silence.'

Denis's other abiding memory concerned an instruction that all electric light bulbs in the Musikhalle had to be soldered into their sockets to prevent them from being stolen. In 1947, one bulb could be exchanged for 250 gm of butter. Looking back he felt his colleague Leon Griffiths, who went on to write the scripts for *Minder*, was inspired by the versatility of Hamburg's black market.

Another BFN broadcaster who started out as an engineer was Alastair McDougall. Although he failed a BFN voice test, he was so determined to get into broadcasting he said he would accept any job in the Musikhalle. On 24 February 1946 he started work in the Presentation Department and moved on to the gramophone library before becoming a programme engineer. Through his many contacts in Hamburg, Alastair became known as 'Mr Fix-it'. He claimed he could organize a telephone call to anywhere in the world and was put to the test when Wilhelm Furtwängler brought the Berlin Philharmonic Orchestra to Hamburg for the first time since the end of the war.

When he explained to Furtwängler during the rehearsal that the concert was going to be broadcast 'live', the famous conductor said, 'I wish I had known about this earlier, as I could have written to my wife and told her to listen.' At the time Frau Furtwängler lived in Switzerland and Germans were not allowed to make overseas calls. 'No problem', said Alastair. 'We'll go to my office and give her a call'. However, Frau Furtwängler was out but would be back later. 'If you get through, come and interrupt the rehearsal', said Furtwängler. Shortly after this, Alastair made contact and with a certain amount of fear and trepidation, went on to the stage. 'The orchestra was aghast – no one interrupted Furtwängler during a rehearsal, but the Maestro put down his baton and took the call.'

Fred Hunt, who had been with the Royal Signals on D-Day, had applied to join BFN at the end of 1945, when he was diagnosed as having diphtheria. After a period of convalescence he arrived at the Musikhalle and started work as a programme engineer, although he had no official posting order. In the meantime, his former unit had been disbanded. Then he received an official posting to a unit in Wilhelmshaven, but he ignored the letter and continued at BFN. Within days, the RMPs arrived to escort the 'deserter' to his new unit, where he was to remain until his official posting to BFN came through.

His two greatest fears as a programme engineer were trying to read the musical scores for the Sunday afternoon orchestral concerts – and mice! Apparently BFN was overrun with them. 'I remember them running along the gram-banks during the programmes and when the German engineers prepared cheese on toast for our supper, the mousetraps were going off like small-arms fire.' Alan Bedford, another programme engineer, remembers a mouse running across his control panel as he was about to join the BBC for the pips. In his panic, he closed his fader and omitted two of the pips. The next day, the Station Director was telephoned from Rhine Army Headquarters and questioned about the missing pips. Bernard Denn, who joined the Presentation Department in 1946, recalls seeing very little for sale in the local shops except piles of primitive mousetraps.

In February 1947 the *BFN Bulletin* announced: 'Many people have visited Broadcasting House to see our shows being broadcast. Now, we will be visiting you and for 30 minutes the BFN microphones will be "On Parade" in your unit. Flt Sgt Steve Palmer will be asking you for your favourite tune. The first programme will come from The Middlesex Regiment.' The programme was very successful. The programme engineer, Ron Chown, remembers a visit to No. 3 Military Corrective Establishment where they met a ten-year-old schoolboy, Douglas Creur, who had won two prizes at the BAOR Hobbies Exhibition. Steve Palmer decided to interview him about his achievements: 'What does your father do?' 'He's in prison,' answered the boy. The interviewer was speechless until Douglas explained that his father, Maj Creur, worked there!

On 18 April 1947 the BFN engineers put the finishing touches to the equipment for a most unusual outside broadcast – the second demolition of the fortifications on Heligoland. Their assistance had been requested by the BBC to install and operate the equipment for an extremely complicated outside broadcast. After eight months of planning by the Royal Navy, approximately 6,700 tons of TNT and Cyclonite were to be detonated, thus destroying a large quantity of German ammunition and explosives which were either too unstable to move or could not be dumped due to lack of transport. At the same time, fifteen miles of tunnels and former U-boat pens had to be demolished. Richard Dimbleby was on the destroyer, HMS *Dunkirk*, and would be commentating on the explosion and its immediate effect. Stewart Macpherson was at Altenwalde, near Cuxhaven, to record the effects as seen from the land, and Charles Gardner would observe the demolition from a height of 8,000 ft in a Mosquito aircraft. BFN's technical team was led by Sgt 'Fergie' Ferguson with Sgt Johnny Ammonds (who later went on to produce the 'Morecambe and Wise Show'), in charge of mixing the output and Sgt Keith Scanlon, Cpl 'Bart' Bartholomew and Cpl Ron Cass looking after the various recordings.

Originally, BFN was not allowed to carry the broadcast for policy reasons, but with fifteen minutes to go, the C-in-C gave permission for BFN to relay the programme. The BBC Light Programme handed over to Stewart at 12.45 p.m., who ended his description of the situation with, 'and now over to Richard Dimbleby'. Nothing happened. After a long pause, he repeated his handover and at the last moment, Johnny finally got through to HMS *Dunkirk*. Richard, whose headphones had failed at the critical moment, eventually came in and continued the build-up. He was joined by Charles Gardner, who described Heligoland from 8,000 ft as 'an island in apparent peace', and then it was back to the *Dunkirk* for the final moments before the explosion. On the third pip of the time signal, at 1 p.m., the explosive charges were detonated and Richard said: 'The island seemed to take off in a sheet of flame.' For BFN it had been a dramatic outside broadcast and its efforts were much appreciated by the BBC.

Five years later, when Heligoland was handed back to the Germans, Alexander McKee returned to the island and produced a feature based on the story of Klaus Störtebecker, a notorious pirate who, in 1402, fought his last battle off its shores.

An extra piece of paper was now appearing with the staff's AB 64. With hindsight it looked more like James Bond's proverbial 'Licence to Kill' or Monopoly's 'Get Out of Jail Free' card; but it meant freedom from parades, kit inspections and, for the recently arrived L/Cpl Nan Pomeroy, being marched with escort to and from the Musikhalle: 'This is to certify that 328669W L/Cpl Pomeroy N is employed by the British Forces Network on programming duties. In the event of a CMP (Camp Military Police) routine check-up or charge against her not involving her being placed in close arrest, may her particulars please be taken and she be released immediately if she states she is due at the studios for duty. In these cases will the CMP please report details to BFN as soon as convenient. If the CMP for any reason decide to place her under close arrest will they please telephone Hamburg 343156 and inform the Duty Officer in order that a replacement may be arranged.'

The authorities kept a close watch on the three servicewomen who worked at BFN. As they were in hostile surroundings they were not allowed out unaccompanied after dark. The last duty bus left the Musikhalle at 10 p.m. and if Nan was working on the late shift, she would have to ask a colleague to see her home. Now, with her slip of paper, she could order transport from the car pool whenever she required it. In her spare time Nan and her colleagues would visit the Urania cinema. The shrapnel holes in the roof had not been repaired and the building was unheated. So they took blankets with them; not only did they keep them warm but they were able to hide their cigarettes when the MPs tried to discover the source of the smoke wafting through the auditorium.

BFN's 'man at the movies' was Sgt Geoffrey Webb, who later wrote the scripts for the BBC's 'Dick Barton' and 'The Archers'. Each week he would go to the AKC cinema armed with a stop-watch and a notebook and check out the latest films. He would arrange for an engineer to dub the clips he wanted and, back at Broadcasting House, he would write up his illustrated reviews for his Sunday morning show 'Coming Shortly'. Bob Boyle remembers that Geoffrey produced the shortest 'crit' on record. It concerned a film called *The Blue Dahlia*. He closed his programme that week with, 'finally, the *Blue Dahlia* is a fahlia [failure], and until next week – goodbye'.

John Jacobs, after failing to make the grade as a continuity announcer, had been sent to the Variety Department. There he helped to prepare and present record programmes and look for new talent. Among those he spotted at the Garrison theatre was a young comedian called Peter Sellers. John recalls: 'He was very funny and I invited him to come to the Musikhalle to make his first broadcast. However, some weeks later I saw another young comedian who didn't impress me, and so I turned him down. His name was Harry Secombe – just how wrong can you get!'

On another occasion John invited Tod Slaughter, who was playing 'Sweeny Todd' at the Garrison theatre, to come into the studio and take part in one of his programmes. At the time BFN was using the powerful Norden transmitter and could be heard in England. John, who was partnered by Jimmy Kingsbury, was in full flow when Tod delivered his famous line 'I'm going to polish you off'. John gave a strangled 'ugh', which was followed by the thud of a body hitting the continuity desk. After a brief pause, Jimmy Kingsbury came in with, 'I'm terribly sorry about what has happened to John Jacobs, but in the meantime here is a piece of music.' After about ten minutes of apologies the telephone in the studio rang. It was the station director. 'What's going on? What's happened to Jacobs?' When the joke was explained to him he was not impressed. 'I've got his mother on the telephone and she thinks he's dead, so if he's not back on air in the next few minutes, he's fired.'

Before the start of the BFN Production Unit, on John McMillan's instruction, plays were put on in the Musikhalle. Inge Stolten was a 24-year-old German girl who had been an actress before the war. Within days of the surrender, she found herself working for the army as an interpreter. She was asked to go to BFN for an audition: 'There were a large number of people in uniform in the studio. One gave me a script and I remember being asked to stand nearer the microphone. I was in a complete daze but I do recall that the audition was part of a love scene. Obviously they were very happy with the result because they asked me back the following day for a recording session. They gave me a new script. It was only when I got outside the Musikhalle that I realized the play was *Macbeth* and I was to be one of the witches.' When Inge came in the next day she found the other actors had been flown out from London. 'They told me the play, which was being recorded by BFN, would be broadcast by the BBC. The producer wanted to know where I came from and told me it was unlikely I would be paid. I was not allowed to go into the English canteen with the rest of the cast, but the soldiers took pity on me and brought me several nice meals with plenty of coffee and cigarettes. The food was most welcome as we Germans could get little from the local markets. I was given a bar of soap and asked if there was anything else I wanted. I explained I was short of underwear and what little I did possess had been repaired many times. The next day one of the soldiers gave me some very elegant new underwear. Later I discovered that he had taken quite a risk on my behalf. He had gone into the Winkelstrasse and had exchanged cigarettes for my underwear.' At the time the Winkelstrasse was in the Red Light district and was out of bounds to all British troops.

The posting of Cpl Margaret Potter, WAAF, to BFN Hamburg coincided with Trevor Hill's move to the Features and Magazine Department. Trevor had been with the BBC as a sound-effects boy on Tommy Handley's show 'ITMA' and later a programme engineer. He was on duty in the studio the day the AEF programme began, and was at the control panel when John Snagge introduced Eisenhower's historic broadcast on D-Day. In 1944 he had been asked by John McMillan if he would like to join the Army Psychological Warfare Unit. When this fell through, after a brief spell as a Bren-gunner with the 1st Battalion The Royal Scots, he was posted to BFN where he met up with John once more. Margaret, who had been spotted by Geoffrey Webb at an RAF debating society at Wandsbeck, was persuaded to come for a voice test at BFN. She introduced some programmes for the station, but was far happier sitting at a desk and writing scripts. Together these two were to become the 'Perry and Croft' of BFN with a touch of Lloyd Webber thrown in.

First off the Hill–Potter production line was the serial, *The Island of Moressa*. Originally broadcast in the 'Family Magazine' programme, it was taken over in January 1947 by the 'Children's Magazine'. In an effort to keep the audience listening week by week, the co-authors wrote such cliff-hanging lines as 'How are we supposed to get off this 'ere island of yours, Professor Selby?', spoken by Cpl John Jacobs playing the Cockney Dave Trevellyan. The professor played by Sqn Ldr Jimmy Urquhart, John's real-life CO, was supposed to reply: 'If you've finished your drinks, gentlemen, come out to my workshop.' During a long lunch-break the squadron leader had gone to the Four Seasons Officers' Club for drinks, and when the recording session re-started, he was heard to say: 'If you've finished your drinks, genelmun, come oot t' ma workhoose.' All the astonished John Jacobs could say was, 'You're drunk – er, sir!' The serial also featured Jimmy Kingsbury as the villainous Meldano. Later, *The Island of Moressa* was bought by the BBC.

Staff Sgt Tom Cousens, one of the BLA
engineers who took over the Norden transmitter
(Alexander McKee)

Sgt Geoffrey Webb, BFN's top scriptwriter,
who later joined the BBC to write 'Dick
Barton – Special Agent' and 'The Archers'
(Lady Evans)

To find out what the youngsters wanted in their programme, BFN interviewed a cross section of their younger listeners. The replies staggered them. One eight-year-old girl said: 'I do not want to listen to fairy stories, but a good detective thriller would be all right.' A twelve-year-old boy wanted plenty of Tchaikovsky. However, they were all keen on quizzes provided they could take part.

Next, the Hill–Potter combination produced a late-night drama series called *The Man with a Limp*. Raymond Baxter played the lead, and in the episode called 'The Henley Street Mortuary' he was carted away screaming about 'bodies in baskets'. Probably the most famous Hill–Potter production was *The Adventures of Robin Hood*, written and produced for the Children's Magazine. It ran for sixteen episodes. Nigel Davenport played Robin Hood with Cliff Michelmore as Little John, and Raymond Baxter as a superbly sinister Guy de Guisborne. Brian Matthew was cast as King Richard and Geraint Evans played the part of the minstrel Blondel. (Although Geraint had returned to the UK, he had recorded several Elizabethan madrigals for Margaret Potter's women's programme and she fitted them in to the Robin Hood script.) Tom Singleton was the Sheriff of

CQMS Jack Pickering preparing a young contributor for 'Children's Corner'

(Alexander McKee)

Trevor Hill and Margaret Potter – the BFN playwrights

(Alexander McKee)

Nottingham, Keith Fordyce played Will Scarlett, Bryan Forbes and Roger Moore of the Combined Services Entertainment Unit and Gordon Savage, Nigel Davenport's room-mate, played the Foresters. So successful was this production that the BBC decided to purchase and produce its own version for the UK audience. When Trevor suggested they should consider using his original cast for this production, he was astonished when they informed him, 'But we only use members of Equity – and they are *all* established actors'. Nigel Davenport, who later became president of Equity, sent Trevor a Christmas card in 1994. On the front was a robin and inside he wrote 'from the original Robin'.

Trevor remembers producing Roger Moore in a radio adaptation of the current Garrison theatre production of *The Shop at Sly Corner*. This play was to be taken by the BBC Home Service, and the part of an eager young naval lieutenant was played by Lt Moore. When it was all over Trevor took Roger to one side and told him he looked marvellous in the naval uniform and despite the fact that he was the number one pin-up of the girls in the Ivy Benson Band, which he was currently escorting around Germany, 'he should give up any thought of acting and take up modelling, perhaps, something like sweaters!' Roger took it well and years later after he had appeared as 007 he wrote to Trevor, 'Still can't act but I'm not doing badly!' 'We were given a lot of licence and freedom in our choice of material – providing BFN didn't have to pay,' recalls Trevor. The same went for casting. Young national servicemen such as William Eedle took the lead in *The Island of Moressa*, and Michael Malnick appeared in *Journey into Darkness*. Trevor and Margaret wrote the latter, the story of a young ballerina who was involved in a serious car accident, with Pat Selby playing the lead. They asked Axel Alexander, the BFN Theatre Orchestra arranger, to compose the music and Trevor was delighted when the BBC bought this production and decided to use Axel's music.

Although BFN had the full BBC sound effects library, if Trevor or his colleagues required extra sound effects, they had to go out and record them. Nan Pomeroy recalls a discussion about whether an egg being broken could be faked realistically. After several failed attempts, Trevor paid out some of his cigarette ration to purchase an egg on the black market. He experimented with cracking the expensive egg, but it sounded more like a bomb exploding, so he went back to crumpling a matchbox, which sounded much more realistic. When he required the sound of a motorboat engine, Trevor almost overbalanced into the Alster while hanging perilously over the back of a moving boat. When Nan wanted the sound of a motorbike to mark the change of scene for a series she was producing on the history of the towns in the British zone, Bob Boyle rode his BSA around the car park using various gears to achieve an authentic effect.

Nan appeared in the children's play *The Mystery of Bendreda*, the sequel to *The Island of Moressa*, as Professor Selby's Scottish housekeeper. During one episode she had to say the word 'meteorologist'. After several attempts to get the word right, Nan gave up and said: 'Och, the weather man'. In another episode which involved a scene in a cave, they decided to use the echo chamber (the famous downstairs toilet). All appeared to be going well with the recording until Alastair McDougall rushed out of the control cubicle and berated a German member of staff who, despite the notices of '*Eintritt verboten*', had used the toilet for its prescribed purpose and had pulled the chain! Sadly, the tape of this unusual recording was not kept for posterity.

During the recording of another episode, Capt Ken Mitchell-Taylor, one of BFN's variety producers, was persuaded to play the part of a villain. He was required to die with a suitable scream of anguish followed by the sound of a body falling, and then gasp out his last words. After several rehearsals, Ken promised the actual broadcast would be his best ever sperformance. He put so much effort into his dive on to the floor that he twisted his hand behind his back and sprained his thumb. In the spirit of 'the show must go on', the rest of the cast ignored the fact that he was obviously in considerable pain and dragged him to his feet so that he could finish his last line. Later on they took him to hospital for an X-ray!

CHAPTER THREE

Lilli Marlene, Furtwängler and the Duke

Little did I realize it at the time, the move to BFN changed the whole pattern of my life.

Sir Geraint Evans

When Lale Andersen gave a concert in Hamburg with Milo Karacz's White Ravens and the Karl Rading Sextet, her audience was surprised she did not sing the song that had made her famous. On that evening in October 1945 she sang songs by George Gershwin, Cole Porter, Sammy Kahn, Berthold Brecht and Kurt Weill.

Lale had recorded 'Lilli Marlene' in 1938, but the song failed to register with the public. However, when the Germans used it as the signature tune of their radio station in Belgrade, 'Lilli' became popular with both the Afrika Korps and the Eighth Army. By the time Tripoli fell everyone was whistling 'Lilli Marlene'. There is a story about an American correspondent who was jealous of the success of 'Lilli Marlene' so he filed a story that the real North African hit was 'Dirty Gertie from Bizerte, Miss Latrine of Nineteen Thirty'. If such a record existed, no one could remember it! Lale was to make several visits to Hamburg and the BFN studios and no matter what she sang for the British troops, she was always the girl who had introduced them to 'Lilli Marlene'.

One of the first departments to be organized at BFN was the Music Department. Originally it was to have been headed by Joseph Cooper, but because his unit, the Control Commission Germany, refused to release him he recommended a friend from his BBC days called Captain Trevor Harvey. Before the war Trevor had been Chorus Master at the BBC.

When Trevor arrived at the Musikhalle he was shown into a fairly spartan office and told to organize the music side of BFN. His first recruit was Sergeant Arthur Langford, who had been a schoolteacher before the war, and would later join the BBC. Between them they set up the Monday auditions and placed a notice in Station Routine Orders: 'Are you a good singer? Can you play a solo instrument well? Have you any experience in acting? Have you an entertaining speciality of your own? Would you like to be heard on Radio? If so write and tell us. Actors and actresses to the Features and Drama Department, all others to the Variety Department, BFN Hamburg. BAOR 3.'

LAC Geraint Evans from RAF Oldenburg had seen the notice but didn't give it a second thought. However, a colleague had volunteered a young pianist called Eddie Peters and Geraint Evans to attend the audition. As far as Geraint was aware, he was going along to keep his friend company. After listening to Eddie Peters play, Arthur Langford asked, 'Where is the singer?' Geraint said, 'I told him I had no music and I wasn't prepared for an audition, but he would not take no for an answer and produced some ballads from BFN's small library. So I sang "Arm, Arm Ye Brave", "Honour and Arms" and Vaughan Williams's "The Vagabond".' Geraint returned to Oldenburg and a few days later received a signal inviting Eddie to record a series of 'Piano Playtime' and Geraint to become the soloist in the BFN Choir. Now all he had to do was survive the six-hour journey there and back between Oldenburg and Hamburg.

Years later in his book, *A Knight at the Opera*, Geraint recalls a slightly embarrassing situation. He had struck up a friendship with a German waitress in the NAAFI and after loading up his lorry, went across to the girl's house and gave her family some cigarettes. He was invited in and they asked, 'Where do you stay at the weekends?' 'In the transit hotel', he replied. 'Why don't you stay with us?' they suggested. After a few weeks of sleeping on a settee, he was offered a bed upstairs. He was just dropping off to sleep when the daughter of the house started to get into bed with him. 'I have only come to keep you warm, we do not make love.' Apparently the girl was as good as her word and she kept the bed warm, but Geraint found himself unable to sleep. Next day he discovered the family came from a part of Germany where sharing a bed with a guest in the interests of warmth and hospitality was an accepted custom. The following weekend Geraint stayed in the transit hotel!

Soon the long journeys began to take their toll. When a vacancy in the Music Department appeared, Trevor Harvey offered Geraint the position. He made his debut on BFN on Armistice Sunday in a programme called 'LAC Evans Sings'. As well as singing he became involved in producing music programmes, reading poetry and taking part in the various drama series. Living in Hamburg gave Geraint the opportunity to go to the opera. It was in the Garrison theatre he first heard Theo Hermann in *Der Rosenkavalier* singing Baron Ochs. Geraint wrote on the souvenir programme, 'Gosh, what an evening – great'.

Theo Hermann was to play an important part in Geraint's development as a singer. Arthur Langford was convinced he was not making the most of his voice and suggested he went to Theo for lessons. Three times a week Geraint did nothing but breathing exercises and scales. If Geraint did something that pleased Theo, his tutor would immediately embrace him and sometimes give him a kiss. If he got it wrong, he often received a slap across the face. However, the tutor had to be paid and Arthur had a whip-round among the BFN staff, who donated twenty-five cigarettes each per week, a fee Theo was happy to accept. When the time came for Geraint to be demobbed, he extended his service by another two months to complete his training with Theo.

By the time the first *BFN Bulletin* (BFN's *Radio Times*) was published, classical music was beginning to feature in their schedules. One of the regular contributors was the North West Germany Radio Symphony Orchestra. When the British authorities took over the direction of the German broadcasting system in the zone, it was decided that the network should have a permanent first-class symphony orchestra. Not only the zone but practically the whole of Germany was combed to find players of the highest quality and slowly the orchestra took shape with Hans Schmidt-Isserstedt as its conductor. Other orchestras to play in the Musikhalle during the last weeks of 1945 included the Hamburg Philharmonic (the orchestra of the Hamburg Opera).

The BFN Classical Music Department. Geraint Evans, Frank Daunton at the piano, Tony Foreman and Arthur Langford   (*Frank Daunton*)

Pte Frank Daunton was serving with the Middlesex Regiment at Mill Hill when he spotted the Army Welfare Service notice asking for volunteers to join Forces Broadcasting. He applied, took the course at Eaton Square, and was sent to BFN Hamburg where he was seconded to the Music Department. After a week's probation he was asked to stay on as the station pianist. As well as accompanying the BFN Chorus (which now included Geraint Evans), he became involved in 'Piano Playtime' and presented the Saturday night classical request programme called 'Orchestral Fanfare'.

Frank, who shared a room with Geraint, remembers him, 'blessed with an enormous voice which he used with terrific passion. He had a great feeling for music, but at this stage in his career, he could not sing softly. It was only after his lessons with Theo Hermann that he mastered the art of voice control. He had great presence and when he was around, you knew it.' Like the rest of his

Lale Andersen after one of her many recordings for BFN at the Musikhalle (*Alexander McKee*)

Sgt James Gibb, who replaced Frank Daunton as BFN's station pianist, was chosen to accompany Elisabeth Schumann on her Hamburg, Kiel and Berlin tour   (*Lady Evans*)

colleagues he spent many hours listening to the great orchestras performing in the Musikhalle and wondering how, on their meagre diet, they could cope with such major works as Verdi's 'Requiem'.

On 23 June 1946 Frank Daunton, Arthur Langford and Geraint Evans performed a concert in the School of Social Studies at 13 Neue Raben Strasse for the Army Educational Corps. Frank played Beethoven's Sonata in D Major, Opus 28 ('Pastoral'), Geraint Evans sang a group of Welsh folk songs and with Arthur Langford sang Purcell's 'Sound the Trumpet' and 'It Was a Lover and His Lass', by Thomas Arne. On another occasion the BFN Light Orchestra, conducted by Trevor Harvey and featuring James Gibb on piano, gave a concert of music by Bach, Sibelius and Vaughan Williams. When Frank was demobbed, he was replaced by James Gibb and in 1947 teamed up with James, Geraint and Arthur Langford for a concert at the Royal Empire Society's Hall in London.

Sgt James Gibb of the Royal Artillery had gone to the Musikhalle with some friends to listen to Beethoven's Choral Symphony played by the Hamburg Philharmonic and conducted by Eugen Jochum. Shortly afterwards he returned to Hamburg to hear the Army Chamber Music Pool perform. Among the musicians were artists he had known but had not seen for several years including Edmund Rubbra and William Pleeth. After the concert he discovered they had recommended him to Trevor Harvey as a possible performer. Unlike Geraint Evans, he was not asked to audition and shortly afterwards made his debut playing the piano. When his unit split up, he was posted to BFN's Music Department, and under the eagle eye of Arthur Langford he began to give talks about music and was soon helping to plan the serious music output.

He recalls his first winter at BFN. 'It was bitterly cold and Major Howard Hartog was running some excellent concerts for the servicemen. He had arranged for one of the principal German sopranos to give a recital. However, at very short notice I was asked to accompany her as her own accompanist had refused to play unless he was paid in coal. In those days everything was run by the Control Commission, who refused to authorize such a payment.' A similar request was made by the German soprano Margot Guillaume after she had sung Mozart's 'Exultate jubilate' with the BFN Light Orchestra, and again the request was rejected.

The bitter winters of 1946 and '47 finally brought about a cancellation of the Sunday afternoon concerts in the Musikhalle. BFN discovered that its heating had been cut off and the orchestras found it impossible to play in such conditions. When Elisabeth Schumann came to Hamburg in June 1946 to sing Lieder, James was asked to play the Sonata in F Sharp, Opus 78 by Beethoven before she sang. James recalls, 'She looked radiant from the moment she stepped on to the stage and when the concert was over she came across to me and put her arm round my shoulder and said, "James, concerts are only nice when they're over".' Working with Elisabeth Schumann was an experience which for James Gibb was to continue in Kiel and Berlin. On another occasion he was asked to accompany his friend Geraint Evans in one of his very rare Lieder recitals. James remembers that he sang 'Die Krähe' and 'Aufenthalt' by Schubert.

On 23 June 1946, in a Sunday concert, James Gibb played Mozart's Piano Concerto No. 23 in A. The concert was a real BFN affair with Capt Trevor Harvey conducting the North West German Radio (NWDR) Network Symphony Orchestra. When James Gibb was demobbed, he left BFN and later became Head of Piano Studies at the Guildhall School of Music.

When Sgt Ted Nash of the SIB was posted to the Music Department of BFN in 1945, he was asked to concentrate on the light music output. At the time, BFN had a light orchestra made up of thirty-five, often very cold and hungry, German musicians who were glad to come to the Musikhalle to keep warm, as did their German audience. When BFN had announced they were going to form an orchestra over 500 musicians applied, and the task of selecting the best fell to Trevor Harvey and Doctor Milo Karacz, who was to become the Orchestra's conductor.

Before the war Milo had been a lecturer in medicine at the Berlin University and an eminent consultant. He was a fine violinist and in his student days had his own orchestra called the White Ravens. This orchestra was re-formed in Hamburg in 1945 and accompanied Lale Andersen in her first BFN concert.

BFN Theatre Orchestra with conductor Milo Karacz   (*Lilo Karacz*)

After the war the Americans asked him to create an Opera Orchestra and to play concerts for the American troops. At one of these concerts he was seen by two British officers, John McMillan and Trevor Harvey, and was asked to form an orchestra for BFN Hamburg.

After Trevor left BFN, Ted Nash suggested that the name BFN Light Orchestra should be changed to the BFN Theatre Orchestra and should pursue a more popular line in music, and in March 1947 the new Theatre Orchestra began appearing at the Musikhalle in a series of concerts. Later these concerts would come from the Forces Club in Hamburg. Sometimes Ted would take an outside broadcast team to suitable locations. On one occasion in Wolfenbüttel, the Brunswick State Orchestra had decided to perform Tchaikovsky's Concerto in B flat minor in the Lessing theatre. When they arrived to rehearse they found the only available piano was the best part of half a tone sharp! Ted recalls, 'We persuaded the orchestra to tune their instruments accordingly and the soloist, Ferry Gebhardt, agreed to use the piano. We presented possibly the only performance of the Tchaikovsky Concerto in the key of B minor instead of B flat minor.' Nevertheless, the concert was much appreciated by the forces audience.

Ted arranged for the BFN Theatre Orchestra to give a concert in the repaired Opera House in Hamburg. They engaged the services of a beautiful young soprano called Anneliese Rothenberger, just setting out on her career which was to take her to many of the great opera houses of the world. Shortly after this they persuaded NWDR to become involved in a joint production of Kalman's operetta, *The Gypsy Princess*. Surprisingly, this joint production was only broadcast by BFN!

Ted Nash still recalls his first meeting with Wilhelm Furtwängler, who was returning to Hamburg for the first time since the end of the war. Dr Furtwängler's first question was 'What is BFN?' Ted explained what it was all about, but was somewhat staggered to hear that the great man was planning five days of rehearsal. This particular concert was recalled by Trevor Hill, who remembered looking out of his office window at an enormous queue of people who he assumed were queueing for food. Later he discovered they were waiting for the box office to open. In some cases the Germans were trying to sell some of their possessions to raise enough money to buy tickets to see Furtwängler.

Cpl Eric Blake RASC arrived at the Musikhalle to take up the post of Record Librarian on the day of the concert. He recalls, 'The Hamburg Philharmonic Orchestra responded magnificently, and the highlight of the programme was 'Death and Transfiguration' by Richard Strauss, the symbolism of which was not lost on the mainly German audience, who gave Furtwängler the longest standing ovation I've ever heard' – an ovation which according to Nan Pomeroy and Denis Shaw included a deafening chorus of 'Sieg Heil'.

Cliff Michelmore remembers another visit of the Maestro to the Musikhalle: 'He had asked to be collected from his hotel for his rehearsal. The only vehicle available was the station Volkswagen. After the rehearsal he complained bitterly to Alec Sutherland, the station director, and said he would not go back to his hotel in a "Beetle". We pointed out to Wilhelm Furtwängler that it was either the Volkswagen, the tram or he could walk! At this point we got in the car and started to drive away. As we looked back, we could see him jumping up and down in absolute fury. We circled the Karl Muck Platz by which time he had calmed down and he accepted our offer of a lift back to his hotel.'

Andy Warhol maintained that people were famous for fifteen minutes. This point was borne out by the number of servicemen and women who applied to BFN for an audition. To put the applicants at their ease, special blinds were fitted between the studio and the control room, where the producer sat unseen. The successful ones were given a fifteen-minute spot, either singing, playing a musical instrument or even the spoons! Margaret Yates, of the Control Commission Germany, was very friendly with its welfare and entertainments officer, Joseph Cooper, and they used to compete for a chance to play the only piano in the local Toc H club. Margaret had become a keen BFN listener and when she saw the notice asking for announcers at BFN, she went to the Musikhalle for an audition. She was not accepted but when she mentioned that she sang, she was auditioned again and offered a fifteen-minute recital which was scheduled to be broadcast on 18 December 1946. She was so nervous she did not tell her colleagues about the proposed broadcast and was very relieved when the producer at BFN decided to record the recital instead of letting her go 'live'. As she was staying overnight in Hamburg, she had no access to a radio, so she persuaded the manageress of the YWCA to let her listen to the broadcast. 'I was so shy I couldn't bring myself to admit I was on the radio, so I told her it was a friend singing. It was quite a shock to hear my voice for the first time, but my colleagues back at the CCG thought it went very well.'

Sgt Stanley Wyllie of the RAF was stationed at Air Division Headquarters, Detmold, when he was posted to the Variety Department in BFN at the end of 1945 as the staff organist. He often represented the department at the Monday auditions. He remembers one particular act which surprised everyone: a young serviceman, who had travelled quite a way, was asked which instrument he played. 'The spoons', he replied. At this point Stanley was asked to go into the studio and accompany him on the piano. Although he was very good, he did not pass the radio audition, but he would have gone down well if only BFN had had television!

Stanley's main duties were to present organ music programmes. The concert organ in the Musikhalle was not amenable to the lighter repertoire required, and so he was given permission to use the theatre organ in the Radio Hamburg

Sgt Stanley Wyllie at the BFN concert organ   (*Crown Copyright/MoD*)

Studios. However, it was impossible to rehearse during the daytime and Stanley could only use the organ after midnight. 'It was a rather eerie experience as, apart from the German caretaker, I appeared to be the only other person there. On finishing, it was back through the deserted streets of Hamburg to the BFN Sergeants' Mess with my Sten gun over my shoulder!'

There were three organ recitals a week called 'Theatre Organ Playtime', 'At the Theatre Organ' and 'The Organist Invites'. Among the many interesting guests Stanley had for 'The Organist Invites' was trombonist Don Lusher, who was playing with an army band that was broadcasting at BFN that week. He agreed to appear on the programme and he chose to play Schubert's 'Who is Sylvia?' and 'The Holy City'. 'I remember the Music Department were rather dubious about this unusual mix of organ and trombone, but they were the first to congratulate us upon hearing the result.'

The Berlin Philharmonic made their first visit to the Musikhalle in May 1948 when their conductor was Sergiu Celibidache. However, a problem occurred after the energetic Sunday morning rehearsal. The orchestra's spokeman approached Cpl Bryan Hodgson, of the Music Department, to check on catering arrangements. When Bryan pointed out that the canteen at BFN was only really geared up to provide light snacks and not the German version of a Sunday roast, he was told: 'Feed us or we will not play.' It was a demand that had to be met as the concert was a sell-out and the audience was already on their way to the Musikhalle. Somehow the canteen managed to produce enough food to satisfy the orchestra but not their conductor. Celibidache announced that he was going to change the running order of the concert. BFN was flexible enough to adapt the 'live' broadcast, but all the programmes for the audience had been printed. Ron Balaam, also of the Music Department, confronted Celibidache and told him he would have to stick to the agreed running order. 'He simply said, bitterly, that the players weren't getting enough to eat, and therefore could only perform the 'Pathétique' before the interval while they still had the physical strength for it.' That afternoon they played the overture to Weber's 'Oberon', Ravel's 'Rhapsodie Espagnole' and Tchaikovsky's 'Symphony No.6 in B Minor Opus 74'. It was interesting to note that the very comprehensive notes for the programme had been written by BFN's Music Department, which also arranged for the printing of the programme.

Ron Balaam found the actual participation as a producer of live programmes invigorating and occasionally hair-raising. 'We were broadcasting a concert, when I had to clarify something with the conductor about the second half. I just had time to dash down to the conductor's private room, only to be asked to leave because I had our young secretary with me to do the translation. Unfortunately the conductor was in the process of changing his trousers.' On another occasion Ron put himself at risk of a court-martial by indenting for an army truck and swearing it was for genuine service purposes. He got away with it, for the emergency was perfectly genuine as far as the Music Department was concerned. The BFN Theatre Orchestra's bass clarinettist was needed for one of the concerts and his village did not have a Sunday bus service. However, the military got their own back on the day that Ron had official clearance to move a harpsichord. Instead of a 15-cwt truck, they sent him the smallest vehicle in the unit.

If classical music had dominated BFN schedules in the early days, every effort was now being made by the programme planners to bring other kinds of music to the listener. The '1600 Club', created by Johnny Brandon, with its theme 'Bakerloo Non-stop', was proving one of the most popular request shows on BFN. John Jacobs, who had persuaded the composer of 'Bakerloo Non-stop', Ted Heath, to become president of his BFN Swing Club, also hosted the equally popular

'Saturday Night Swing Shift'. When Derek Jones took over the programme, he blended the music of Duke Ellington and Tommy Dorsey and added a weekly fifteen-minute special called 'The Kenton Korner'. So popular had the programme become with both British and German listeners that he was often asked to go to German youth clubs to talk about jazz and swing music. Many top British bands visited Hamburg during the late forties, including Geraldo, Eric Winstone, Teddy Foster, Vic Lewis and Ivy Benson. Derek recalls the rumour of the time was that Ivy had to sign an affidavit that her girls would not get involved with the British servicemen during their visit, much to the troops' chagrin.

When Derek came to present the '1600 Club', he recalled playing a request on the programme which caused a great deal of consternation. 'The card arrived asking for the very popular "Don't Smoke in Bed", by Peggy Lee. It had been chosen by three unit clerks and was dedicated to Charlie "Fuzzy Bristle" Britton. I played the request complete with dedication and thought nothing more of it.' Next morning, the telephone lines from Rhine Army were red hot.

After the concert in the Musikhalle, Duke Ellington joined some of the members of BFN at a party at the Bocaccio Club. Left to right: Billy Strayhorn, Jack Martin, Al Celli, BFN's Station Director Leslie Perowne, the Assistant Station Director Dennis Scuse, Joyce Scuse, The Duke, Hilda Pacey, Capt Neville Powley and King Stassio   (*Dennis Scuse*)

It transpired that 'Fuzzy Bristle' Britton was the OC of a unit in BAOR who, following a barrack-room fire, had banned smoking in bed! The Station Director of BFN issued a note: 'Unfortunate repercussions in official circles mean that, in future, no requests can be played unless a rank is given.'

Because of a boxing commitment, Derek was unable to attend a BFN Duke Ellington concert, which proved to be a smash hit. Duke Ellington was accompanied by Harry Carney, Ray Nance, Sonny Greer and Don Byas and they played to a packed Musikhalle. After the concert, the Duke accepted an invitation to join BFN for a party at the Bocaccio Club. As this club was a popular haunt of the members of BFN, loudspeakers relayed the output of the station into the bar. Every night BFN closed down with the National Anthem and as soon as the first notes of 'God Save the King' sounded, Duke Ellington was on his feet followed rather sheepishly by the rest of the Brits.

BFN's visitors book began to read like the *Who's Who* of show business. Benny Goodman, Dorothy Lamour, the Vienna Boys Choir, Danny Kaye, Donald Peers, Anne Shelton, Tino Rossi, Yehudi Menuhin, the Dagenham Girl Pipers, Leopold Stokowski, Carole Carr, Ted Ray, Sir Adrian Boult, Gracie Fields and Kirsten Flagstad, to name just a few.

In June 1952, the Swedish soprano was giving a recital based on the songs of Richard Wagner, accompanied by the NWDR/Hamburg Symphony Orchestra conducted by Hans Schmidt-Isserstedt. Kirsten Flagstad had received a bad press from the West Germans because she had visited East Berlin, but when Alastair McDougall, who was producing BFN's 'Mid-week Magazine', asked her to give an interview, she agreed. Alastair had assumed that the interval would be at 9 p.m. so went off for an early meal, only to discover that the interval had been re-scheduled for 8.30 p.m. When he returned, it was nearly over. He apologized profusely and suggested that they did the interview after the concert. 'No', said Kirsten, 'we will do it now and they [the audience] will have to wait.' It turned out to be an excellent interview!

Vernon Rees, who became head of the Music Department in 1950, remembers a recital given by Walter Gieseking when he stopped in mid-flow. Apparently a woman in the front row was turning over the pages of a different edition of the score. It so distracted Gieseking that he lost his concentration, walked down to the front of the stage and said: 'Madam, if you have to do that, do it somewhere else – I know the music!'

In those days, BFN had a small section responsible for copying scores for the instruments of the Theatre Orchestra. The members of this section doubled as performers. Gerhardt Kunisch was the orchestra leader, Leonora Gray was a singer with the orchestra when required and Axel Alexander, the chief arranger, was a fine pianist in his own right. There was also an elderly German lady

Yehudi Menuhin being interviewed by Chris Howland   (*Alexander McKee*)

affectionately known as Mutti, who in the beginning refused to speak a word of English but was won over by Trevor Hill.

The BFN Theatre Orchestra at this time consisted of thirty-five musicians. There were two conductors, Milo Karacz and Kurt Thiem, who were quite at home in the symphonic field where the smaller orchestra was sufficient. The orchestra had a sound similar to Mantovani's, with relatively small woodwind and brass sections. The Theatre Orchestra gave a considerable number of broadcasts for the BBC Light Programme. Occasionally, the orchestra was used for variety shows and was augmented to introduce a 'dance' or 'swing' element. When Donald Peers came to the Musikhalle, the Theatre Orchestra was conducted by Rae Jenkins.

Not everyone who came to the Musikhalle agreed to the BFN request to broadcast their concerts. The great Italian tenor, Beniamino Gigli, refused to allow BFN to make a recording unless his impresario was paid an exorbitant fee. Needless to say BFN, already known as 'bands for nothing', could not afford to pay. So great was the pressure for tickets that seats were placed on the platform, just allowing room for the singer and the piano, with a narrow corridor for Gigli to advance to and retreat from his singing position.

John Grey clearly remembers the night of a long-awaited Danny Kaye show: 'Danny Kaye was extremely famous through his films and his show was a 100 per cent sell-out; even the orchestra pit was full of standing customers packed cheek-by-jowl like sardines. He gave a magnificent one-man show, including all the well-known songs from his many films. It was a long show and nobody could blame him for instituting a break in the proceedings by moving down-stage to the roof of the prompt-box, sitting down, and inviting the audience to throw him a cigarette. He received more than one! There followed a stream of anecdotes until, rested, he resumed his performance.'

Shortly after Danny Kaye's visit, Bob Hope arrived in Germany to entertain the American troops. Cliff Michelmore was invited by the CO of AFN Bremerhaven to come along and record the show. Hope would not agree to the recording, but offered to do an interview with Cliff instead. In the quiet of his dressing room, Cliff recorded thirty minutes of brilliant non-stop humour and recalling it nearly fifty years later he can still remember the close of the interview:

> 'The camel as he turned around,
> Surveyed the mess upon the ground,
> To think that when I see it next,
> 'Twill be inside Camel cigarettes.'

When L/Cpl Philip Towell, REME, gave a talk in Studio E of Broadcasting House to the Anglo-German International Music Club, he did not realize that within a matter of weeks he would become a member of BFN's Music Department. Now he was able to listen to and watch such famous artists as Shura Cherkassky, Alfred Cortot and Walter Gieseking. Like all the staff at the Musikhalle, he would wander into the Concert Hall to hear these great musicians during rehearsal. He still recalls a row between Herbert von Karajan and BFN's station director, Leslie Perowne. Von Karajan had a rule: no visitors to the Concert Hall during rehearsals. Chris Howland, one of the Music Department's senior producers, had gone to listen to the orchestra (the Vienna Symphony Orchestra), when he was ordered out in no uncertain manner. Chris was furious and reported the matter to the Station Director. When Leslie entered the hall he was ordered out in the same rude way. At this point Leslie made it clear to von Karajan that the British Forces controlled the Musikhalle, and unless he apologized to Chris, the rehearsals were over. Initially, the German refused, but after thinking about it, relented and then got on with the rehearsal.

If von Karajan was difficult then Hans Schmidt-Isserstedt was the reverse. A man of infinite charm, he had spent the war in neutral Sweden before being brought back by the British authorities to build up the North West Germany Radio Symphony Orchestra. Philip Towell still remembers Dr Schmidt-Isserstedt fingering his sports jacket and commenting on the 'real Harris tweed', something which had not been seen in Germany for many years. Philip also recalled Wilhelm Furtwängler. 'This tall thin man seemed to control his orchestra by shaking his arms. There appeared to be no discernible direction to the musicians but on the night of a concert, he and they were brilliant.'

One Sunday afternoon, Philip and his Music Department colleague, Vernon Rees, were involved in an attempt to pre-empt NWDR. Normally on a Sunday, BFN would record the NWDR Symphony Orchestra's final rehearsal (before an audience) and broadcast the concert the following week, while NWDR would broadcast their concert 'live' the following evening. Philip had produced copious notes on the orchestra, the guest conductor, and the composers. All was ready for the 'live' junction, but something went wrong. What should have been a two-minute introduction lasted thirty minutes. The conductor, Sergiu Celibidache, a Romanian, had failed to turn up! The theory is that NWDR had found out about BFN's attempt to upstage them and reacted accordingly.

The Music Department often used the continuity announcers and presenters to introduce their various classical programmes. Bob Boyle recalls being asked by Trevor Harvey to introduce a programme of chamber music 'But I know nothing about chamber music', protested Bob. 'Don't worry,' said Trevor. 'I'll write the script for you. See you next Wednesday night in Studio B.' Came the fateful Wednesday and Bob, instead of being in Studio B, was at the local cinema with Nan Pomeroy. Next morning, he offered profuse apologies to Trevor Harvey. 'Don't worry', said Trevor. 'Same time next week?' Bob forgot again and never did introduce the chamber music programmes.

Nan was producing a 'live' concert with the BFN Theatre Orchestra. 'I was having a little trouble with my stopwatch, with the result that we were into the final number with about four minutes to go. I made frantic signs to the conductor, Milo Karacz, and with that magic a really good conductor can conjure up, he sent the orchestra back to a repeat halfway through the item and he managed to keep them playing for the full time without missing a beat. I think of that moment whenever I hear Leroy Anderson's "Fiddle Faddle".'

The tune 'Melodia' will always bring back memories of Hamburg for Trevor Hill. It was late in the winter of 1947 when he and his colleague Cpl John Weekes were returning from covering 'Operation Woodpecker' – an exercise in felling acres of trees in the Uelzen/Celle areas to provide timber for the people of Hamburg. They decided to stop for a cigarette when they heard the sound of a pipe-organ. It took them some time to find the source of the music, but after wandering through the rubble-strewn streets, they found Ferdinand Busso playing '*Hoerst du mein heimliches Rufen?*' (Do you hear my secret calling?). After exchanging several cigarettes, they persuaded him to play the tune again while they recorded it. A week later, Busso came to the Musikhalle and re-recorded 'Melodia' in the studios. It became the signature tune of BFN's late night show 'Slumbertime' which Trevor devised and introduced, with the Karl Rading Sextet providing the music and Tony Friese-Green reading the poetry.

The original pipe-organ recording of 'Melodia' was to feature three years later in one of the *Adventures of Samuel Poppleton*, originally written for BFN listeners by Margaret Potter. One of the episodes was set in Hamburg in 1913, and making his acting debut for the BBC in the role of young Poppleton was a Manchester Grammar schoolboy named Robert Powell. By chance this episode was heard by former BFN colleague Ray Martin, now conductor of the BBC Northern Variety Orchestra, whose vocalist at the time was a certain Jimmy Young. On hearing 'Melodia', Ray borrowed the original pipe-organ recording, which was then released by Columbia records in an orchestral arrangement by Norrie Paramor.

Mistakes sometimes happen in the best regulated circles. In 1948 the BFN duty engineer recorded in the station log-book: '22.18. Break in transmission. Main fuse gone in Studio E. Filled from Continuity. "BFN Music Shop" transferred to Studio B.' The drama began when the guitarist plugged his recently repaired amplifier into the studio power point. The German bass, who was making a guest appearance, was in full flow, but when the guitarist switched on his equipment, the studio went dead. The Engineering Manager dashed into the control room just in time to hear the duty announcer fill with a disc that sounded very like the original programme, so he assumed everything was back to normal. In the meantime, the musicians were rushing from Studio E to Studio B dispersing on the way the choir who had been working on Beethoven's 'Choral Symphony' only minutes before. Halfway up the stairs Neville Powley's xylophone disintegrated, the crooner, who was making his debut, almost passed out and the bass player suddenly developed a violent nose-bleed. Somehow they made it to Studio B and, as the red light went on, Leonora Gray, the soprano, tilted back the bass player's head and held up his music to the ceiling. The rest of the team carried on as if nothing had happened and the programme finished on time! For Corporal Trevor Holdsworth, the BFN pianist, now the chairman of National Power, it was a night to remember.

CHAPTER FOUR

Berlin – the Divided City

Berlin is a forgotten city – sadder still, Berlin is a prostrate and forgotten capital. A capital city in premature retirement, pensioned off before its time.

Alexander McKee – 1949

In 1945 Berlin was a shattered city. Its water mains had over 3,000 fractures and the emergency gas and electricity supplies worked intermittently. The centre of the city was a pile of rubble and splintered fragments of wood where once beautiful trees had stood. (Some of the linden trees in the Unter den Linden had been destroyed on the orders of Adolf Hitler in 1935 causing the Berliners grave concern as their unofficial anthem had predicted that, 'as long as the trees bloom on the Under den Linden, nothing can defeat us'.)

Berlin was a city where no bird sang, a fact that made an everlasting impression on the new arrivals. When Alexander McKee paid his first visit to Berlin in 1949, it was an experience that inspired him to write a series of talks for BFN called 'Outpost of the West' in which he described his first meeting with the Russians. 'As our Humber rolled towards the Red Flag hanging limply over the border post at Helmstedt, we would soon meet Ivan as an army: not as an individual or as a fantastic aberration conjured up by German soldiers. Here come the first two – ragged, brown greatcoats, brown fur caps with a red star, slung rifles with leather slings – they looked sloppy and scruffy; and eminently capable of living in the open fields in this bitter winter after the Blockade. The Russian post contains a neatly dressed officer, Lenin and Stalin in oil reproductions on the wall; on the table the Red Army version of *Soldier* magazine. There's a quick glance at our papers: two passes with a rubber stamp, a salute, and we are back in the Humber and on our way behind the Iron Curtain. Then we realized their radio had been tuned to the British Forces Network.'

Before he became BFN's record librarian, Eric Blake had served in Berlin since August 1945, as a member of 784 Car Company RASC. One of his first duties was to drive senior civil servants around Berlin as they searched for suitable accommodation: 'I remember visiting a house owned by a frail elderly

The Berlin postcard

(*Ken Scarrott*)

German couple and, as I spoke reasonable German, I had to give them notice to quit, telling them that they could take only what they could carry – a bizarre experience for a nineteen-year-old private soldier.'

The sector boundaries in Berlin were totally ignored by the Russians who toured the city helping themselves to anything that took their fancy. One such target was Eric's Humber Snipe staff car which they towed away from the British sector into East Berlin. 'There was a Court of Inquiry but as I still had the rotor arm it was accepted as proof that I had obeyed Military law and immobilized my car – I ended up with a token fine "pour encourager les autres". Despite representations being made, the rest of my car was never seen again!'

As in Hamburg, Berlin's black market thrived on anything that could be exchanged, from German army binoculars to the ubiquitous cigarettes. Wristwatches were the ultimate in luxury and a status symbol for the average Russian soldier. At the time, it was rumoured that the Russians would pay hundreds of Allied military marks, the Occupation currency, for a watch, only to throw it away once it stopped! It appeared that the Russians had no shortage of these marks because they had acquired duplicate plates for printing them.

Opposite Eric Blake's mess was a small public garden about the size of a London square. One day his lunch was interrupted by the arrival of some Russian lorries which proceeded to unload a number of rough wooden coffins. Russian soldiers quickly dug some shallow graves into which the coffins were bundled. The soldiers then drove back to East Berlin. The British protested and later the coffins were disinterred and reburied in the Russian sector.

Until the BFN engineers had installed a transmitter, the British troops had either the cinema or the theatre for their entertainment. Eric remembers the Sadlers Wells Ballet with Robert Helpmann and Margot Fonteyn performing dances from *Les Sylphides*, *Les Patineurs* and *The Rake's Progress*. When he left Berlin, after a spell in Neumünster, he received a letter from a former colleague, Patrick Wallace, about a vacancy at BFN and was duly posted there in 1947.

Two years earlier Ken Scarrott had finished installing the equipment in the Musikhalle when (in mid-November 1945) he was detached to Berlin to set up a transmitter for the British Forces. The old BLA 3 transmitter was installed in some fields in Ruhleben but the output came from BFN Hamburg, not by landline, as the Russians would not permit landline communications across their zone, but via

The British sector noticeboard   (*Alexander McKee*)

an FM link courtesy of the Americans through Hanover. Although there were turntables and a microphone available, as the unit lacked gramophone records and was out of the range of the BBC transmitters, BFN Berlin could not be operated independently. It would be another sixteen years before this would be achieved.

Just after Ken arrived in Berlin he was woken up by a rather wild-eyed colleague, who said he could not start up the transmitter because there was a body under the vehicle: 'I didn't believe him, but when I went to look there was a naked female body, so I put a blanket on her and went off to report the matter to the RMP. Their only interest was whether she was British! I pointed out that, as she had no clothes on, it might be difficult to say. Eventually the medics came and removed the corpse. Berlin was a wild place at the end of 1945, with shootings going on all around us.'

Douglas Brown was to take over the operation of the Berlin relay transmitter and was due to travel to Berlin in early December 1945. Previously he had been involved, as the programme engineer, in a series of recordings and programmes in the Musikhalle featuring Dr Milo Karacz and his Orchestra including, on 16 October, a concert with Lale Andersen. The day after the concert, Milo's wife arrived from Berlin. Travel through the Russian Zone was forbidden to Germans and those who did make the journey had to use clandestine methods. It certainly was not a journey to be undertaken lightly. When Lilo Karacz left Berlin, it took her two days of hitching rides on trucks and a night crossing of the border before she reached Hamburg. Learning of Douglas's impending departure for Berlin, Milo requested a favour: 'He asked me if I would take his wife back to Berlin.' There were two reasons for this request: one, her mother and small children were still there and two, he wanted his music, which was stored in Berlin, brought to BFN Hamburg. This request placed Douglas in a quandary. Although the fraternization ban had ended, the transportation of German civilians in military transport was certainly not encouraged. Douglas referred Milo to John McMillan. After listening to the request, he issued and signed the necessary movement orders and asked Douglas to arrange for Milo's music to be brought back to Hamburg on the vehicle's return journey.

On Wednesday 5 December, Douglas Brown, Vernon Clements and the driver set off in a 15 cwt Fordson Utility. Frau Karacz was in the back of the vehicle with Vernon. They travelled via Celle and Hanover to Helmstedt, the border post, where the British Military Police were not at all impressed with John McMillan's movement orders, but finally said: 'Be it on your own head, if you are caught by the Russians, we don't know you!' With Frau Karacz hidden beneath a pile of luggage and blankets, they set off for the Russian border post. After a rifle had been pushed through the window of the cab and much distribution of largesse in the form of cigarettes, chocolate and soap, which Douglas had had the foresight to carry with him, the Russians lifted the rear flap of the vehicle, saw only Vernon and waved them through. With much relief they set off up the autobahn and as there was so little traffic about, they were able to stop for sandwiches and coffee, finally arriving in Berlin just as it was getting dark. 'We dropped Lilo Karacz at her home, with a promise to call back for the music in three days time.'

With Berlin now part of the network, teams from BFN arrived to set up a series of outside broadcasts. In February 1946, Geoff Pexton came down from Hamburg to record the Berlin Philharmonic Orchestra which was using the church hall in Dahlem-Dorf, a suburb of Berlin, as a rehearsal room, and with Douglas Brown recorded Prokofiev's First Symphony, the 'Classical', on acetate discs. At the end of March 1946 Douglas returned to Hamburg after handing over the Berlin Relay Station to the Control Commission.

Ken Scarrott and Jimmy Urquhart covered an athletics meeting at the Olympic Stadium where they watched an unknown athlete win his event by a lap; his name was Emil Zatopek and in 1948 he won the Olympic 10,000 metre gold medal – again by almost a lap! Their other memory of this particular meeting was taking evasive action when a javelin went off course!

At the beginning of 1948 the Russians began to step up their pressure on the Allied zones in Berlin. American trains were stopped and searched and on 24 January the Berlin to Bielefeld train was held up for eleven hours. Road traffic was also halted. The reason given by the Russians was 'irregular documentation and other technical difficulties'. Next they accused the Western Allies of aiding and

Nick Bailey, the Berlin representative, with one of his many visitors, Miss UK – Carolyn Seward
(*Crown Copyright/MoD*)

abetting illegal traffic into Berlin. In April all secondary rail routes from Hamburg and Frankfurt were closed and all rail traffic had to be re-routed through Helmstedt.

Only one thing remained common to the four Occupation Zones – the Reichsmark and the hyper-inflation that went with it. On 18 June the Western Allies unveiled their plans to replace the Reichsmark with the Deutschmark. Gen Sir Brian Robertson, British Military Governor, wrote to his Russian counterpart, Marshal Sokolovsky: 'The economy of the British Zone is suffering acutely from the evils of inflation, and of economic stagnation, which our quadripartite proposals for financial reform were designed long ago to eradicate, and I feel that I am not justified in waiting any longer before taking remedial measures. I have, therefore, decided to include the British Zone in a scheme of currency reform to be introduced in the Western Zones on Sunday, 20 June 1948. Advance copies of the relevant laws will be sent to you. The British Sector of Berlin will remain unaffected by this decision.'

Sokolovsky replied: 'You have informed me of the decision taken by you to carry out a separate currency reform in Western Germany almost simultaneously with its practical implementation. This undoubtedly puts the Soviet Occupation Authorities in a very difficult position, and forces me to carry out urgent and necessary measures to safeguard the interests of the German population, and the economy of the Soviet Zone of Occupation in Germany.' The Russians acted, and carried out 'the urgent and necessary measures', and at midnight on 18 June the Soviet authorities closed their normal frontiers to all incoming passenger traffic from the West. The Soviet authorities then announced a currency reform in their own zone. Financial experts from the Four Powers met but they could not reach a satisfactory agreement.

Meanwhile the Russians announced that the railway line between Berlin and Helmstedt was in urgent need of repair. No freight or passenger trains would be able to travel on it until the repairs were carried out. On 26 June Sir Brian Robertson sent a letter of protest to the Russians: 'Under arrangements in force among the Occupying Powers, the British Authorities are responsible for contributing supplies for the population of Berlin. I am able and willing to discharge this responsibility, provided that my freight trains and barges are free to pass between the Western Zone and Berlin.' Two days later the Soviet Commander replied: 'As regards the railway line, Berlin–Helmstedt, the work on which has been temporarily suspended in view of technical defects, all measures in their power are being taken by the Soviet Transport Organisations, in order to eliminate these difficulties. I trust that this important railway line will recommence its work as soon as possible.'

The Services were able to follow the build-up to the Airlift through the BBC news bulletins carried by BFN. Cpl Nigel Davenport, who had become BFN's chief announcer, recalls that the Berlin Airlift provided him with one of his most exciting moments in radio. 'In those days, an announcer did three night shifts in a fortnight. He closed down the station, slept in the studio and opened up the following morning. I had just completed my last night shift when Alec Sutherland, the Station Director, called me in and told me that I was doing that night's shift. I tried to protest, but he ignored my comments. "As chief announcer, you *will* do the shift and I will come in at 6 a.m. tomorrow and give you a special announcement to broadcast." The next morning he arrived carrying a bulky envelope which contained the announcement that the Berlin Airlift was about to start.'

'Operation Knicker', the original codename for the Berlin Airlift, got under way. On Day 2 Trevor Hill, then in charge of the Features and Drama Department, decided that the event must be covered by BFN. Cliff Michelmore and Raymond Baxter were his reporters using, for the very first time, two of the German portable tape recorders since there was no room to fly in the mobile disc recorders which BFN had used up to this time. His feature on the Berlin Airlift was hastily assembled back in Hamburg and then broadcast by the BBC.

As there was still no sign of the vital railway line being reopened, the tempo was speeded up. In the beginning, the Allies estimated that West Berlin had just enough food to last one month and they would need to airlift 2,500 tons of food a day to meet the Berliners' requirements. By September, the Allies were flying in 7,000 tons daily – an average of 895 flights per 24 hours. To BFN this was still a major story and Trevor planned a documentary to be called 'Operation Plainfare'. Raymond would fly with the Royal Air Force from RAF Wunstorf and cover the land-based operation and at the same time Cliff would make the journey from the Elbe to the Havel in Berlin with the Hamburg-based 201 Sunderland Flying Boat Squadron. Cliff still recalls this flight into Berlin: 'I recorded a piece on take-off from the Elbe and another when we entered the corridor, with a final piece as we landed on the Havel. It was a bright moonlight night with wispy cloud, what we used to call a typical "bomber's moon", and the night sky was alive with aircraft. On the return journey we brought out people from the city.'

With the Airlift in full swing, the BFN reporters asked the Berliners what they thought about 'Operation Plainfare'. A young typist remarked: 'I have heard on the radio and seen in the newspapers about the planes which the Western Authorities are sending to Berlin, and I'm amazed at the great numbers which arrive.' A Berlin doctor said: 'In the Communist press the absurd idea exists that the Western Allies are not putting anything into Berlin but are removing everything they can by taking out machinery and all other valuable goods that are still here.' A Berlin housewife commented: 'I have two children, my husband was killed in the war. Can the British and Americans continue to bring enough food to feed my children? All we want to do is to try and rebuild our country like people in other countries. We want the four Allied Powers to come to an agreement, but we must never have another war.' 'Operation Plainfare' was the most important event to be covered by BFN since the war ended and it was the first time that BFN reporters had been given free access to cover a world event.

One of the most unusual stories to come out of the Berlin blockade concerned a colleague of Raymond Baxter, who woke up one night thinking he could hear the trains running again. When he went to his window all he could see in the pale lamplight were groups of Berliners, mainly women, moving bricks in a never ending stream, from one end of the street to the other. What he had taken for the sound of the train was the chorus of 'danke schön – bitte schön'. The Trummerfrauen's contribution to the rebuilding of Berlin was vital.

As news of the ending of the Blockade reached BFN Hamburg, Flt Lt Fred Pacey and Cpl Douglas Cooper of the Engineering Department made their way to the Helmstedt checkpoint and arrived at 3.30 a.m. on 11 May 1949. After discussions with the BBC, NBC and AFN it was agreed that the various teams would leave for Berlin at midnight on 12 May. As the barrier was raised, all the vehicles started off rather like a Le Mans 24 Hour Race. The BFN Humber 4 x 2 was full of outside broadcast equipment, and with Fred Pacey driving like a young Stirling Moss arrived in Berlin at 2 a.m. Although eighth in the overall dash, they had the privilege of being the first military vehicle to arrive.

In 1951 Flt Lt Ralph Barker, then on the strength of BFN, wrote a dramatized documentary called 'Airlift Anniversary' based on his experiences as an RAF public relations officer during the Blockade. Some of the facts and figures he produced made fascinating listening. During the airlift two RAF Yorks flew the Berlin Philharmonic Orchestra to Britain for a concert tour and then flew them back to Berlin as an airlift load. A Dakota from Lubeck carried, as part of its load, 'Taffy the Sixth', a goat, mascot of the Royal Welsh Fusiliers; a pedigree boxer dog, trained in Berlin and separated from its blind master by the Blockade, was flown out to Western Germany. With aircraft landing every three minutes, Ralph pointed out that if an aircraft was over thirty seconds late and could not catch up on its schedule, the pilot would have to turn round and fly back to his base as it was considered better to send one aircraft back rather than risk holding up the others. Coal made up 67 per cent of the total combined lift, and Ralph captured some of the airlift humour with a comment made by an American pilot over the R/T as he approached Berlin: 'Here comes a Yankee with a blackened soul, heading for Gatow with a load of coal.'

The Berlin Blockade had cost the Allies $200,000,000. One of the BFN announcers was also counting the cost of the blockade. Cpl Ron Balaam had left the 'comfort' of the RAOC depot at Glinde for BFN Hamburg. Instead of a barrack block, he had been living in the Kronprinz Hotel in the centre of

Hamburg with a chambermaid to clean his room and a private restaurant on the ground floor. With his weekly issue of free cigarettes, worth a lot of money on the black market, life was good, so he signed on for an extra year.

Three months later the Russians blockaded Berlin and the Reichsmark had been replaced by the Deutchsmark. For Ron, it was back to barracks because an organization considered to be more important than BFN took over the Kronprinz and in the new financial climate, his cigarettes had lost their value. He could no longer afford to go to the opera three times a week! 'The start of the economic miracle was good for Germany, but it meant extra greyness for me.' However, he still had his official title at BFN – NCO i/c Classical Music Department, BFN Hamburg.

Although the Forces in Berlin wanted their own radio station, this was not possible for a variety of reasons. In the late fifties, Ian Woolf, who had replaced Dennis Scuse as Station Director, realized that the Forces withdrawal from the Cologne area created a dilemma for BFN: 'The station was ill-placed from the point of view of audience involvement and local programme origination.' Therefore a studio was set up in the Signals Barracks in Herford followed shortly by one in Berlin. 'I wanted to set up more of these "collecting points" but shortage of money and staff were ever in the way.' Manning the studios was a major headache, but initially, Herford was operated by a member of the Royal Signals, Sgt Tony Plummer, on a voluntary basis. 'The same went for Berlin when Vic Andersen, who had helped out in Cologne, was posted to the city.' Until the MoD could be persuaded that a permanent member of the BFN staff should be posted to Berlin, Vic kept the supply of news items flowing down to Cologne.

On 13 August 1961 West Berlin taxi drivers complained that they were being stopped and questioned every time they entered or left the Soviet sector. It appeared that the freedom of unrestricted travel was in dispute. Later that same day, Berliners and the Allies alike looked on aghast as East German workers began to unroll barbed wire from lorries, under the watchful eyes of East German soldiers. The attempt to halt the flow of East German refugees had begun. Thirteen crossing points had suddenly been reduced to seven and the East Germans announced that the only Allied access point would be at Friedrichstrasse, to become known as Checkpoint Charlie.

By now 'The Wall' was dominating life in Berlin and during the Cuban Missile Crisis in October 1962, Berlin and the zone waited with bated breath. Alastair McDougall, whose posting to Berlin had finally been agreed with the MoD, had been joined by Alan Grace, who was covering a sports meeting at the Olympic Stadium, and they spent the night of 22 October listening to the activity just over the Wall. So grave was the crisis that children in Berlin were being prepared for evacuation while staff at BFN Cologne were facing a similar dilemma. On the

28th, the world stepped back from the brink when Mr Khrushchev promised that the Russian missiles based in Cuba would be dismantled and shipped back to Russia. For the Berlin representatives, life could now return to normal.

In July 1963, President Kennedy came to Berlin and visited the Brandenburg Gate and Checkpoint Charlie. He boosted the morale of the West Berliners with his 'Ich bin ein Berliner' speech. Four months later on 22 November Alastair McDougall had just got out of the shower and was listening to a non-stop music programme from AFN Berlin, when the programme was interrupted. 'News is coming through that an attempt has been made on the life of the President.' This was followed by an announcement that President Kennedy had died. Alastair's first reaction was: 'What a pity, I've already recorded Roving Report'. His next was to ring Peter Buckle, Senior Programme Director, in Cologne and alert him to the situation. At Alastair's suggestion, BFN's schedules were changed. At 8 p.m. they joined 'Radio Newsreel' and later AFN, who by this time had a direct line to America, and for the rest of the evening, BFN's programmes took on a more sombre sound.

The next day the BBC, which had changed its programmes as a mark of respect, reverted to their normal broadcasting and BFN did the same. This move caused an outcry among BFN's German listeners and Cologne was deluged with irate telephone calls. At one point the British Embassy in Bonn rang up and suggested that BFN's programmes should show more respect.

By the late 1960s the Berlin studio situated in the education block at Spandau was considered too far out from the centre of Berlin, and it was decided to move to Theodor-Heuss Platz, once known as Adolf Hitler Platz. Before the decision was finalized, Bryan Cave-Brown-Cave, the new Director of BFBS, decided to visit Berlin to see what the Military were offering as an alternative location. During the inspection of what had once been the officers' club shop, John Russell, the Senior Programme Director of BFBS Cologne, suddenly realized the director was no longer with them. Looking back, he spotted him on his knees, with a corner of the carpet turned back, busy counting the knots. 'Who owns the carpet?' asked Cave-Brown-Cave, 'The Military', came the puzzled reply. 'Well, when you move out all the other fixtures and fittings, can I put in a bid for the carpet?' According to the director, the carpet, so recently walked over by servicemen and their families, was priceless and Persian. Within days, it had vanished and no one knew of its whereabouts!

In September 1968 BFBS Berlin's Eddie Vickers produced a documentary called 'The Walled City', in which he talked to Berliners about their memories of the Blockade, and to the British Military Government experts who gave their view of the economic and political situation. He highlighted Berlin's success with some unusual statistics; every fifth electric light bulb, every fourth dress, and every third cigarette sold in the Federal Republic was made in Berlin. He ended his programme with the words of the late President John F. Kennedy and the famous quote: 'Two thousand years ago the proudest boast was "civis Romanus sum" [I am a Roman]. Today, in the world of freedom, the proudest boast is "Ich bin ein Berliner."'

Four years later, BFBS decided to mount a special Berlin week with a range of programmes culminating in the annual international carol concert from the Kaiser Wilhelm Gedachtniskirche involving choirs from America, France, Germany and Britain, singing their own carols to a congregation of around 1,000 people. The 'Six-Thirty' magazine programme, introduced by Don Durbridge, produced three special editions: 'Germany Bandstand', presented by Dick Norton, featured the Band of the 1st Battalion Worcestershire and Sherwood Foresters; Peter McDonagh's very popular Saturday show came from the Berlin studios and the 'Wednesday Folk' programme with Guy Francis featured a group called Terry Brenchley and the Boys.

Nick Bailey, now the Breakfast Show presenter with Classic FM, was posted to BFBS Berlin in 1977. 'Although the posting was fascinating, it was never going to be an easy one. Officially I was Cologne's Berlin representative, but I was conscious that the Berlin audience wanted more local material.' Like other reps before him, he found the quality of stars available for interview was staggering – from Liza Minnelli to Rudolf Nureyev to Peter Sarstedt.

During the winter of 1979 the temperature in Berlin dropped to -25°C. The West came to a standstill, but in the East they kept going. Something had to be done if the West was not to lose face, and it was decided that the school buses would operate regardless of the weather. All units were asked to co-operate and Nick Bailey suggested that BFBS Berlin should open up at 6 a.m. with a special breakfast show full of information for the families.

To Tony Orsten, the new BFBS reporter, Berlin was the most exciting city in the world, but then he was twenty-three, single and ready for anything! He could not believe that a city could be cut down the middle by a wall. How could the Germans on one side be so happy and contented, while on the other be so poor and wretched? 'I remember on my first day standing on a viewing tower looking over the Wall at the dismal grey buildings and the timid people. It was all too much. For the first time since my childhood, I cried – in public.'

BFBS Berlin ran a series of competitions for listeners with prizes donated by local German companies. These ranged from holidays to a hi-fi, or even a car. The most popular competition was 'Radio Roulette'. All the listener had to do was to select a number between 1 and 100 and when the wheel was spun, and a prize or forfeit was chosen at random, the listener had to answer a series of questions. On one occasion a young soldier chose the number which corresponded to the Star Prize, which was an all-expenses-paid holiday for two in Eilat, Israel. His first question was, 'Name the three seas which border Israel', and back came the answer, 'Red, Dead and Med'. The second question was, 'What is the name of the ceremony celebrated by Jews at this time of year?'; the caller replied, 'The Passover'. So to the final question – by now the young soldier was beside himself with anticipation – 'So for your holiday for two in Israel, please tell me the name of the communal family camps which are so popular in Israel?' After a long pause the would-be winner shouted out 'Kebab'!

When Chris Russell arrived in Berlin from BFBS Cologne in March 1983, he found Berlin had a remarkably different atmosphere from what was still known, in British military circles, even in the eighties, as The Zone (meaning the former occupation zone of Western Germany). It was an island life with memories of the Berlin Airlift still conjured up by the continued existence of the ration system, which was still strictly maintained in case the Soviets tried to cut West Berlin off again. The system run by the RAOC maintained a minimum of supplies and kept them topped up by selling off – at favourable rates – products of limited shelf-life.

Because Berlin operated at every level on a different scale from elsewhere, every BFBS Berlin representative was able to draw up an impressive sounding guest list of interviewees. Chris Russell's varied from George Segal to Pérez de Cuéllar, Edward Fox to Teddy Tinling, Sir Colin Davis to Salman Rushdie (before the fatwa).

Berlin's unique situation was often used by visiting politicians to the BFBS Berlin studios to make political statements, usually about the evils of communism and the dangers of the Soviet state. Michael Heseltine, then Secretary of State for Defence, during an interview, referred disparagingly to the peace protesters at Greenham Common (there had been a resurgence of anti-nuclear protests) and said, referring witheringly to the East: 'You won't hear much protesting over there.' At least the lift serving the fourth floor of Summit House was functioning when he visited but this was not always the case as, for instance, when James Callaghan, the former prime minister, visited Berlin to give a keynote speech to the British Chamber of Commerce. The interview was arranged for Saturday morning, the sniffer dogs had been to search for explosives and the route from the car park checked out – Saturday morning was going to be difficult with all those NAAFI shoppers sharing the building with BFBS. Because of security, the main lift was declared out of action and the former Labour leader had to be brought in with the Wrangler jeans and jars of Marmite via the NAAFI goods lift. Fortunately he took it well and the interview proceeded in a jocular fashion.

In 1987 Berlin celebrated its 750th birthday and was also the European City of Culture for that year. There was so much going on that the BFBS Berlin weekly programme meetings found the hardest decisions were what to leave out.

When the Queen visited Berlin for the first time in ten years, Her Majesty took the salute at the Queen's Birthday Parade. BFBS Germany covered the event and advised listeners to tune to German TV, which was also covering the parade, and turn the TV sound down and the radio sound up. Jon Bennett and Charly Lowndes commentated throughout with one eye on the Maifeld and the other on their portable TV. This was BFBS Berlin's first 'simul-cast'. Jon Bennett recalls looking across the Maifeld at the splendid sight of the 14th/20th Kings Hussars, who were formed up in line in front of the Olympic Stadium, while the queen's landau made its way to the dais. Jon's co-commentator, Charly Lowndes, remarked on how beautiful the grass at the Maifeld looked, particularly as the Military had manoeuvred their tanks across it. Jon kept quiet: 'I happened to know that the Garrison Sergeant Major had sent out a fatigue party early that morning armed with tins of paint and an order to cover up the tracks made by the tanks and paint the damaged grass green!'

In 1988 the Berlin Breakfast Show presented by Baz Reilly won the Small Market category at the Bicentennial Pater Awards organized by the Australasian Academy of Broadcast Arts and Sciences. In the best Small Market Local News and Current Affairs category, Jon Bennett's programme shared the award with ABC Radio Sydney.

BFBS Berlin had, for some time, been the envy of the other BFBS stations when it came to exclusive interviews. Robin Merrill, one-time lead singer with the Pasadena Roof Orchestra, was now working for BFBS as a reporter. In March 1989 Elton John came to Berlin to play the Deutschlandhalle and everyone wanted an interview with the star. Robin, along with the rest of the press, was backstage hoping for an interview before the sound checks got under way. Suddenly six 'heavies' appeared and moved everyone out of the dressing room area and ushered Robin into the inner sanctum. Apparently, what the rest of the press did not realize was that the Pasadena Roof Orchestra had once played for Elton John at one of his private parties. Robin recalls that Elton, unlike many celebrities who only talk about their latest record or book regardless of the question, listened to his questions and answered them in full.

The visit of the legendary Johnny Cash provided BFBS Berlin with one of its unusual stories. When he arrived at the studio, he was suffering with a bad case of flu but insisted on doing the interview, which was part of the BFBS London production, 'Simon and The Squad'. Also taking part in the programme was Stan Lee, the creator of Marvel Comics (Spiderman, etc.), and it appeared that Johnny was a big fan and was thrilled to be on the same show, albeit in a different country. Although his manager tried to get him to leave and rest before his concert that night, he would not go until the programme was over.

After Jon Bennett had interviewed Meatloaf, he was asked to organize a game of golf at the RAF Gatow golf club for the rock star and his manager. When word of Meatloaf's arrival at the Golf Club got around, he was besieged by autograph hunters and, unlike some stars who went to Berlin, he signed every single one.

On the 28th anniversary of the Berlin Wall going up, a West Berlin group called a press conference at the Checkpoint Charlie Museum. Just yards from East Berlin, the assembled journalists were suddenly introduced to thirteen young East German border guards who had escaped to the West. Patrick Eade, the BFBS Berlin rep, spoke to a nineteen-year-old called George: 'He told me that he felt the time had come to strike out for a better life. He had thought about the consequences on his family but decided that he would get away and hope for a reunion somewhere, someday.' When BFBS Berlin ran the interview, it stopped people in their tracks. Questions were being asked: 'Is this the start of a whole new era? Were the young of the East really going to decide their destiny? Could the communist ties be broken?'

The answer to this question began to unfold on the streets of Dresden and Leipzig that autumn. Tens of thousands took to the streets, inspired by the sight of other young people pouring into West Germany from Eastern Europe. They

Alan Phillips and Patrick Eade reporting from the Brandenburg Gate on the day the Wall came down   (*Charly Lowndes*)

were being welcomed as heroes. If the Hungarians and Czechs could do it, why couldn't they? The British in Berlin were concerned that the street protests could provide as big a challenge as the stand-offs between the Americans and the Russians in the early sixties. What could they do if the protesters rushed the Wall or Checkpoint Charlie and how would the East Germans react?

In the second week of November Erich Honecker, the East German leader, stepped down and Egon Krenz took over. On the Thursday evening a press briefing was enlivened when a government minister casually announced that travel restrictions for East Germans were being lifted. 'Did this mean that the people were free to leave East Germany?' The official replied that yes, he supposed it did. In a flash, that quote was broadcast. Thousands of people took to the streets and headed for Checkpoint Charlie. It was early evening and against this human torrent the East German guards were powerless. The German radio and television began broadcasting newsflashes and people were on the move. The West Berliners rushed to the Brandenburg Gate to see the East Berliners climbing on the infamous Wall and on to Checkpoint Charlie to welcome the 'Ossies' who were pouring through.

The full impact of this momentous occasion hit the BFBS Berlin team the following day. Patrick Eade recalls: 'It was a beautiful winter's morning and as far as I could see up the 17 Juni Strasse to the Victory column, hundreds of cars crammed with people were watching history unfold. On the eastern side, the sun's rays formed a cross on the glass of the radio tower. Was this an omen? The East Berliners had always maintained that this would be the sign that their city would be united once more.'

BFBS Berlin began to plan its coverage of the 'Fall of the Berlin Wall' at 10 a.m. Each reporter was given an area of the city to cover with the brief: 'Be back with something for the one o'clock news.' Alan Phillips had been on the breakfast show and had gone to bed early the previous evening and so slept through the excitement of the breaching of the Wall. Now he was to see the drama at first hand. His first deadline was to get the story from Checkpoint Charlie back to the studio in time for the one o'clock news. By now, Berlin was experiencing an enormous traffic jam. Car journeys that should have taken twenty minutes were now taking at least two hours. So Alan abandoned his car at the Hallesches Tor U-bahn and walked and ran to the Checkpoint. When he arrived, he found hundreds of people cheering the long line of East German Trabants and Wartburgs as they were driven into the West, even though by now this had been going on for about fifteen hours.

Having recorded a short descriptive commentary on what was happening, he realized that he could not get back to the studio in time for the news deadline, so he headed back to Checkpoint Charlie. The building on the Allied side was little more than a portakabin in the middle of the road with counters inside for

British, French and American Military Police, but it did have what Alan needed, a telephone. As BFBS Berlin had a high profile with the Allied community, he had little problem in persuading an RMP corporal to let him use the telephone. He called Summit House and prepared for his report. Just before he went on air, the feed of the station output disappeared from his telephone earpiece. He was able to confirm that the line to the studio was still there, and as the RMPs had their radio tuned to BFBS, he took his cue from the radio, and delivered his piece. Baz Reilly had taken off with Major John Ley in a 7 Flight Army Air Corps helicopter. From their vantage point 1,000 feet above the city, they could see the pages of history unfolding beneath them.

Meanwhile back in the studio, the atmosphere was electric, the phones and the faxes would not stop. Could BFBS help IRN, or BBC Radio Leeds, or Thames TV or BBC Radio Solent, who had a ten minute question and answer session with Patrick Eade at the Brandenburg Gate? BBC Radio 1 rang to enquire whether Simon Bates could present his morning show from the BFBS studios the following Monday.

Also in action were Cathy Hulett covering the Staaken Crossing and June Wilde, who had gone for a walk on the Glienicker Bridge, past the spot where the spies were exchanged at the height of the cold war, with her Berliner husband. She reported on the opening of the bridge for the first time in 40 years. Normally you couldn't get near the Glienicker Bridge for border guards and barriers, but now all had changed. As June reported: 'One man from East Berlin is riding a horse across the bridge, while others are making the journey on foot.'

That lunchtime news bulletin was compelling listening. The only story was Berlin. Patrick Eade recalls: 'The Brigade Chief of Staff came on the air to appeal for calm in the British Sector. "There is still a job to be done and we must all be watchful and steadfast." At the time, I thought how very British!' Later, assorted politicians and diplomats would have their say.

After Checkpoint Charlie, Alan Phillips set out for the Brandenburg Gate. Along the way 'wallpeckers' were already at work chipping away at the concrete with hammer and chisel. The stretch of the 17 Juni Strasse leading up to the wide semi-circle of wall in front of the Brandenburg Gate was packed with people. The Wall here was five or six feet wide and not as tall as elsewhere, so he was able to climb up and see both sides of Berlin. After his return to ground level, an RMP captain gave him the lead he needed for his report from the Brandenburg Gate. Former Chancellor Willi Brandt was standing in the middle of a group of people on a small platform which had been set up by one of the television companies. Willi Brandt had been Governing Mayor of West Berlin when the wall went up in 1961, so his appearance was a radio-man's gift. When he spoke to Alan Phillips, his voice

A 'wallpecker'

(*Andrew Carnall*)

was full of emotion as he stood close to the Brandenburg Gate with the excitement and the cheers all around ringing in his ears.

Once again, Alan's problem was to try to get back to the studios through the traffic, which was getting more congested as the hours went by. He decided to take a taxi and the normal ten-minute run took just an hour, but sitting in the back of the cab he was able to mark the tape inserts and write his script. Although that was his last report for the day, he continued to soak up the atmosphere of this historic occasion. He went to the Falkenseer Chaussee to see a West Berliner doing a bit of DIY on the Wall with his power drill. The man managed to knock out one section before being stopped by the West Berlin police.

Alan then drove to Bernauer Strasse, one of the most moving places in Berlin. Here, when the wall was erected, the border ran along the pavement on one side of the road, so the line of tenement buildings just inside the East became part of the wall itself, while the edge of the pavement was in the West. The first person to die because of the Berlin Wall died here. Twenty-eight years later the Wall at Bernauer Strasse was coming down, the air was full of the sound of pneumatic drills, hammers, falling scaffolding, and cheers whenever something happened. Over in the East, Alan could see residents in the blocks of flats watching with candles burning in their windows. At around 10 p.m. the first section of Wall was lifted.

That weekend, the Wall continued to fall, with pieces being extracted like bad teeth as the Berliners hammered away at the remnants. In Potsdamer Platz, the centre of pre-war Berlin, Robin Merrill interviewed the West Berlin Mayor, Walter Momper, by standing in front of the door of his car so he could not get in. As the East German border guards put down their weapons, roses and carnations were placed in the barrels of their rifles. Later Robin recorded an interview with Crosby, Stills and Nash, who had travelled from a concert they had given for UNICEF in the United Nations building in New York, to witness history being made. In the shadow of what was left of the Wall, they spoke to Robin: 'For too long we have all lived under the shadow of this apparition but now it's gone. Not by a tank, or a B52 bomber or an army, but by the people.' Later they sang their old 1983 hit 'Chipping Away' against the backdrop of the Brandenburg Gate.

On that Saturday lunchtime the whole BFBS Berlin team was still buzzing with excitement. Mary Walker reported from the Ku'Damm that many of the shops were accepting East German marks. Baz Reilly still recalls the postcard from Kurt Lehmann which read: 'British friends! We don't want to miss thanking you for your interest and Mrs Thatcher for her will to help the refugees from the DDR. We know where our friends are. Sooner or later we'll make it up to you. The best of luck to you all!' By Monday most of the East Berliners had returned home and the streets of West Berlin were empty of Trabants and Wartburgs. For Baz Reilly and the team the next project was the

Simon Bates Show, which was carried by both BBC 1 and BFBS. After that BFBS resumed what might be called 'normal service'.

The Berlin Wall disappeared as if rubbed out by magic and BFBS could continue with its normal run of stories. During the days that followed, BFBS Berlin produced a number of special programmes: 'The Rise and Fall of the Berlin Wall', the following June, 'Charlie Comes in from the Cold – the Closure of Checkpoint Charlie' and in October 1990, 'Unity Day'.

In a letter to *Sixth Sense*, the Forces newspaper, Angie Dring summed up the feelings of many of the listeners to BFBS. 'The team, Baz, Alan, Patrick, Robin and Jamie managed to convey a lot more than the facts. They succeeded in getting across the sheer joy and amazement that most Berliners must have been feeling.'

On 15 January 1991, the Gulf War started and the Headquarters of Berlin Brigade was concerned for the morale of the wives whose husbands were serving in the Gulf. 'BFBS Germany decided to go "live" on a twenty-four-hour basis with each of the smaller stations, Hohne, Osnabrück, Paderborn and Berlin providing a presenter for the "grave-yard" shift.' Richard Jones, who had arrived a year earlier, found himself presenting the midnight to 4 a.m. programme on a Saturday night/Sunday morning. At the time BFBS Berlin was waiting to move from Summit House to the new studios in Spandau. The NAAFI had already left Summit House, but the tills and shelves were still in place, giving it an air of the *Marie Celeste*. The response to Richard's late night show was excellent, but most of the calls came from Berliners, who were rather taken with the idea of a 'live' late night voice.

When BFBS Berlin moved back to Spandau, it was to the old officers' block that had been used by Rudolph Hess's guards. The architect was given a free hand and the result was certainly the most luxuriously appointed studio that BFBS had. All wooden fixtures were solid oak and the main door handles were specially cast replica nineteenth-century fittings which cost hundreds of marks each. The building was affectionately known as the 'Hess Hess Vee See' and it was close to the new NAAFI, which in turn was known as 'Hesco's'. As soon as the restoration was completed, the news came that within two years everyone would be moving out of Berlin.

Aidan Donovan arrived in Berlin in January 1992 and found the staff in buoyant mood despite the threat of redundancy. Although July 1994 was still a long way off, the record company representatives were no longer as keen to get their stars on a radio station that was preparing to leave Berlin. However, the listeners remained loyal and their enthusiasm never waned. Former East Germans who had listened to BFN when the Wall divided the city were among the station's many visitors. BFBS Berlin had started in Spandau in Schmidt-Knobellsdorf Strasse in 1961 and ended on 15 July 1994, three hundred yards away in the warder's block of Spandau Prison.

For Peter McDonagh, SSVC's Director of Broadcasting, it was a very sad occasion. He had been born in Spandau, had lived in Berlin for his first twenty years, had cut his broadcasting teeth in Berlin in 1969 and met his wife Moo in the city that he had come to know as his home town. 'It was inevitable following the disappearance of the Berlin Wall and German unification, the four post-war powers agreed a timetable to pull out of Berlin. The schedule allowed for occupation costs for the Allied Forces to be paid until the last Russian, and therefore the last Allied serviceman, had left the former divided city. As we in BFBS had a remit to broadcast to HM Forces – when they left, we had to go, too.'

When he arrived in Berlin for the closedown Peter found that his Berlin pedigree ensured a great deal of media interest. 'My German had become a bit rusty after many years away and suddenly I found myself in the TV studios of the Sender Freies Berlin giving an interview about my life and times in "Jinglish", a mixture of English and German, overlaid with a very thick Berlin accent. The interviewer was amazed and just wanted to hear this strange Irishman continue to murder his language!' Afterwards Peter went back to the BFBS studios where he was the subject of the last interview on BFBS Berlin. 'Most of what I said is a blur. I tried not to sound over-nostalgic but when Aidan asked me what my most memorable experience of the Berlin studios was, I told him my first child had been conceived in BFBS Berlin! Our MD almost choked on his beer! My real problem was what to say at the end. I told the audience that to say Auf Wiedersehen – see you again – would not be proper, as it implied that we would be back, and of course we could only come back if our troops were stationed in Berlin again. Luckily, there was a light-hearted way of saying goodbye – more like cheers – which I thought would fit the bill. So, as the studio filled with people, we had a count-down, the champagne corks were popped, and I said a final "Tschuss". The second that BFBS went silent, the engineers were already dismantling the microphones which had broadcast a "Very British Service" to thousands of troops and millions of Berliners for over thirty-three years.'

BFBS Berlin had reflected the dramatic history of the city. As the cold war years drew on, the station became a vital element in West Berlin's identity as a small pocket of freedom behind the Iron Curtain. BFBS Berlin captured a huge audience beyond the British garrison, playing the latest UK hits and interviewing almost every notable visitor to the city from Ray Charles to Peter Ustinov and Margaret Thatcher. They had all shared their thoughts with the BFBS Berlin listeners. Whenever Berlin was in the news, from President Kennedy's visit to the city in 1963 to the fall of the Berlin Wall in November 1989, BFBS was there.

All that was left was to return the equipment to the Berlin Senate, the governing body, for auction, and dispose of the record library. Many of the archive tapes were donated to the German Historical Museum, so in the years to

Baz Reilly with Robin Merrill interviewing top pop group Bros   (*Crown Copyright/MoD*)

come visitors to Berlin would be aware of the part played by BFN and BFBS. To the Germans, the passing of BFBS Berlin was a sad occasion and their letters bore a testimony to the station's popularity. Bernd Beyer wrote: 'There were no walls when there was BFBS and it is, for me and my friends, a great tragedy that after 15 July there will be no more BFBS Berlin. Thank you for making the darkness brighter, keeping our spirits up and giving us a sense of well-being.'

Heidi Brauer was one of the many East German listeners: 'As an East German, BFBS opened up a whole new world. Of course I could not physically leave East Germany, but every time I listened, I was spiritually in the "Free West". No East German policeman or Stasi official could get in the way of this feeling.' At the time Heidi was living 60 kilometres from Berlin and at times, reception was poor. To keep in touch with the Free West, she recorded the output on cassettes and because of the constant threat of a visit from the Stasi, she wrapped the tapes in tinfoil and buried them in the garden. 'Whenever I wanted to listen, I dug them up again.'

Although the studio had closed, the transmitter was to remain 'on air' for another five months. On 12 December 1994, Richard Hutchinson introduced the last programme that would be heard by the Berliners. The last request in that programme went to all members of 16 Regiment RA and raised 606 DM for the Wireless for the Blind Fund. Its title was very apt – 'The Long and Winding Road' by the Beatles. Richard's closing announcement expressed BFBS's thanks to all the people of Berlin for their support and friendship over the years. After bidding them all a fond farewell, he ended the programme with the BFBS theme – 'Force One'.

CHAPTER FIVE

Hamburg – the Final Years

I felt BFN was classless, and apart from submarines
I have never known an organisation to pay less attention to rank.
It was a case of what you could do, not who you were.

Sir John Harvey-Jones

When I asked Raymond Baxter which of his many BFN broadcasts he could still remember I fully expected him to mention his reporting of the Berlin Airlift in 1948. However, it was his coverage of the return to Hamburg of a Jewish refugee ship that had the biggest impact on him. 'They had left Germany so full of hope for their new home in Palestine, now, dejected and bewildered, they were ferried by British soldiers from the docks to their next home – another displaced persons' camp.'

For the serviceman in Germany 1948 not only saw the start of the Berlin Airlift, but the arming by the Russians of the East Berlin Volkspolizei. Elsewhere British troops left Palestine for the last time. In December of that year, National Service would be increased from 12 to 18 months. The ATS and the WAAF had become the WRAC and the WRAF. The first Oxfam shop opened in Britain and BFN's sports programmes reported the 'failure' of Don Bradman in his final test match at the Oval and that a new sporting heroine had arrived on the scene. The Dutch housewife, Fanny Blankers-Koen, won four gold medals in the London Olympics – the games to which the Germans had not been invited. Geoffrey Webb, who had until recently been looking after the BFN Film programme, was now working on the script of 'Dick Barton – Special Agent' and was faced with the new BBC guidelines: 'No swearing, the hero must not tell lies, only clean hits to the jaw and sex would play no part in the production.'

Alec Sutherland had taken over as Station Director from John Humphreys and he followed many of the policies laid down by John McMillan. Although never very keen to face the microphone, his was the voice that announced the currency reform details and took the part of 'Jock' in the educational programme, 'German Without Tears'. One evening, shortly after he arrived, he was working late in the

Musikhalle with Cliff Michelmore. As Cliff recalls: 'Alec heard a strange noise which seemed to be coming from below his office in the region of the Transport Department, so he decided we should investigate. A check on the transport area revealed nothing, but the noise continued. This time we were convinced that the source lay below us in the cellar. As we descended the stairs we could see a chink of light beneath a door. We went in and found a group of mothers and their children. At the end of the room was another door and inside we found a man in a white coat examining a child. All he had was a single light and an enamel bowl which he filled from a cold tap. Alec asked him who he was and what he was doing. "I am a paediatrician and I have nowhere to practise. My friend, Dr Milo Karacz, the leader of the BFN Theatre Orchestra, said as no one used this part of the cellar, I could set up here." Alec Sutherland's comment was typical of the man: "Don't worry, we'll see what we can do to help." The next morning, the Quartermaster, Captain Jim Coles, was tasked with giving the doctor hot water, heating, tables and chairs. The surgery continued for several months. The Military never discovered the "extra welfare" provided by BFN Hamburg.'

Alec possessed an impish sense of humour. BFN had its own rather special gremlin called 'Athelstan Gurney Smeed', who usually appeared on shift with

Alec Sutherland, BFN's Station Director during the Berlin Airlift   (*Alexander McKee*)

Anne Shelton being interviewed by Keith Fordyce   (*Keith Fordyce*)

Nigel Davenport – BFN's Robin Hood
(*Gordon Savage*)

Sgt Bob Boyle, one of the first servicemen to be recruited by BFN, better known today as Robin Boyle, presenter of 'Friday Night is Music Night'

Tim Matthews and entries would appear in the log book explaining that only five pips had gone out because 'Athelstan' had swallowed the sixth! Ron Balaam recalls his demise: 'Athelstan brightened our lives because he alone carried the can for every blemish in any broadcast. Not even the "powers that be" dared to interfere with our gremlin until the tragic day when the log book was opened and we saw (in the writing of Alec Sutherland) the sad announcement of Athelstan's passing away, authenticated by a sketch of his tombstone.'

Gordon Savage had been serving with the RAOC initially at the Volkswagen factory in Wolfsburg and later at Bad Oeynhausen, when he spotted the advertisement in *Soldier* magazine inviting interested personnel to apply to BFN for an audition. As he had a hankering for the entertainment business, he applied and was successful. In 1948 the news pattern was: news from the UK via the BBC link, the CCG (Control Commission Germany) news followed by the BFN news. Gordon remembers the day when everything changed in Germany: 'The CCG newsreader came in with a sealed envelope and a guard. His instructions were to open the envelope when the microphone was "live", which he did. He then informed our listeners that the Reichsmark would no longer be legal tender after midnight. Holders of the Reichsmark would be able to go to their banks the next day and exchange a certain number for the new marks, but many, especially the black marketeers, were stuck with millions of worthless Reichsmarks.'

The advent of the Berlin Airlift meant that all staff were working long hours, but as Gordon recalls: 'We found them enjoyable because the camaraderie was excellent.' After a time Gordon was introducing the excellent Saturday night concerts from the Musikhalle and his career as an announcer appeared to be going well until one Sunday night when the lines failed, just before the start of a 'live' church service. 'In the studio we kept a spare church service for just such emergencies. I grabbed the reserve, apologized for the loss of the "live" service and spun it in. To my horror, what the listeners heard was a programme by Fred Waring and his Pennsylvanians. Unfortunately Raymond Baxter was listening and I was relegated to become an assistant in the Presentation Department under Kit Plant.'

Gordon shared a billet with Pte Nigel Davenport, who had been serving in the orderly room of an RASC unit near Dortmund when he too spotted the circular asking for volunteers to join BFN Hamburg and he decided to apply for the audition, which was conducted by Raymond Baxter. To his delight, he passed. Although Nigel had no previous knowledge of radio he quickly became aware of the expertise of those around him, many of whom had BBC experience. He began to feel that he was taking the first steps on the road to acting. His breakthrough into radio acting came when he was chosen to play the part of Robin Hood in the serial, 'The Adventures of Robin Hood'. It was so successful that when a party of schoolchildren visited the studios at BFN, their first request was to meet Robin Hood. 'At the time I was suffering from a bad attack of acne and so Trevor Hill, the producer, felt it would be kinder all round if he made my apologies whilst smuggling me out of the back door. A spotty-faced Robin Hood would shatter their illusions.'

Today he is known as Keith Fordyce, but in 1948 as LAC Keith Marriott of the Hamburg Movements Unit, he was posted to BFN Hamburg. Up until this point the highlight of his service career seemed to consist of counting crates of Bovril destined for the NAAFI. When it was decided that BFN would increase its number of RAF personnel, Keith applied for a post and was sent to BAFO for an interview with several senior RAF officers and Raymond Baxter. He felt he had done well until he was asked whether, instead of going on to university, he might like to consider a full-time career with the Royal Air Force. When Keith declined, he thought his chances of joining BFN had gone. However, like Sgt Bill Crozier, he was successful and was soon being greeted at the Musikhalle by Sgt Kit Plant. At the time, Keith wanted to go into 'features and drama', which he considered to be the creative side of radio, but as Nigel Davenport, Brian Matthew and Kit Plant were going on demob, he was earmarked for 'continuity and news reading'. Keith still remembers Raymond Baxter's words after his news-reading audition: 'You're not exactly God's gift to radio, but we'll make something out of you.'

Keith felt you were expected to be perfect from day one and any young announcer who made a mistake on air was moved into a non-broadcasting part of the organization. He recalls one announcer who was making his first continuity announcement. He was expected to go from the padre's talk straight to the BBC Home Service for the news. The padre was a poor broadcaster. There was no script or timing with his tape and as he droned on towards the pips, the young announcer realized that he would have to cut the padre if he was to get into the news on time. He managed, by the skin of his teeth, to join the BBC, but unfortunately in his panic he had omitted the pips and the actual broadcast had gone: 'And Jesus said to the Disciples – this is the BBC Home Service'. That young announcer was removed from continuity and sent back to writing scripts.

During the early part of Keith's time at BFN the black market was still in operation and on one occasion local dealings got in the way of programme making. Keith was in the continuity studio when he realized that the programme was under-running and he did not have a suitable piece of music to fill the gap. He phoned the Record Library and spoke to the German assistant librarian and explained his problem. 'Otto, I need the record right now.' 'Herr Marriott, I'm very sorry but I cannot come now as I am selling cigarettes and chocolate for the Religious Department!' Like many other members of BFN, Keith used the black market to buy new tennis racquets.

Raymond Baxter referred to Padre Bob Crossett as the man who invented the art of religious broadcasting. The charismatic Ulsterman became an integral part

Padre Bob Crossett, head of BFN's Religious Department   (*Alexander McKee*)

of life at BFN Hamburg. He could be found not only looking after religious broadcasting but recording poems for 'Poets' Corner', playing cameo parts in Alexander McKee's productions and producing his own programme called 'Anthology'. He knew the word anthology would be associated in most people's minds with a collection of verse, so he set out to feature what he described as beautiful, helpful and cheering quotations, ranging from Homer and the Song of Solomon to modern-day philosophers. As with most of his work, the programme was an immediate success.

Throughout Bob Crossett's time at BFN the OB teams could often be found broadcasting church services from around the zone. Douglas Cooper, who was one of the OB engineers, recalls a church service in the Garrison Church in Hamburg when the Chaplain to the Forces, Bishop Cuthbert Bardsley, was visiting Germany. 'It was quite a complicated microphone set-up because church dignitaries usually like to have colleagues giving different readings, etc. I was in the vestry with an unseen array of microphones and trying, for once, to follow the proceedings. After the service the bishop came in to see me and said: "How did it all go?" I assured him that it went very well, and then, to my amazement, he slipped me two half crowns as a tip!'

In November 1948 BFN conducted some listener research and the top six programmes were: '1700 Club', 'Family Favourites', 'Have A Go', 'Saturday Swing Shift', 'Tango Time' and 'Round the Records'. Other programmes popular with the Forces listeners were 'ITMA', 'Variety Bandbox', 'Much Binding in the Marsh', the two early morning programmes 'Wakey Wakey' and 'Sunrise Serenade' and two programmes with the unusual titles of 'Hill Billy Gasthaus' and 'Canteen Break'. Several listeners remarked there was not enough dance music on BFN, and one irate female producer on the BFN staff complained the listener research forms seemed to encourage certain members of the audience to return anonymous and crudely written forms which, she pointed out, 'would fascinate any psychiatrist'!

At the end of the war Bill Crozier, along with seventy other members of 2805 Squadron RAF Regiment, found himself guarding around 2,000 members of the German Luftwaffe, most of them women! During the days that followed, Bill's biggest problem was keeping the RAF boys away from the German girls! Shortly after this he was posted to RAF Schleswig and in the evenings used to entertain the patrons of the Malcolm Club at the piano. News of his prowess quickly spread and, following a visit to BFN, Bill was invited to return for an audition conducted by Pte Laurie Gray and was passed as suitable for broadcasting, but before he could record his first series of 'Piano Playtime' he was posted back to the UK on a SNCO course.

When he returned to Germany in 1948 he joined 2817 Squadron at RAF Wunstorf. For a man who was later to be recognized as having one of the quietest

Bill Crozier   *(Joan Crozier)*

voices on radio, he quickly became known as the 'Little Bastard of Wunstorf' for his ability to be heard across the parade ground. In his spare time he continued playing piano in the Malcolm Club and was once again recommended for an audition with BFN. However, when he arrived in Hamburg, Bill pointed out he had already passed an audition in 1946, so was immediately signed up for 'Piano Playtime'. At the same time Raymond Baxter told him BFN was about to increase its RAF establishment and he should apply for a full-time posting.

As 1948 drew to a close BFN produced a Christmas Special linking the various parts of the zone. The programme was called 'Christmas Among Ourselves'. It started with a visit to Prince Rupert School at Wilhelmshaven, on to Hameln to meet members of the CCG, then to a link with the Americans who were working on the Berlin Airlift at Fassberg. Next the programme called up British servicemen stationed in Berlin before moving down to Cologne to hear about the completion of the first permanent bridge across the Rhine and a Christmas message from the Archbishop of Cologne. This was followed by Christmas greetings from the Army Commander, Lt Gen Sir Charles Keightley. The final message in the programme came from the C-in-C, Sir Brian Robertson. Cliff Michelmore, who was producing the Special, recalls how they came to link to the C-in-C. 'We had decided that we needed a "squaddie" in the programme, so Gunner Jimmy

Cliff Michelmore recording Gunner Jimmy Cabane's Christmas message   (*Crown Copyright/MoD*)

Cabane, a Cockney from Plaistow, was chosen. After explaining how he and his friends would be spending their Christmas, this chirpy Cockney introduced the C-in-C. "As well as wishing everybody a Merry Christmas and a Happy New Year, I want to say a special Merry Christmas to the Military Governor and Commander-in-Chief. To Sir Brian Robertson, from all the lads down in Düsseldorf, the Ruhr and the Second Div. – a real good Christmas".' The programme ended with a carol from the children at Prince Rupert School.

After two years as station director, Alec Sutherland returned to the BBC and was replaced by Leslie Perowne, one of the original pioneers of Forces Broadcasting in North Africa. Leslie had also served with Forces Broadcasting in Italy, Greece and Austria. He was a lover of classical music and in 1950 he covered the first post-war Passion Play in Oberammergau.

In 1949 the BFN programme schedules included the new series of 'Dick Barton – Special Agent', 'The Adventures of PC 49', 'Hi Gang' with Ben Lyon and Bebe Daniels, 'Stand Easy' starring Charlie Chester, 'Twenty Questions' and Valentine Dyall's 'Appointment With Fear' (billed in the *BFN Bulletin* as 'spinal refrigeration'!). The visit of T.S. Eliot to BFN resulted in a fifteen-minute special in which the distinguished poet recited part of 'Wasteland', 'The Hollow Men', and 'How Unpleasant to Meet Mr Eliot'. The programme, introduced by Cliff

Michelmore, was a coup for BFN as T.S. Eliot had been on a tight schedule. Another special came from the Garrison Theatre in Hamburg, when Vera Lynn and the REME Band put on a concert for the Forces. Finally, one of the more poignant highlights of the year was Frank Gillard's commentary on the return of HMS *Amethyst*, of Yangtse fame, to Plymouth, which was carried 'live' by BFN.

Following a suggestion by the headquarters at Bad Oeynhausen, BFN's Features and Drama Department began a series called 'Services Spotlight'. The first programme called 'Missing Persons' investigated the difficult task of identifying the bodies of airmen who had been killed during the war and were buried in unmarked graves. The central story of this programme was based around a piece of flower pot which had been buried with an airman. Apparently the Germans had removed his identity discs but a Pole, who had been part of the burial party, had managed to scratch his number on to the piece of flower pot and so identification was possible. Trevor Hill, who produced the first programme, had Leon Griffiths and Alexander McKee as his scriptwriters. In subsequent programmes they visited No. 1 Mobile Field Bakery, the Amphibious Training Centre near Kiel and the Aquatic Training Camp near Eckernförde.

Sgt Alexander McKee, known to his colleagues as Mac, was a Normandy veteran who had found time during the lulls in the fighting to write a series of poems, some of which he later submitted to BFN for 'Poets' Corner'. When the war was over he found himself as a clerk in the quartering offices of the Town Major of Düsseldorf, but he had a desire to return to journalism (before the war he had been a freelance journalist, writing for aviation magazines) and so he joined the Divisional newspaper, *Keynotes*. Here he was to become reporter, cameraman, sub-editor, proof-reader and part-time compositor. When *Keynotes* folded in 1948, he applied for a post with BFN and submitted a suggested script for a dramatized feature programme. As a result he started work at BFN on 14 August 1948. He was still writing poetry and one of his most successful was called 'Dortmund' – a long poem about the ruins in which the dead come back and tell how they lived and how they died.

> I was a soldier, from the wars returning,
> This I found, but there was no sky,
> Only smoke,
> And the curtains of the shattered windows
> Rattled in the rain . . .
>
> This was a City and is no longer,
> These were homes but death is stronger,
> And more than the dead

Leon Griffiths, one of the scriptwriters for 'Services Spotlight', who later went on to create the TV series 'Minder' (*Gordon Savage*)

> Were slain, this place
> Is a void and a vacuum,
> There lives no trace
> Of the sum of human happiness.

The response to this poem was tremendous and it was even taken up as a subject for discussion at Hamburg University.

At the time Alexander was fascinated by the interplay between the civilian members of staff, who had varying amounts of broadcasting experience, and the young National Service announcers. He felt those who had been trained by the BBC looked down upon the rest and, in a wicked moment, he produced the following creed: 'In the beginning God created the BBC, from whom descendeth all wisdom (for an adequate salary); those who follow the BBC's footsteps shall be great and walk in righteousness.'

Alexander was asked to take over a programme called 'Nocturne', which in the past had consisted of a piece of music, followed by a poem followed by music, etc. He felt the programme needed a new direction and so in 1949 wrote a feature called 'They Came from the Sea', based on D-Day, the landings, the beach-head and the breakout, and in it he resurrected many of his original battlefield poems. His choice of music to complement the narration was dramatic. He used part of Beethoven's 7th Symphony as a theme, and backing the description of a Panther tank riding out from behind a farm 'Massive; invincible; with its distortedly long gun and hot watchful eyes behind the Spandaus', he used 'The Catacombs' from Mussorgsky's *Pictures at an Exhibition*. The reaction to this programme was sensational. As Alexander was to remark; 'The Padre Bob Crossett, Derek Jones, and Don East with their reading and interpretation of my poems made all the difference.'

As Alexander's interest in photography grew he made the first ten in the advanced class of the Rhine Army photographic competition, and many of his photographs appeared in the *BFN Bulletin*. It was in the world of the feature programmes that he was to make his mark at BFN Hamburg. In 1950 he wrote 'Squadron X', based on Guy Gibson's book, *Enemy Coast Ahead*. In 'Walpurgis Night' he used a blend of fact and fantasy to weave stories of the witches and the devil. In a programme called 'The Man from Neandertal', he built a word picture of the spirit of a man who had lain undisturbed for 60,000 years in a cave near Düsseldorf.

His speciality was writing and producing documentaries on military subjects, 'The Tiger and the Rose' (the history of the Royal Hampshire Regiment), 'Postponement Indefinite' (the story of the Battle of Britain), and 'Smith, Our Brother' (a documentary on the Air/Sea Rescue Service). On 20 September 1952 his programme 'Total Immersion' was broadcast by BFN. The original idea was that Michael Baguley would make the first dive wearing old–fashioned diver's equipment including the helmet, into which the engineers had fitted a small microphone. As Michael recalls: 'It was very scary, and at 30 feet I could see nothing at all and felt my feet sinking into a carpet of mud. When I surfaced, "Mac" suddenly announced he was going to have a go.' So he too entered the underwater world of the River Elbe. Little did he realize at the time that this programme would shape the rest of his life. After he left BFN, he became a very successful military author and was to spend hundreds of hours in the Solent searching for, and eventually finding, the *Mary Rose*.

A new programme started on 5 December 1949. It was called 'Women's Notebook' and was compiled and edited by Nan Pomeroy. Its aim was to answer listeners' queries ranging from medical matters to cookery, pets and servants! Within two months a small editorial appeared in the *BFN Bulletin* asking women to fill in a questionnaire regarding the type of information they wished to hear in their programme. However, 'Women's Notebook' became one of the first casualties of the Copenhagen Plan, with its last edition being broadcast on 13 March 1950.

In November came the first indications of what might happen to BFN at the Copenhagen International Radio Conference. In an article entitled 'Good Listening' listeners in Herford, Hanover and Cologne were informed of an

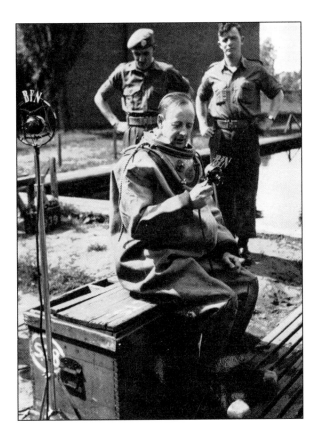

Alexander McKee about to
descend into the River Elbe for
his programme – 'Total
Immersion'   (*Alexander McKee*)

experiment that would involve them in listening to extensive transmissions of the
BBC Light Programme. In addition, other tests would involve BFN originating
its own programmes while the BBC was transmitting on the same wavelength.
The idea was to check whether listeners in Germany could get strong enough
reception to hear BFN without the Light Programme in the background.

The tests ended on 20 December, and BFN returned to its old wavelengths.
However, from 15 March 1950, BFN gave way to the BBC Light programme at
5.15 every afternoon. In his front-page editorial in the *BFN Bulletin* for that week
Leslie Perowne, who had replaced Alec Sutherland as Station Director, made the
point: 'BFN has not packed up, nor is it going to pack up, but it has altered its face a
bit. Why? Because of the Copenhagen Plan. At the conference at which the Plan
was formulated it was decided that BFN would share the same wavelength as the
BBC Light Programme. The tests carried out in the autumn of 1949 found that
BFN could broadcast its own programme during the hours of daylight without
interfering with (or being interfered with by) the BBC Light Programme. Because

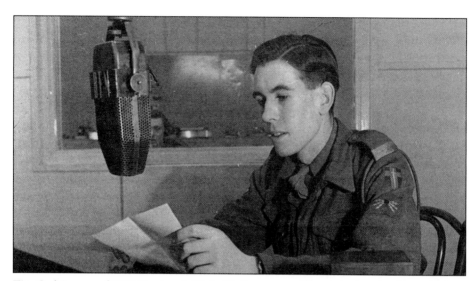

Tim Gudgin, one of BFN Hamburg's 'Early Bird' presenters. He can be heard today reading the sports results on BBC TV's *Grandstand*   (*Alexander McKee*)

of BFN being unable to originate any of its own programmes during the evening hours, many of your favourite programmes have had to be moved to new times during the day.' Leslie ended his editorial: 'Nobody regrets these changes more than we do, but we feel sure you will appreciate their inevitability. Please study your *BFN Bulletin* carefully each week. There are many changes now and there are bound to be many more.' From this moment on, the sound of BFN would change forever.

The BFN schedules for 1950 had to absorb the BBC Light Programme's output and, according to the listeners, many of their favourite programmes came from the BBC. Among the most popular were: 'Much Binding in the Marsh' with Kenneth Horne and Richard Murdoch, 'Ray's A Laugh', 'Top of the Form' and 'Have A Go', produced by a former BFN Hamburg producer, Barney Colehan. The local favourites were: '1700 Club' and Neville Powley's 'Old Comrades', which this year included a visit to the Royal Navy Rhine Flotilla. A little piece of history was made when BFN stayed on air until 4 a.m. to bring its listeners the results of the general election. The BFN Theatre Orchestra was now featuring on the BBC Light Programme in a series recorded at the Musikhalle called 'Moonlight on the Alster'. Günter Meyer-Goldenstädt had just joined BFN as an engineer, and he recalls sitting in the control room which overlooked the back of the stage and watching the BFN Theatre Orchestra's pianist, Lucie von Reibnitz, knitting during piano breaks. At the same time, the chief percussionist was managing to read the *Hamburger*

Morgenpost while continuing to play. All of this was happening without the conductor being aware he had not got the orchestra's full and undivided attention! A new programme started up in the autumn of 1950. 'Calling All Forces' was introduced by Ted Ray and was designed to give the British Forces, wherever they happened to be serving, a taste of home. Freddie Mills, the former world light-heavyweight boxing champion, answered questions on sport, with the difficult ones being passed on to Leslie Welch, the 'Memory Man'. Petula Clark brought messages from the families in the UK to the Forces overseas, and the programme, as expected, was an instant success.

By now demobilization was playing havoc with the BFN staff and no sooner had a serviceman settled in than it was time for him to go. The advertisements inviting interested servicemen and women to apply for an audition were being distributed in Germany and the UK. Tom Stephenson was just about to leave RAF Cranwell when he saw the notice and applied for a post at BFN. He had been studying singing in the UK and so on his arrival at the Musikhalle he was sent to the Music Department and in time took over managing the BFN Theatre Orchestra. His announcer was Chris Howland. Like Geraint Evans before him, Tom took the opportunity of continuing his musical studies under the guidance of Rudolph Bockelmann, the great Wagnerian bass. His first impression of the Musikhalle was that it had a tremendous atmosphere and impressive acoustics. He recalls seeing a relatively unknown Dietrich Fischer-Dieskau singing on stage: 'He was very relaxed and almost draped himself over the crook of the piano, but what a voice and what a pleasant unassuming man.'

Chris Howland had been serving with the Royal Artillery when he was posted to BFN Hamburg in 1948: a year later he was demobbed and joined BFN as a civilian. He came from a radio background. His father, Alan Howland, had been one of the BBC's most popular announcers and wartime news readers. He had been playing the part of Columbus in 'Children's Hour' when his son was born and that is how Christopher got his name. Chris went to school at Blundells and showed a talent for music at a very early age; he wrote his first composition at school. While he was waiting to be called up, he took a job as a cinema organist. Originally a continuity announcer, he went on to manage the BFN Theatre Orchestra as well as to take part in a variety of programmes, ranging from the 'AKC Film Review' to 'Two Way Family Favourites', which he began presenting in 1950. During the late forties and early fifties many famous artistes visited the Musikhalle and Chris was often given the role of 'minder' to such personalities as Peter Ustinov, Peter Lorre, Dorothy Lamour and Yehudi Menuhin. It was during this time that Chris became aware of the sheer professionalism of some of the stars. When Dorothy Lamour came to Hamburg, she was taken ill on the day of the concert and was advised by her doctors that under no circumstances should she leave her bed and go on stage. Miss Lamour was determined not to let the servicemen down and so arrived while the concert was in progress. On stage at the time was a relatively unknown German singer called Anneliese Rothenberger, who brought the house down and took several encores. When Dorothy Lamour went on stage, she was helped on by four soldiers and although she gave of her best, the audience, not knowing of her illness, was unforgiving.

Another newcomer to BFN was Tim Gudgin, who had been called up for National Service. After completing his basic training at Catterick, Tim was posted to Hohne to join the 5th Royal Tank Regiment. Shortly after his arrival he too saw the now-familiar notice in Rhine Army Orders, 'As the result of demobilisation, BFN Hamburg need people for a variety of posts including announcing.' Tim had always wanted to be a radio announcer, but his careers master had maintained: 'To be a broadcaster, you require a first-class degree.' Along with 200 other young hopefuls he went for the audition and was selected. When he arrived he was sent to the Presentation Department and learned the art of news reading under the eagle eye of Robin Boyle. Before Tim was called up he had been interested in amateur dramatics, so he wasted no time in becoming involved with the BFN Drama Club. His best role was as Wing Commander Guy Gibson in Alexander McKee's 'Squadron X'. Playing the part of Flt Lt Hoppy Hopgood was a young trooper from the 9th Lancers called Christopher Headington, who managed to convey all his intercom messages by talking into a tumbler!

Christopher was serving in Edinburgh when he spotted the notice in Squadron Orders and duly applied for an audition to join Forces Broadcasting. He was offered either an announcing post in Trieste or a place in the Music Department in Hamburg. He decided on the latter and was soon at BFN where he started by writing scripts for classical music programmes, followed by taking part in 'Poets' Corner' and later on joining Peter Paxton's drama group. With Bill Crozier he was to feature in a series of programmes in a lighter vein: 'I can't remember who suggested that Bill and I should play together on two pianos. As I recall we hardly ever used music, just played by ear after agreeing on the key! It always worked, I think I usually played the upper part and Bill the bass. Bill was very musical and a naturally expressive and spontaneous player, who always listened to what his piano partner was doing.' At the same time Christopher was introducing 'Tuesday Pop', a selection of popular classical pieces.

Christopher's first outstanding memory of BFN was, after being told about the ghost of Johann, who played his violin in the Brahmatorium, he found that he had to spend his first night on duty sleeping in the Brahmatorium! The second was being given the chance by Leslie Perowne to play one of his own compositions with the Hamburg Symphony Orchestra. His 'Variations on an Original Theme

Opus 11' for piano and orchestra was well received by the local German press. In the *Hamburger Abendblatt* under the heading, 'Gifted young English composer', its music critic wrote: 'The "Variations on an Original Theme" by the English composer, Christopher Headington, could be characterised as a divertimento for piano and orchestra. The composition, performed by the Hamburg Symphony Orchestra with the composer at the piano, received spontaneous approval. This was owing to its new style, the concentrated form and lively scoring, and the excellent balance of contrasting passages within the "Variations".' Quite an accolade for a twenty-year-old National Serviceman.

Michael Baguley had started his Forces Broadcasting career in Trieste, and after he was demobbed was posted to BFN Hamburg as a War Office civilian. As a former actor he found himself in great demand for Alexander McKee's dramatic features and for Peter Paxton's drama group. In those days BFN Hamburg was producing a play every two weeks and this put considerable pressure on the staff, especially on those who were committed to other departments. Michael found relaxation in writing short stories for BFN, a talent he would continue at the BBC. In 1951 he produced and presented a series called 'Actors Are Come' which was designed for lovers of Shakespeare. He wrote a children's serial called 'Cut and Run', about smuggling in the west of England, and joined Tim Gudgin and Don Moss as an 'Early Bird' presenter. In 1953 the rumours of staff reductions at BFN plus a possible move were gaining strength and as he had an offer to return to the theatre, he went back to the UK.

When Gunner Bill Utting was posted to BFN Hamburg in 1950 he thought his role would be either a studio sweeper or the station messenger, but from the beginning it was made clear to him that if he was interested in broadcasting, the sky was the limit. He started by shadowing Tim Gudgin on continuity, and he can still recall his first words on air on 3 August: 'And now the time is half-past three, this is the British Forces Network'. Next, it was on to writing and translating short stories, from Guy de Maupassant's 'A Question of Guilt' and the Grimm Brothers 'The Nose', to his own compositions 'In the Beginning' and 'Little Children Suffer'. Soon he was appearing in the BFN Drama Club's productions, first as a taxi driver in 'Souvenir' and then as Doctor Hardie in 'The Key'.

Working for BFN in the early 1950s meant putting in a six-and-a-half-day week, and Bill's diary for 1951 shows that in one month he did sixteen continuity shifts, produced and presented three 'Services Cinema', introduced two military band concerts, took part in four feature programmes, two plays, four miscellany programmes, presented two 'Early Bird' record programmes and continued to write and record 'Morning Story'. The result of this hard work was that he came out in boils and joined an ever-growing list of BFN staff who had been taken ill. When examined by the MO, Bill was informed that he appeared to be fitter than most of his colleagues, but appearances could be very deceptive. On top of his broadcasting duties, he was still required to keep up his military skills.

Another member of the BFN Drama Club was Betty Harvey-Jones, whose first appearance on the stage in Germany was with the Control Commission Germany's Theatre Club and its production of 'Night Must Fall', in which she played the part of the housekeeper complete with blacked-out teeth. After this performance it was suggested that she applied to BFN for an audition to join its drama club. In her letter she gave the impression that she had worked with Yvonne Arnaud, although it might have been more accurate to say that her mother was the link with Madame Arnaud. Obviously the name-dropping did the trick, and Peter Paxton, the producer of the BFN Drama Club, invited her to join.

As BFN had no funds Peter Paxton either wrote the play or persuaded the author to waive the fee. Sometimes whole families would be enlisted to read parts for the weekly BFN Playhouse. His invariable remark to an unsuitable candidate was: 'I'm afraid the mike doesn't like your voice, darling.'

'In those days,' Betty recalls, 'we would get together for a rehearsal which would be recorded and work late into the night to get it ready for broadcast. Usually we would get by with one take, but there were times when we had to make several recordings to gain the producer's approval.' Betty's husband, John Harvey-Jones, was a lieutenant commander in the Royal Navy. 'I was drawn into the BFN circle through Betty, who had become a member of the BFN Repertory Company. Our house was always full of BFN people and because they liked the sound of my voice I was roped in to present the BFN Book Review.' Later John would appear in several of Peter's plays.

To John, BFN was in tune with its listeners and was more relevant to the service audience than the BBC, but more importantly it helped to build bridges with the German population: 'The Germans who listened, and there were many, obtained a softer view of Britain. When I first heard BFN I was responsible for a team of Russians working in Wilhelmshaven and they too were very keen on BFN. What stood out was that BFN was not broadcasting an endless stream of pop music, but producing schedules which were well-balanced. Finally, my experience with BFN helped to break the ice when it came to public speaking. It was a gentle introduction into the art of radio. After BFN, radio and TV held no fears for me.'

One of the highlights of the year had been the visit to BFN by Orson Welles, fresh from his triumph as Harry Lime in *The Third Man*. Despite a busy schedule, he gave a talk on the AKC Film Review programme and then with the rest of his company recorded half an hour of Shakespeare for the BFN Radio Playhouse series.

As 1950 drew to a close, it was obvious to Leslie Perowne that many listeners still did not understand that BFN had to relay the BBC Light Programme from

BFN drama group with Peter Paxton, Michael Baguley, Don Moss, Bill Utting, Tim Gudgin, Betty Harvey-Jones and Titus Brindley *(Alexander McKee)*

one hour before sunset to closedown. In another editorial he made the following point: 'When once we have gone over to the Light Programme, we are unable even so much as to make an announcement at our own microphones, let alone (as some people suggest) relay the Home Service or the Third Programme. So please don't ring us up to complain that we are not broadcasting a rugby international (from the Home Service) at 16.15 hours on a Saturday afternoon, or ask why you have to endure "Woman's Hour". It's all part of the Copenhagen Plan and once again, we assure you, there is nothing we can do about it.'

However, the listeners were still not happy. On 18 November 1951 in the *BFN Bulletin* under a 'Chad-like' heading 'Wot! No Home Service', BFN reiterated that since the Copenhagen Plan had come into effect, it had to share its wavelength of 247 metres with the BBC Light Programme. 'If BFN were to relay a programme from the BBC Home Service or originate its own programme in the evening, very bad interference would result. That is why BFN could not bring its listeners sports flashes and results after dusk.'

Understandably this was a frustrating period for BFN, which still had a large staff and the potential to produce a full broadcasting schedule. A partial solution to the problem was the introduction by the BBC of a joint identification so that listeners often heard during the course of an evening the announcement, 'This is the BBC Light Programme and the British Forces Network in Germany'. Some of the evening programmes were broadcast direct from the BFN studios in Hamburg and they included the popular Donald Peers, Frankie Howerd, Calling All Forces and Rhineland Serenade programmes.

There were still some areas where BFN's signal was fairly weak. In order to identify these, one of the German engineers was sent out on a fairly regular basis to carry out signal strength checks. He would set off on a Monday morning for one of the large garrison areas where he was supposed to check with the unit and monitor the strength of the signal before returning to Hamburg. However, this engineer had a girlfriend at the Forces Leave Centre in the Harz Mountains, so instead of driving around recording signal strengths, he would head straight for the Leave Centre. On arrival, he would hide his army vehicle in a local farmer's barn, turn the speedometer forward to cover the miles he should have travelled, and then siphon off the petrol he should have used and sell it on the black market, before settling down to a few days of passion. On Friday he would return to BFN and hand in his signal strength returns with sufficient variations to ensure he would be required to go back again and continue his checks.

There was no lack of characters applying to join BFN. LAC Don Moss was a self-confessed radio buff. After completing a wireless course at RAF Compton Bassett, he went for an interview at Eaton Square and in due course was posted to BFN Hamburg. He began as a trainee announcer, but after several attempts at broadcasting the station idents, it was decided his accent was so pronounced he should be sent back to his former unit. He was saved by the intervention of Hedley Chambers, who needed someone to look after his office administration. Don decided to take every opportunity to practise his reading and he could often be heard in the toilet reading aloud from a newspaper. His perseverance paid off and after six months he was posted back to the Continuity Department. From there, he became involved with 'Midweek Magazine' and the morning show called 'Early Bird'. Don, however, was accident prone and on one occasion was preparing to introduce Padre Bob Crossett when he looked up and saw the chair was empty. Thinking he had pressed the talkback switch, he enquired: 'Where's the bloody Padre?', a comment that was heard by the whole of BAOR, as he had pushed the 'live' microphone switch by mistake. When the rundown of staff began to take effect in Hamburg, Don was posted to BFN Austria.

Another character was John Mead, who had failed his officer training course. When asked to give the names of two current generals in the British Army,

John could only think of the general whose name was on the entrance to the barracks in which he was billeted – unfortunately, General Buller had died in the Boer War! It was obvious that the army would have to find something special for John. Having heard about BFN, he actually posted himself to Germany where he was sent to a Scottish Infantry Regiment in Dortmund. After convincing his commanding officer that he was close to useless, he managed to get his posting to BFN.

One of his colleagues at BFN was Oliver Reinganum, whose father was a famous illustrator with the *Radio Times*. Like John, he did not fit into the army's idea of a typical 'other rank'. Oliver spoke fluent German. He was a brilliant trumpeter and got a job playing from midnight to 5 a.m. on a floating German nightclub on the Alster. One night, coming back over the wall, he was arrested and confined to barracks. He was then apprehended again, this time for sitting on a pile of ammunition, smoking! He was sent to the military prison near Bielefeld and was never heard of again. Another of his room-mates was Titus Brindley, who used to move slowly round the room with a black cloth on his head reciting the death sentence! Everyone thought he would become a leading QC.

Along with Don Moss and Chris Howland, John became expert at a game they had invented using the windows of the Musikhalle canteen which were set high in the eaves of the building. The roof was infested with pigeons and the game consisted of taking the tops off the NAAFI trifles, each top consisting of a pat of cream with a cherry in the middle. These portions were then flicked through the air and landed on the German businessmen below who would take off their Homburgs, examine the white mess with the bright red centre and look with deep misgiving at the circling pigeons above.

The BFN schedules in 1951 saw the start of 'The Archers – an everyday story of country folk', 'Paul Temple and the Jonathan Affair', and Jack Jackson's 'Record Roundup'. After several months 'off air' the '1600 Club' returned, hosted by Derek Jones and Don Moss. The BFN Theatre Orchestra began a series of programmes from the Four Seasons Hotel called 'Teatime on the Alster' and Frankie Howerd's 'Fine Goings On' and 'Educating Archie' were attracting good audiences. At 10 a.m. each weekday morning, BFN Hamburg produced and presented its own version of 'Morning Story', with Tim Gudgin, Bill Utting, Michael Baguley, Titus Brindley and Peter Paxton among its readers.

In July 1951 David Porter, who had a very distinguished career in broadcasting, took over as the Station Director from Leslie Perowne. Following a spell as a prisoner of war, he ran the British-controlled German radio station in Cologne and later moved to Berlin. A fine linguist, he translated Goethe's 'Egmont' into English and produced it for the BBC. Although he did not have the same interest in classical music as his predecessor, he continued to encourage the Music Department and was a stimulant for Alexander McKee, in his various productions. However, his time at BFN was not destined to be easy.

Flt Lt Ralph Barker had been the public relations officer for the Berlin Airlift and had first met Leslie Perowne while commentating at an air display in Germany. 'Leslie was obviously impressed with my commentary and made the suggestion that I should join BFN. Because of my interest in cricket, I began covering the various matches that involved touring sides and the Army and RAF cricket teams. Not long after this I was posted to BFN as the Admin. Officer. One of my memories was planning an open day at the Musikhalle and making sure we had sufficient notices for the toilets!'

The effect of the Copenhagen Plan was beginning to demoralize the staff, especially as BFN was not broadcasting during peak time. Ralph Barker was becoming increasingly concerned: 'The talk of redundancies made many of the German staff very worried and I took part, with David Porter, in much of the correspondence appealing for BFN to stay in Hamburg and continue on a permanent basis in support of the Army Welfare Service. I remember writing some fairly strong letters when David Porter was back in the UK and in the end I believe we obtained a better deal than was originally expected, and although we could not stay in Hamburg, BFN was guaranteed a future.'

The late 1940s and early '50s were the halcyon days of the BFN demob parties. These ranged from boat trips on the Alster and the Elbe to good old-fashioned drinking sessions in the various messes. Raymond Baxter was one of those seen off in style on the Alster while Alec Sutherland, Karl Miller and Cliff Michelmore were dined out by the rest of BFN. Alexander McKee could always be relied on to come up with a nice turn of phrase, and for Keith Fordyce's farewell he wrote a poem entitled 'Lines Written in a Booze-Uppe on the Imminent Departure of a Most Smooth Announcer', which ended: 'But we'll not mourn too much our loss,/ For we the water too shall cross . . ./ For epitaph, we'll say once more:/ Not dead, but merely gone before!'

For another demob party, Alexander wrote a lengthy poem based on the assumption that the world had come to a violent end and the various members of BFN were now meeting at the Pearly Gates. Leslie Perowne's arrival in heaven was recorded: 'When the dust cleared away and the ashes had flown,/ The first at the Gate was Leslie Perowne,/ St Peter was shaken, but cried out with glee:/ 'You're the first we've had from the BBC.' For Bill Crozier he wrote: 'And so they entered, thus and thus/ And Crozier after, there was a bit of a fuss./ But even the Angels couldn't very well carp/ At the way he played boogie on the red-hot harp.'

In 1952 the economy measures began to bite and many at BFN felt that there was no future in broadcasting in Germany. Alastair McDougall and Tim Gudgin were posted to FBS Trieste and Don Moss to BFN Austria. The German staff numbers were decimated.

Dennis Scuse, who replaced David Porter as Station Director, had realized that BFN's Hamburg days were numbered. 'We had accepted the Copenhagen Plan with its reallocation of medium wave frequencies, but then the powers that be began to question the need for a separate BFN. If we became a BBC Light Programme relay station, then staff reductions could be made. However, at the same time, plans were being discussed to move the British Headquarters administration to the other side of the Rhine. As it looked as though we would have to move, I suggested that BFN should take advantage of the new German radio system called VHF. Instead of getting rid of all our staff, we could continue to fulfill our role and provide a better service. It took a lot of persuasion but in the end we won through. Once we had decided to move from Hamburg, the problem was where? We looked at various properties within striking distance of the new headquarters and these included old radio buildings, offices, warehouses, a chocolate factory and even a disused dairy. In the end, the solution was literally under our nose. When our Technical Officer, Pip Duke, and I went to Cologne we stayed in the Civilian Officers' Mess in Parkstrasse. It suddenly dawned on me that this splendid house would make an excellent studio centre and it would give us all the broadcasting facilities we required. The main drawback was that, by itself, it wasn't large enough to provide all the necessary offices and storage accommodation that we needed. However, luck was on our side because at the bottom of the garden there was a similar large house, which had been used as an Officers' Mess and if we could have the two, we would have exactly the right amount of accommodation. After a few enquiries, and a certain amount of discussion, it was agreed we could have both buildings.'

Several months before the move, new staff were employed in Cologne and sent to Hamburg for training. They included Herbert Hawellek and Hans Brylka from the Cologne Workshops. The Military suggested that BFN Hamburg should close down on 31 December 1953 and reopen the following day in Cologne. The idea was rejected by Dennis Scuse because his small staff would be working non-stop over the Christmas period and he felt it would be unfair to ask them to undertake a major move as well.

With exactly one month to go before BFN Cologne came on air, Alastair McDougall and Eric Hamer were sent to the new studios to begin the programme integration. When they arrived they found they had one chair, one desk and one telephone. The idea was that Alastair would introduce the housewives' programme called 'For You At Home' 'live' from the Cologne studio, but without making reference to its new location. The requests were still going to Hamburg and were being sent by express post to Cologne. In order to

Dorothy Lamour being interviewed by Chris Howland on her arrival in Hamburg

(*Chris Howland*)

cope with any last-minute delays, the programme, which was normally on air from 9.10 to 10 a.m., was now going on air one hour later.

The last programme to come from BFN Hamburg was introduced by Bill Crozier, but the closing announcement was made by Dennis Scuse. The next day the rest of the team set off for the new station in Cologne leaving behind a host of memories.

When John McMillan and his team arrived in 1945 they found their new location was surrounded by some rather unusual buildings, the pathological laboratory, the prison, the police station and the boarded-up road to Winkelstrasse. As Cliff Michelmore remarked in later years: 'The Musikhalle was a bit of culture surrounded by sin!'

CHAPTER SIX

With a Song in My Heart

There was no script for 'Two-Way Family Favourites' and no rehearsal. The result was simply a conversation between two friends interspersed with records.

Jean Metcalfe

'The time in Britain is twelve noon, in Germany it's one o'clock, but home and away it's time for "Two-Way Family Favourites".'

That was probably one of the most famous announcements on radio during the 1950s and '60s. At its peak, the programme had an audience of 16,000,000 in Britain alone, but it had not always been like that. Before 1941, there had been no concept of a record request programme for the Forces, but after receiving a postcard from three Army sergeants serving in the Western Desert, Tom Chalmers, at the time head of presentation for the BBC's General Overseas Service, had suggested the schedules should include a record request programme for those personnel serving overseas. He therefore set up 'Forces' Favourites'. The presenters were Marjorie Anderson, Joan Griffiths, Barbara McFadyean and Jean Metcalfe and the programme was designed to give the Forces the sort of music they wanted to hear.

Tom had come across Jean Metcalfe by accident. 'I was trying to get hold of Cecil Madden at the BBC's Variety Department when his telephone was answered by a girl who had a delightful voice. Now bearing in mind that the wartime telephone system between Wood Norton and London was of a rather dubious quality, the voice still made an impact. I suggested to Cecil she might make a good announcer and he should give her a voice test. He did, and she passed.' Jean and her colleagues continued to relay the messages from home until the autumn of 1945.

Following the end of the war in Europe, BFN Hamburg was broadcasting to thousands of servicemen in Germany and the planners felt they needed a link with home. The idea of a request programme was mooted but the problem lay in finding a line of broadcast quality. To assess the situation, Tom, one of the architects of the BBC Light Programme and now its assistant head, flew to Hamburg, and put the suggestion to John McMillan for a Two-Way family request programme.

When Doreen Taylor interviewed John McMillan for her book *A Microphone and a Frequency*, he explained how BFN and the BBC overcame the problem. John had good contacts with the Royal Corps of Signals in Hamburg and discovered there was a direct telephone circuit from Hamburg to an exchange housed in an underground railway tunnel in Goodge Street. At the time it was being used for military traffic between London and the continent. John decided to see whether he could get through to the BBC and was delighted when he was connected to Langham 4468 and was soon talking to Tom Chalmers. They discussed the possibilities of a two-way request programme and Tom, using his contacts, found that it was now possible to get lines of sufficient broadcast quality through to Hamburg. It was decided that a new request programme, called 'Family Favourites', would start in October 1945. In London the presenter would be Marjorie Anderson and Sgt Alan Clarke would host the Hamburg end.

The signature tune, 'With a Song in My Heart' by André Kostelanetz, which was to become synonymous with the programme, was discovered by Trevor Hill when he was working for the BBC in the 1940s. Earlier Trevor had been asked to find a fanfare for the North American Service editions of 'Radio Newsreel' in the same key as its signature tune, 'Imperial Echoes', and found what he was looking for on a 12-inch Columbia record. By chance, he played the other side of the record and was so impressed with what he heard that he suggested to Tom Chalmers that this could be used as the signature tune for the new request programme. Tom agreed, and at 11.15 a.m. on Sunday 7 October 1945 listeners to BFN Hamburg would hear the melody for the very first time. The first request on that first 'Family Favourites' had a special place in the affections of the British soldiers, but instead of the Lale Andersen version of 'Lilli Marlene', they played the one by Geraldo and his Orchestra. This was followed by Richard Tauber singing Handel's 'Largo', Bing Crosby's 'Sweet Leilani' and the Boston Promenade Orchestra with Ponchielli's 'Dance of the Hours'.

The programme was an instant success, but its very success was causing Tom concern. During the days of 'Forces Favourites' he had become aware that some of the presenters had begun to feel that they were more important than either the programme or its content, and as a result played fewer requests than they should have done. So on 27 November he issued a 'Family Favourites' directive. In it he explained he was concerned that unless the producers kept a firm grip on the programme, it could become unmanageable. Based on his long experience with 'Forces' Favourites' he considered that, as the title itself suggested, the programme was there to link family with family and not the girlfriends or fiancées of those in the Services, and the selection of music should reflect family rather than individual tastes. The directive he issued also suggested that the presenters, both in London and in Hamburg, should concentrate on the listeners and their messages, rather than on themselves.

The rules were still in operation when BFN celebrated its first anniversary. On the front page of its programme sheet the editor had written: 'Family Favourites – Sundays from 11.15 to 12.30 – still seems to be one of BFN's most popular programmes judging by the number of letters which pour in each day. CSM Brian Whittle, who presents Family Favourites, would like to be able to play all these requests, but this is of course impossible. However, don't let this discourage you – if you write in, you might be one of the lucky ones. Remember, we can play requests for your wives and families, but not girlfriends or fiancées.'

The *Radio Times* gave the progamme the following billing: 'From London the tunes you asked us to play, and from Germany the tunes that make them think of you.' But no mention was made of the presenters. The first time their names appeared in *Radio Times* was Sunday 12 January 1947, when Alan Clarke, who had left BFN to join the BBC, presented the London end, and CSM Roy Bradford was in Hamburg. The programme did not have a settled spot for some considerable time and the BFN presenters appeared on a rota basis. At the start of 1947, 'Family Favourites' was on the air at 10.15 a.m. On 30 March, the programme moved to 12 noon. On 27 July 1947, it appeared at 5 p.m., and on 2 November it had moved again, this time to 3.30 p.m. The BFN announcers were credited in *Radio Times* with their rank and unit: so it became Sgt John Jacobs RAF, Cpl Hedley Chambers RAC, Sgt Don Douglas RASC, Sgt Bob Boyle RAC, and Pte Derek Jones REME. One announcer who did not make the 'Family Favourites' list was Nigel Davenport, although he passed Raymond Baxter's audition. Just as his name was being added to the rota, it was discovered that he only had weeks to do before he was demobbed. As Raymond remarked: 'We won't waste our time on grooming you for stardom!'

When Roy Bradford, who later became an MP in Northern Ireland, was producing the Hamburg end of the programme, he was interviewed by *Soldier* magazine. 'We get dozens of letters asking for the same records, nearly every one of them saying this is my sixth time of asking, but we can only play nine records in a programme. Ninety per cent of the requests are for the vocal sentimental numbers with "Bless You for Being an Angel" receiving about fifty requests a week. There are those with a demob angle "Put Another Chair at the Table Mother" and the hackneyed ballads like "I'll Walk Beside You" and "I'll See You Again". These are followed by the holies like "The Lost Chord", "Ave Maria" and "The Holy City". I think that "Family Favourites" runs on a repertoire of about fifty records. Picking out the ones that fit into the programme puts the producer under a great deal of pressure; so many letters have an appeal like "can you play 'Temptation' for my wife" or "my marriage is heading for the rocks unless you play my request."'

At the time John Jacobs was presenting 'Family Favourites', he was also hosting the Saturday late night show. The Military, concerned about scruffy soldiers, had issued an edict that leather jerkins would not be worn 'off duty' in the Hamburg city centre. John was making his way back to his billet after presenting 'Saturday Night Swing Shift', when he was picked up by two RMPs for wearing his jerkin. Back at the guardroom, he was informed that as it was the weekend, he would stay in the cells until Monday morning. 'But I've got to present "Family Favourites" in about ten hours' time', pleaded John. The RMPs were not impressed but they did contact their boss who, having verified that it was *the* John Jacobs of 'Family Favourites' fame, said: ' If Sgt Jacobs will play a record for my wife, who is in England, then he can go free.' By this time John was trembling so much the RMP corporal had to take down the request details for him.

Derek Jones began presenting 'Family Favourites' in 1947. At the time he was still a private but when the *Radio Times* went to print, he had been promoted to corporal. The programme was so popular with the service audience that he was continually being stopped in the street by servicemen who wanted a request played for their mum, cousin, maiden aunt, etc. Derek's policy was that all requests would go into a hat and the lucky ones would be played. Much was written in later years about 'Family Favourites' and Payola, but Derek recalls that the record pluggers would phone him from London asking for his help in promoting this or that record. During his time as a presenter, one of the big hits was Russ Morgan's 'So Tired'.

According to Cliff Michelmore, he became involved in 'Family Favourites' in 1949 as a last-minute replacement for Derek, who had been hospitalized. He can still recall the moments before he went on air. 'Hello', I said, 'My name is Cliff Michelmore.' To which Jean Metcalfe replied: 'What rank are you?' 'I think we'd better dispose of that because I'm a Squadron Leader', and from then on they dispensed with rank forever.

Cliff first saw a photograph of Jean in Trevor Hill's office. 'Who's that?', said Cliff. 'That's Jean Metcalfe' said Trevor. 'She's a bit of all right', remarked Cliff. 'She's more than that, she's lovely' replied Trevor. On his next visit to London, Cliff called in to the BBC to meet his co-presenter, and so began one of British radio's best known romances. In the beginning, the BBC tried to keep it under wraps and only friends and colleagues knew about it. They were not allowed to become engaged until Cliff had left BFN and the RAF.

In their book *Two Way Story*, Jean and Cliff recall some of the letters they received:

Your job is to introduce the artist and not give comment on the weather and finish with childish giggles . . .

Sgt John Jacobs RAF, who was
allowed out of the guardroom to
present 'Family Favourites' on the
understanding that he played a
request for the provost marshal's
wife

(*Crown Copyright/MoD*)

One listener from Bristol wrote, 'I must be frank, I don't like the programme or
the sickly bathos you lay on in those condescending tones, but my wife would
like you to play for her . . .'

The request for 'On the Street where You Live', by Victor Moan, and instead of
'La Golandrina', the card asked for Llangollen Dreamer.

For all members of the officers' mess, a girl called Penelope chose 'The Stripper'
to thank them for such a swinging holiday . . .

The young serviceman called George who had requested 'For Ever and Ever'
for 'my sweetheart Rose'. Just before Cliff was due to play it, a telegram arrived:
CANCEL FOR EVER AND EVER FOR ROSE STOP SUBSTITUTE NO ROSE IN
ALL THE WORLD FOR SHEILA.

Sometimes Jean and her colleagues in Cologne were accused of giggling too
much, but not without reason. Dennis Scuse turned the movement from

Sqn/Ldr Cliff Michelmore and Jean Metcalfe together in the BFN Hamburg studios
(Alexander McKee)

Beethoven's 'Pastoral' Symphony, known as 'The Shepherd's Thanksgiving after the Storm' to 'Thank Heavens, It's Stopped Raining', and Bill Crozier caused more hilarity when he christened Kathy Kirby – Curvy Kirby. However, when Jean mentioned on air that some people were irritated by the giggling, the carry-on-giggling comments flooded in, including one from a chef in the royal kitchens!

Dennis Scuse, who had become the Station Director of BFN Hamburg, had taken over the German end of 'Family Favourites' from Chris Howland. 'My introduction was made so easy by Jean Metcalfe, I had no time to be nervous. In those days, London and Germany were playing eight records each and the mix had to contain popular records of the moment, classical, instrumental, opera and occasionally, comedy. It was a programme about nostalgia. Mothers remembering their sons and daughters who were serving in Germany, and they, remembering their mums' and dads' wedding anniversary.'

The mail response to the programme in Germany was fantastic, even though BFN insisted on postcards only. In 1951 Bill Crozier devised a novel way for listeners to get a record played on 'Family Favourites'. The listeners sent in their top eight records against which they placed any number between 1 and 46. BFN compiled a list of 46 league or cup matches and after the Saturday football

Dennis Scuse, who presented the
programme from Hamburg and
Cologne in the mid-1950s
(Dennis Scuse)

results; based on the pools system of three points for a draw, two for an away win and one for a home win, the listeners' lists were checked against the results and the one with the highest number of points had their request played on the following Sunday's 'Family Favourites'.

When Dennis handed over to Bill Crozier in 1957, it was with a mixture of sadness and satisfaction. Sadness that he would no longer be linking up with Jean Metcalfe and satisfaction for a job well done. 'There was a bonus, being able at long last to have Sunday lunch with my wife, Joyce, and our son.' When he was returning home from Germany, he found the fame of the programme had followed him into the Customs Hall at Dover. 'As I pulled up there was a distinct sound of my duty free slurping away in the boot. The Customs Officer looked interested and when I explained I had been abroad for almost ten years, he looked at me and said "the voice sounds familiar, what's your name sir?" Dennis Scuse, I replied. "Ah," he said, "the Family Favourites man. Go on sir, and welcome home".'

As soon as news of Dennis's imminent departure reached the BBC, they informed BFN Cologne they would be sending out a team to audition the various announcers for this very high profile programme. Bill Crozier decided to run a book on who would get the job, and at the last minute added his name to the list and gave himself the rather generous odds of 10 − 1. Only his old BFN Hamburg colleague Tom Cousens backed him, and when Bill was selected he was the first to congratulate him, and then asked for his winnings.

Bill stayed as the 'Family Favourites' presenter from Cologne for seven years. He and Jean became an institution. Like Jean he received unusual requests. 'One lonely airman wanted me to tell his sweetheart how much he loved her and sent his request on a label tied to an old boot and said that's what I'd get − the boot − if I didn't play his request.' On another occasion, Bill was asked by a boy in hospital to play a record for his father, and to tell him he had just begun to walk again following a serious illness affecting his legs. This request brought a lump to his throat.

When he left Cologne he took with him some of his favourite requests including a cushion, which had embroidered in black letters, 'Send Me the Pillow that You Dream On', a long chain attached to a letter for Sam Cook's 'Chain Gang' and a piece of wood on which was stuck a collection of soles and heels with the painted request for Nancy Sinatra's 'These Boots Were Made for Walking'.

In 1964, after seventeen years of presenting 'Two-Way Family Favourites', Jean retired and was replaced by Judith Chalmers, but she came back to join Judith in May 1965 to dedicate the last record in the programme to Bill, who was leaving BFBS to become a freelance broadcaster. On the turntable in Cologne was a package marked 'Not to be opened until 1.30 p.m. Sunday'. Inside was a massive handkerchief from Jean with the message: 'Dearest Bill, this is the biggest I could find and you're going to need it, have a huge blow on me.' Jean's last record for Bill was 'With a Song in My Heart' and Bill's final record from Cologne was 'So Tired'.

At the height of the programme's popularity Jean was getting 1,000 requests a week and Bill around 800, with the most popular being 'I'll Be Home' by Pat Boone, Doris Day's 'Secret Love', 'Home Lovin' Man' by Andy Williams, 'Every Time We Say Goodbye' by Ella Fitzgerald and 'The Green Green Grass of Home' by Tom Jones. What appealed to both of them was the 'open' card which enabled Jean and Bill to select something they enjoyed playing. For Bill, it could well be a jazz recording; he was the first person to play Dave Brubeck's 'Take Five'. For Jean, the duet from 'The Pearl Fishers' or something by Kathleen Ferrier. It was Jean who invented the expression 'bumper bundle'. She recalls a meeting with John McMillan, then Head of the BBC Light Programme, on how one could link a lot of requests for one record; 'He suggested the phrase − most requested record, but I felt this was not quite right. That evening, while driving home, I got to the Battersea crossroads and was queueing bumper to bumper at the lights when suddenly it came to me, "bumper bundle" might be the answer to our problem', and so a new phrase was written into 'Family Favourites' history.

Joining Judith Chalmers to present 'Family Favourites' from Cologne was Ian Fenner and although the programme still had a large following, the end of National Service and better telecommunications meant the basic format would have to change. In 1968, Michael Aspel was given the chance to present World-wide Family Favourites which now took in Australia and Canada as well as the various Forces Broadcasting Stations around the world. Clearly BFBS Germany did not want to broadcast a two-hour programme in which it featured only every other week. David Lamb, the acting programme director, decided to replace 'Family Favourites' with a new weekend request programme called 'Sounds Like Sunday', which would include the half-hour link with London as and when it occurred, plus links with the various BBC Local Radio stations. His decision was not without controversy and the *Sunday Express* branded him as the man who took away 'Family Favourites' from the troops, but in effect the BBC had already done that. Sandi Jones, who followed Dick Norton as the presenter of the new programme, restored the profile of the link between BAOR and the BBC to such an extent that few noticed the programme had undergone a radical change.

Sandi can still recall her first 'Family Favourites' link. 'I didn't have time to be nervous because Mike was so easy to work with. He had a wicked sense of humour and we just bounced off each other.' Later when Sandi met Michael in London, he said, 'Do you know there are little old ladies across Britain who think you and I are having an affair!' The BBC were impressed with Sandi's style and she was asked to stand in for Michael when he went on leave and this led to her taking over the programme when she moved back to England. Like all 'Family Favourites' presenters, she was inundated with calls from record pluggers. 'In those days there was talk of Payola, but I must have missed something because I never even got an offer of a casting couch.'

Don Durbridge, who was later to make his name with Radio 2, took over the Germany end of 'Family Favourites' in 1969. He recalls sitting in the studio, with his first record lined up and waiting for the BBC news summary, which preceded 'Family Favourites', to end. 'Suddenly I heard a rustle of paper as the news reader concluded the bulletin with the words "and finally, some news just in. The singer and actress, Judy Garland, has been found dead in the bathroom of her London flat. More news in an hour." Immediately in came the familiar strains of the signature tune "With a Song in My Heart" and Michael Aspel's voice introducing the programme and handing over to me. There was nothing for it but to go ahead as planned, with a few off-the-cuff remarks by both of us by way of introduction to that first record of mine. . . . Judy Garland singing "Somewhere Over the Rainbow". I think I can positively say it was the very first tribute to the star, who had died less than an hour earlier.'

The last 'Family Favourites' was broadcast on 13 January 1980 in Pete Murray's Sunday Show. From over 1,000 requests a week at the height of its popularity, it was down to between 20 and 30 and the programme was no longer viable.

On 30 July 1995 as part of the BBC Light Programme's Golden Jubilee, a special edition of 'Family Favourites' was produced with Sandi Jones, the former BFBS Germany presenter, in the London studio and Glen Mansell in BFBS Germany's new studios in Herford. The programme brought back many memories of the years gone by. Sandi's first request went from a Mrs Howcroft to her niece and her husband serving at RAF Laarbruch. Thirty-two years earlier, Mrs Howcroft had a request played on 'Two-Way Family Favourites' when she and her husband were stationed at RAF Laarbruch. From Germany came a request from an SSAFA social worker to his wife in Blackpool with the added message: 'This will bring back memories of the time we listened to the programme back in the sixties.' There was a certain touch of nostalgia in the music with songs by Doris Day, The Beatles and The Carpenters. Phil Harris's 'Woodman Spare That Tree' , reminded the listeners that comedy records had always been popular in the programme. Two other sounds of the past, but brought up to date, were 'Unchained Melody' and 'True Love', the latter featuring Peter Skellern and Mary Hopkin, ending the programme. The easy rapport between Sandi Jones and Glen Mansell was in stark contrast to the rather formal style used in 1945. Then, there was no mention of the weather at the start of the programme, but a cue from John Webster, 'And now Sgt Alan Clarke, it's time to hear what the forces in Germany are asking for this morning.' After a pause, Alan read out two dedications for wives in Hounslow and Manchester and introduced Monte Ray's 'You Belong to My Heart'. When the record had finished, he rather surprisingly back-announced the dedications before handing back to London. One of the requests came from Jack Sheard, who was spinning in the records from BFN Hamburg. There was one major difference with this last edition of 'Family Favourites'. Many of the requests from the UK were going to wives in Germany whose husbands were serving in Bosnia and as the programme was being broadcast there, it had this extra link with home, although Glen Mansell had a request from Vitez school in Bosnia for a soldier's in-laws in Battersea, with the message, 'Thanks for the parcels', a message that would not have been out of place fifty years before.

At the height of its popularity, 'Family Favourites' stood alone with very little competition. Today with multi-channel radio and television, plus an excellent telephone system, the need for the request programme has greatly diminished. It is doubtful whether any other programme in radio history will be remembered for a smell – Sunday lunch with roast beef and Yorkshire pudding!

CHAPTER SEVEN

Living among the Millionaires

The strange world of Astors and Uncle Bill has little to do with the mainstream of life in modern Britain . . . with little publicity, BFBS is performing the vital task of giving 200,000 Britons in an alien environment a morale-boosting link with home.

The Times 1975

On 26 February 1954 BFN Cologne opened its new studios in Marienburg with the same announcement BFN Hamburg had used eight and a half years earlier, 'This is the British Forces Network'. Instead of Sgt Gordon Crier, who had long since returned to the BBC, the honour of making the official opening announcement fell to John Mead. As Dennis Scuse, the Station Controller of BFN Cologne, remarked 'In Hamburg, the opening announcement came from a studio which had once been a dressing room used by world famous conductors in the Musikhalle; now we were using a room which, up until six months ago, had been a bedroom in a beautiful house on the outskirts of Cologne.'

Among the guests who attended the official opening were Kenneth Adam, Controller of the BBC Light Programme, and Brigadier Johnstone, the Deputy Adjutant-General, who had arrived in Cologne by special train and delivered the official opening speech. Later that evening, 'Radio Newsreel' carried an account of the opening of BFN Cologne's new studios, which were located in Parkstrasse in a villa that had once been owned by a Jewish family who disappeared shortly before the war. It was destroyed during an Allied bombing raid on Cologne. When it was rebuilt in 1948 it became the temporary home of a British general, then offices for the MPBW (Ministry of Public Buildings and Works) and later an officers' mess. It was reputed to be haunted following the tragic suicide of an MPBW painter. When it was decided to relocate BFN the house underwent more alterations, but this time under the supervision of British and German radio engineers.

Dennis Scuse and his chief engineer, Pip Duke, had a very good relationship with NWDR: 'They undertook to carry out the entire conversion for us including the technical installation. It so happened they had just completed their own studio complex in Cologne which included all the very latest and most up-to-date electronic equipment, so we had a ball wandering around their Broadcasting House saying – yes, we'll have two of those and one of these and six of those amplifiers. We were rather like children buying sweets in a shop.'

The new station had a unique system of interconnecting studios and a control room, all divided by soundproof glass with a push-button system for communication. Every possible precaution was taken to prevent BFN going 'off air' by accident. If the local power line failed, fifty large batteries, always kept fully charged in the basement, automatically took over. If the breakdown lasted longer than four hours, a diesel generator could provide the necessary power for operating. As with Hamburg, one of the many bathrooms in the house had been converted into an echo chamber, to provide various sound-effects.

Although BFN was now several hundred miles from Hamburg, it had not lost all connection with its original home. From a small studio in the AKC cinema, Chris Howland and Frank Honeyman recorded items for inclusion in BFN's weekly 'Film Review'.

One of the many innovations Dennis Scuse started during his time in Cologne was 'morning prayers' held in the bar in Lindenallee. Over a morning cup of

Studio A in BFN Cologne 1954   (*Crown Copyright/MoD*)

coffee, programme ideas were kicked around, and out of these meetings came two ideas which remain with Dennis to this day. The first was called 'A Day with a Regiment', when BFN spent an entire day on location with a regiment in BAOR. The day would begin with their requests making up the early morning programme 'Wakey, Wakey'. At the same time, the features department was working on a documentary about the regiment's history. The regimental band was recorded for a band concert and if a star such as Petula Clark or Frankie Vaughan was out on a visit, they would join up with Bill Crozier and Dennis Scuse and put together a one-hour variety programme. The programme took a great deal of effort from the BFN staff, but the audience reaction was excellent.

The other programme which grew out of 'morning prayers' was called 'Let's Spend an Evening at Home'. The programme started at 7 p.m. and finished at 10.30 p.m. It carried the news, the weather forecast and had something for everyone, from cooking tips to the latest comedy tracks, from advice for nursing mothers to jazz or opera recordings. Everyone on the station was expected to be involved.

The last *BFN Bulletin* of 1955 contained some good news and some bad news. The good news concerned the arrival of VHF and the bad news the fact that the bulletin, for economy reasons, was being reduced from six pages to four. For several years BFN had been broadcasting on 247 metres in the medium waveband but

John Mead showing Brigadier Johnstone how Studio D works   (*Dennis Scuse*)

from 1 January 1956 it would be heard only on VHF. The editorial explained: The biggest argument against VHF is that some initial financial outlay is required on the part of the individual in equipping himself with a set capable of receiving these broadcasts. To offset this official sets have already been issued and the majority of our listeners who live in barracks should be able to receive us. For those of you who do not live in barracks, a special scheme has been arranged by Headquarters Northern Army Group whereby you can purchase a very good model for a very reasonable price. There is no doubt at all that VHF broadcasting has come to stay and the BBC is already broadcasting on VHF in the London area and soon this coverage will spread through all England. For these reasons by equipping yourself with a receiver capable of receiving VHF you will in fact be ahead of the majority of people in the United Kingdom.'

In the new schedule for 1956 BFN achieved an ambition in providing something for its younger listeners and a 'Children's Hour' was broadcast each weekday evening. Gerald Sinstadt introduced a team of experts to discuss topics of the moment in 'Sports Forum' and at 8.30 on a Thursday night Bill Crozier presented music for jazz fans. 'The Archers', 'A Life of Bliss', 'The Goon Show' and 'Any Questions' continued to be popular with BFN listeners.

On 10 May 1956 after 18 months of planning, BFN reported from Aachen when Sir Winston Churchill received the Charlemagne Prize. The presentation took place in a small room and as there were a hundred steps to climb, Sir Winston was carried up on a chair by the local fire brigade. Only two reporters were present at the ceremony, Gerald Sinstadt for BFN and a German commentator. The following weekend Sir Winston paid a visit to his former regiment, the 4th Queen's Own Hussars. Although it was a private visit, BFN was invited to broadcast Sir Winston's address to the regiment. The BFN engineers had been informed that Sir Winston would give the address sitting down, but at the last minute the great man decided to stand, setting the engineers a problem of how to move the microphone without disrupting the ceremony.

John Harrison was doing his National Service as a radar operator at Lüneburg when he decided to write to BFN regarding a possible posting to Cologne, but to no avail. He then wrote a report on what he thought of BFN's programmes and its presentation and sent it to Dennis Scuse. Finally, he accosted Dennis at the Radio Show at Olympia and as a result was invited down to Cologne for an audition. 'I remember Dennis saying to me on my first day, "For most of us this is a hobby job". Also I was advised not to wear my uniform as it reminded the German staff too much of the RAF's bombing of Cologne'.

Dennis Scuse remained with BFN until December 1957, when he was succeeded by Ian Woolf, whose previous Forces Broadcasting experience had been in Italy and Kenya. 'When I took over on 1 January 1958, I visualized that my

Ian Woolf, who replaced Dennis
Scuse as Station Director in
Cologne, and later became
Director of BFBS
        (*Crown Copyright/MoD*)

contribution to BFN would include improving its programme-gathering reach,
improving reception of the BBC on which we depended totally for world news
and comment, improving the lot of the German staff, whom I felt to be rather left
out of things, and setting up audience research. The latter proved a tall order
because it called for extra money and effort. Naturally, neither was available and
there were doubters who argued that audience research was a frill BFN could do
without.' As Ian quickly found out, there were many who felt that BFN's role
should be to educate the troops. He explained that BFN's mission required them
first to entertain, second to inform and third to educate. 'As I repeatedly pointed
out, unless we first capture the audience (by entertaining it) we could hardly hope
to be able to inform or educate it.' Ian argued that a second reason for mounting a
good audience research was that it provided first class ammunition with which to

convince BFN's backers – the War Office, Treasury and its agencies – that money spent on broadcasting was money well spent.

At the time BFN's staff was too small to meet any extra programme commitments. In 1958 it totalled twelve UKBC (United Kingdom-based civilians) and two RAF attachments. They were expected to broadcast for 120 hours a week – which in terms of basic announcing shifts alone occupied the time of four or five people. This left little manpower to dream up, compile, script, produce and present the sixty-odd hours which had to be provided from BFN's own resources. As Ian Woolf discovered, the 'system' did not allow for improvements to be made. 'Bringing about change proved, if not impossible, certainly a mammoth task. Lack of money and interest vied with one another alternately as reasons for an inability to put the service on a proper footing.'

Ian often quoted the Americans who thought up the idea of Forces Broadcasting in the first place. 'They saw their mission with the emphasis on information . . . to Inform, Entertain and Educate. In other words, whereas BFN gave priority to the welfare side, the Americans saw information as their main goal. As a result, in American Military eyes, broadcasting to the Forces was regarded as important, whereas in British Military eyes, it tended to be treated as a "fun thing".'

Although most of Ian Woolf's team were civilians, BFN Cologne still had its service connection. CSM Charlie Crashley, who had worked with Forces Broadcasting in Austria, was in charge of administration. He was joined by Keith Skues, David Hamilton, Paul Hollingdale, John Marsh and Alan Grace (the author), who were all members of the Royal Air Force.

Paul Hollingdale was a sergeant serving at RAF Bruggen, when he managed to work a posting to RAF Wahn, which was fairly close to BFN Cologne. Like many other young servicemen, he was keen to get into radio and after helping out in the gramophone library, he was offered the chance of producing a half-hour Latin American dance programme. Shortly after this, Paul found himself as the early morning announcer on BFN's 'Musical Clock'. Once the programme was over he dashed back to the Supply Depot at RAF Wahn, to continue his normal day job. He was best known at the time for his film programmes and for an excellent series about Glenn Miller. Most of the background material he used came from some American Armed Forces Radio system discs, which had many tracks not available on commercial gramophone records.

When David Hamilton was called up for his National Service he was asked by the careers officer what he wanted to do. 'Get into radio', he said, so they sent him to become a wireless operator at Compton Bassett! At the time, he had written to Ian Woolf asking if he could work for BFN during his spell of National Service and received a reply to the effect that if he were posted to Cologne, Ian would be delighted to meet him. After completing his training at

David Hamilton, Marian Ryan and Bill Crozier, BFN Cologne, 1958   (*David Hamilton*)

Compton Bassett, David was posted to RAF Digby in Lincolnshire, but following a meeting with an understanding postings officer, he had it changed to RAF Butzweilerhof, on the outskirts of Cologne.

The first thing he did on arrival at Butzweilerhof was to telephone a rather surprised Ian Woolf and inform him he was now in Germany. Ian's suggestion was that he should see whether his new Commanding Officer would allow him to join BFN. As the RAF wanted to make use of David wireless skills, the answer was no! However, this did not deter David and following a meeting with Ian, he ended up working shifts at Butzweilerhof and, in his spare time, recording and producing record programmes for BFN. When David suggested he should be given a regular programme, Ian enquired whether he could undertake such a commitment. David assured him he could. He proposed, if necessary, to pay someone to cover his RAF shift, should it clash with the programme. As rock 'n' roll was all the rage, BFN's programme planners agreed that he could present a programme featuring Elvis Presley, Jerry Lee Lewis and Bill Haley. Based on his knowledge of the servicemen at RAF Butzweilerhof, David was convinced it would be a hit. The programme, called

Keith Skues, one of BFN Cologne's National Service announcers   (*BFBS Archives*)

'Hey There', took off in a big way and very soon he was inundated with fan-mail, most of it coming from young German girls!

However, David's aversion to anything military put him at odds with a certain officer who charged him for being 'scruffy' on pay-parade and told him to report to the RAF police. He quickly discovered that a mention on 'Family Favourites' could get him off all the unpleasant parts of 'jankers'. There is a story, which is part of BFN folklore, that during his incarceration David asked if the OB van could come to the guardroom at RAF Butzweilerhof so that he could present his programme 'live'. According to David it made a good story, but he had recorded a programme in case of such emergencies.

When his time came to leave BFN and Butzweilerhof, he celebrated by burning his uniform piece by piece in the large open fireplace in Parkstrasse, much to the amusement of the German staff. Years later, he appeared on BFBS Germany as a presenter of pop programmes which had been recorded at the BFBS headquarters in London.

Like David, Keith Skues had always wanted to be a radio announcer and after writing to Roger Moffat, who at the time was introducing 'Make Way for Music' with the BBC Northern Dance Orchestra, he was invited along to see the show being recorded. Afterwards, Roger suggested that if he wanted to get into broadcasting he should write to BFN Cologne.

At the end of 1957 Keith received his call-up papers and after a spell at RAF Chivenor was posted to RAF Jever in Germany. Remembering Roger Moffat's advice, he wrote to Ian Woolf and asked for an audition which, to his great delight, he passed and was posted to BFN in January 1960 as a presentation assistant. During the first few weeks he shadowed Bill Crozier and Derek Hale and produced his first programme, 'Canteen Break'. Like many others making their way in the world of broadcasting, he spent every spare moment learning how to operate the studio desk, editing, and various microphone techniques. 'In those days BFN's output was very much akin to an MOR (middle of the road) station, not a lot of pop music, but very strong on instrumentals.' At the time Keith felt BFN spoke to millions of listeners who were 'somewhere out there'. 'I would like to be remembered as an announcer who helped to break down the barriers between listener and radio presenter. Both David Hamilton and myself tried to talk *to* them and not *at* them, plus we were young and spoke the same language. Having said all that, BFN taught me everything I know about radio, it was the best training ground in the business for a fledgling radio announcer and producer.'

Since 1951 the broadcasting service had been split, on the orders of the Army Council, with the Director of Signals responsible for the technical side while the Adjutant-General looked after programmes and staff recruitment. In 1958 a paper from the Executive Committee of the Army Council accepted that Forces Broadcasting needed to be controlled by one department, and in 1960 Jack Knott was seconded from the BBC to produce a report which would later become the foundation for the British Forces Broadcasting Service. For the second time in ten years the morale of the staff was low, with many in the services looking upon Forces Broadcasting as an unnecessary extravagance. Jack Knott's first overseas visit was to BFN Cologne where he and Ian Woolf discussed, among other things, the growing need for television in Germany. This was followed by visits to the smaller stations around the world and in early 1961 his report was finished. His basic recommendations were that the service's name should be changed to the British Forces Broadcasting Service and a charter be drawn up to ensure that BFBS would provide a service of entertainment, information, education and, more importantly, a link with home. There should also be improved salaries and conditions, with a proper career structure for the members of BFBS. Also he recommended that BBC instructors should visit the overseas stations and the BFBS programme staff should return for special courses at the BBC. The staff at BFN, while welcoming the idea of better conditions and salaries, were unhappy with their new title. As one Hamburg veteran put it: 'There has always been AFN and BFN, why have they got to change it?'

With the arrival of Ian Fenner from FBS Cyprus, the jazz experts of BFN doubled overnight. Until then, Bill Crozier had been looking after the Forces jazz interests with his two programmes 'Just Jazz' and 'Kool Korner', but Ian Fenner was a big band enthusiast. Shortly after he arrived Germany, he met Joe Napoli who had been Chet Baker's manager before the war and who wanted to repay a debt to a small village in the Ardennes. Apparently Joe's Division had been rested following the Battle of the Bulge and he was so taken with the kindness he and his comrades received that he promised one day he would return and promote a jazz festival. Because of Joe's friendship with Ian Fenner, BFN was given the sole rights to record the festival, and over the years Ian met and recorded Cannonball Adderley, Jimmy Smith, Johnny Dankworth and Woody Herman and their orchestras. When AFN announced the visit of Stan Kenton, June Christy and the Four Freshmen to an enlisted men's club in Wiesbaden, Ian was invited to go down and record interviews with them. By now, the words British Soldaten Sender or Forces Broadcasting opened many doors in Europe. When Edward Heath was to receive his Charlemagne Prize in Aachen, all it took was a phone call and facilities were made available. Ian will always be remembered as the disc jockey who was the first to play a Beatles record on BFN. He remarked: 'That's a strange name for a group, I don't think they'll make it.'

The state visit of HM the Queen to the Federal Republic of Germany in May 1965 put BFBS Cologne's resources to a demanding test. Ian Fenner, Brian Bass, Alan Parfrey, Pat Pachebat and Alastair McDougall produced a series of OBs along the hectic eleven-day route. These included covering ceremonies at a variety of cities, ranging from Munich to Hamburg, and making everything sound as if it was going according to plan. The royal party was continuously mobbed by enthusiastic spectators. In Koblenz, where the Queen gave her first address to the public, she reminded them that the first steamboat used on the Rhine in 1816 was made in Britain. When she had finished the crowd broke through the police cordon and the Guard of Honour was hastily deployed for crowd control. In Bonn, she laid a bouquet of roses at Beethoven's statue and in Cologne she was presented with a third-century AD Roman glass vessel and invited to sign the City's Golden Book. At RAF Gutersloh, seventy aircraft representing every type in service in Germany, including Hunters, Javelins, Canberras and Pembrokes, staged the biggest flypast in Europe since the Second World War. The next day, BFBS was covering the parade of 7,000 troops and 300 armoured vehicles, including Centurion and Conqueror tanks, in Sennelager. Then it was on to West Berlin where the Queen's Own Hussars fired a 21-gun salute, the first time a cavalry regiment had done so in the presence of a monarch.

Each night, the reports were sent back to BFBS Cologne for broadcast in the news magazine 'FBS Special', produced by Bob Egby. On the final day of the tour, Bob edited twenty hours of tape recordings down to a thirty-minute review and then went 'live' to Ian Fenner in Hamburg for a commentary on the departure of the Queen and Prince Philip on the Royal Yacht *Britannia*. 'It was', said Bob, 'a hectic time. We were virtually working round the clock, and when the Queen left, we were all caffeine addicts bouncing off the ceiling.'

'FBS Special' was a forty-five-minute nightly news and feature magazine which ran for 350 editions. Bob Egby, a former Suez accredited war correspondent, set up a network of correspondents and reporters all over West Germany and West Berlin. He equipped them with tape recorders and sent them off to cover stories in their area. 'We trained service personnel of all ranks – anyone showing promise and enthusiasm – and they responded well and produced some fascinating interviews. We did the programme live because we frequently got feeds from the various locations or a good interview would arrive just as we were going on air.' Bob was impressed with the enthusiasm of his team of reporters. 'Sometimes their enthusiasm went berserk. I assigned a regular member of staff to cover a German wine festival and told him I needed no more than five minutes. Off he went and made the fatal mistake of buying a glass and tasting the wine, which was freely available, before doing his interviews. The result was ninety minutes of rambling, reminiscent of the Goons, and it took half a day to cut it down to a four-minute piece!'

The popularity of BFBS with the German listeners was borne out when it was decided to hold an Open Day on Saturday 30 July 1966. It was only after the event had been well publicized that it dawned on the management of BFBS that 30 July was also World Cup Final Day and when it was realized that England would be meeting West Germany in the final, the big question was, would anyone turn up? As all the arrangements had been made, BFBS went ahead with its Open Day and placed TV sets at strategic points around the studio building and waited. In the event about 1,200 visitors turned up between mid-morning and early evening and while the match was on, every goal was announced over the 'in-house' loudspeaker system. That evening, West Deutscher Rundfunk had invited Pat Pachebat, the programme director, to take part in a 'live' broadcast to talk about the Open Day. 'I hastily scribbled a few notes in German about the day's activities but they were more interested in my views on whether the ball had crossed the line and was the Russian linesman in the right position to give the decision!'

The *BFN Bulletin*, in the mid-1960s, had changed very little from the original format set up in Hamburg. The station opened at 6.30 a.m. with 'Musical

Clock' – the time and a tune, followed by a programme for the housewives called 'For You at Home'. At 5 p.m. Bill Mitchell opened up his 'Kinder Klub', followed by the very popular '1800 Club'. 'The Archers', 'The Dales', 'Woman's Hour', 'Sunday Half-Hour' and 'Any Questions' were the top programmes relayed from the BBC. However, a closer look at the *Bulletin* reveals several former members of BFN Hamburg presenting programmes from the UK. Trevor Harvey, BFN's first head of music, was introducing 'Concert Hall', Don

Bill Mitchell, creator of the 'Big Wood' stories, working on his map   (*BFBS Archives*)

Moss – 'Pops at Your Place', Brian Matthew with 'Top of the Pops' and Alan Clarke commentating on many of the top football matches in England. David Hamilton, now of Radio 1, was introducing 'Mid-day Spin'.

Bill Mitchell, better known as Uncle Bill, was without doubt BFBS's greatest eccentric and was well known for his 'Big Wood' stories with Owl, Badger, Hedgehog, Constable Otter, Captain Rook and Water Rat, the villain. His sedate style of broadcasting would have been more suited to the BBC in the late 1940s, but children and adults alike adored him. Bill was a brilliant mimic; he read all his stories 'live' using seven or eight different character voices in each episode, and he never made a mistake. His performance was all the more astonishing because his scripts appeared to be a series of sentences with no notation as to which character was to say what. When quizzed about his ability, his favourite expression was 'It's all in my mind'.

At first Bill occupied a small office, but his legendary 'Big Wood' railway took up so much room that Pat Pachebat moved him into a larger office where the railway and later the 'Big Wood Tramway' blossomed, and it became the Mecca for all visitors to BFBS Cologne. However, woe betide any visitor who referred to 'his train set'. Bill would look at them like a Victorian grandfather: 'This is not a train set, it is a model railway.' Pat recalls visiting a transport unit and being invited to the officers' mess for tea: 'Imagine my surprise when I heard majors and captains making remarks like "pass the sugar, Owl" and "after you with the milk, Otter". At first I thought they were setting me up, but I was assured that they called each other by the names of the "Big Wood" characters because they had become such fans of the programme.' It was not just the British who were fascinated by 'Big Wood'. When Pat attended a lunch party at the British Embassy in Bonn, he met a German admiral who had a very British sense of humour. 'He often listened to BFBS, especially for the news and then he surprised me by saying, "Every day, when I leave my office, I sit back in my car and listen to Uncle Bill".'

Although his 'Big Wood' stories were brilliant, Bill was not suited to the new style of presentation. He could sound very superior and made anything near to pop music sound distasteful. He never saw himself as a music presenter – to Bill a DJ was something one wore to a 'posh do'! In the end, as BFBS Germany moved into the 1970s with its new sound, Bill decided to take early retirement.

When John Russell arrived in Cologne in 1968 he found, despite the changing world of broadcasting, BFBS Cologne was still steeped in the past. The German staff had formed few close relationships with their English colleagues, while some of the British staff had little or no concept of their real audience. This was due to the location of BFBS. Once surrounded by Army and RAF units, now the nearest serviceman was many miles away. He knew the older members of staff would oppose his radical plans, but he felt it was time to axe some of the 'sacred cows'. The evening request programme, the '1800 Club', which began in 1946, was the first to go and 'Family Favourites', the flagship programme of the BFBS schedule, was, in John Russell's eyes, past its sell-by date. He was convinced that the listener should not dictate what was broadcast, but should accept the announcer's choice! Another programme that suffered was 'Kinder Klub'. Although it had become a BFBS institution, he felt the programme was losing touch with its audience, and so it was cut from a daily show to thrice weekly. The old-fashioned announcer's shift pattern was the next to go and the Radio 1 style of presentation took over. Surprisingly, the biggest stumbling-block to the changes was found among the engineers, who were against self-operation by presenters.

The first major change was seen in the evening's broadcasting when a music and speech programme called 'Time Out' took over from the '1800 Club'. John Russell's brief to the producers was: 'Make the programme interesting, entertaining and relevant, and increase the serviceman's awareness of what is going on in Germany.' Soon the 'Time Out' team, which included David Davis and Keith Rawlings, were spreading their wings and covering such events as the Eurovision Song Contest, the Nijmegen Marches, visits to Antwerp and Brussels for British Week and from the beaches in Normandy on the 25th anniversary of D-Day. 'Time Out' was also invited to cover the floodlit Military Tattoo in Arnhem to celebrate twenty-five years of friendship and co-operation in NATO. Don Durbridge recalls an international incident. 'When the Turkish contingent came into the arena with their unusual marching routine, which appeared to be two steps forward and one to the side, with a simultaneous knee-bend action, the British participants standing off-stage fell about laughing. However, their amusement was cut short when a few minutes later, it was the turn of the British army to do its stuff. As luck would have it, we were represented by a famous Highland regiment, resplendent in their kilts and accompanied by the pipes and flutes. To the Turks, these men in women's skirts playing penny whistles was the funniest thing they had seen for some time. Now as we all know, the Jocks [sic] have a marked aversion to being laughed at, so as they completed their tableau, they marched off and straight away got stuck in to the Turks, who were gathered around in the dispersal areas. Our Turkish allies, as history has shown, are no mean performers when it comes to a bit of fighting and in no time at all, a fair old punch-up was in progress. It so happened the Americans were responsible for the Provost arrangements for that evening, and so not for the first time in the twentieth century, Uncle Sam had to wade in and pull warring Europeans apart! Their Marine Corps major, who was sharing the commentary box with me, put it rather succinctly – and I think accurately – when he turned to me and muttered: "Holy shit, God help the enemy if you guys ever get involved in the real thing!"'

Another member of the 'Time Out' team was Sandi Jones. Within a few weeks Sandi had not only caused controversy with several senior officers, who complained about a woman reading the news, but her first solo continuity shift brought with it a diplomatic problem. 'Saturday Night Theatre' was on a BBC transcription disc and about half-way through the programme the telephone rang. It was an irate German listener who, after living for several years in the United States, had returned to Germany and switched on BFBS to hear: 'The only good German is a dead German'. Sandi spent some considerable time placating him!

Sandi was interested in most things mechanical and could fix a broken tape deck with a paper clip as fast as any of her colleagues. However, being the only woman reporter she found she was in great demand. 'One of the most exciting broadcasts I ever recorded was with the King's Own Scottish Borderers. There were fourteen burly Scotsmen and I with my portable tape recorder, launching a mock attack on an "enemy" bunker during an exercise. We were helicoptered in and the moment we hit the ground, we were off and running. There were smoke bombs going off everywhere and explosions all around. It sounded very realistic but then as we charged over a hillock, we fell headlong into a very wet marsh. I kept the tape recorder going but the trouble was, even though I couldn't understand what the Jocks [sic] were saying, I was told later it wasn't really suitable for transmission on a family station.'

On another memorable occasion Sandi, Don Durbridge and David Davis were sent to interview the inhabitant of a massive and most forbidding castle overlooking the Rhine. As David recalls: 'It was straight out of a Hammer production. The door creaked when opened and after a tramp through huge halls and corridors, I met the owner. The interview was little short of a disaster because not only was the owner of great and venerable age, but he did not speak one word of English. However, some common ground was found when he took us on a tour of the dungeons, where I was shown armour, weaponry and some unpleasant instruments of torture, including a remarkably sturdy and extremely uncomfortable looking chastity belt which I was invited to try on! It proved to be a fascinating experience and we got an acceptable piece for "Time Out". However, since that day Sandi has always referred to me as Dr Drackenstein.'

Nigel Gillies had been a provincial newspaper reporter before joining the MoD as an assistant information officer. He was posted to the 4th Division PR Office in Herford. In the process of looking around the area, he discovered the old BFN studio on the top floor of one of the blocks in Hammersmith Barracks. The studio, complete with a full console, two microphones, three record decks and two reel-to-reel tape recorders, was not used apart from a couple of young subalterns who were using the facilities to transfer the latest pop records on to tape.

From the Herford studios, two or three evenings a week, came stories for 'Time Out' of events and personalities from the central region of BAOR. Nigel, with his BFBS microphone, was on board the first M2B bridge vehicle of the Royal Engineers to splash into the River Weser at Hameln. On another occasion an army cook, a native of Glasgow, had been preparing mountains of haggis for British Airways at the special launch of their new service from Düsseldorf to Scotland. After he had described, in detail, the ingredients and explained the method of cooking haggis, Nigel asked him: 'What is the most difficult part of preparing the haggis?' Without pause came the reply: 'Opening the tins!'

The BFN bulletin for 31 May 1971 highlighted a new programme – 'Ulster Calling' – which linked the men of 1st Battalion the Welsh Guards serving in Northern Ireland and their families back in Germany. Two weeks later a second request programme involving the Welsh Guards was broadcast, and it was presented by a new name to the BFBS Germany listeners – Gloria Hunniford. In the weeks that followed, Gloria spoke to men of 1st Battalion Light Infantry, 21st Engineer Regiment RE, 1st Battalion Royal Green Jackets, 45 Medium Regiment RA, 39 Missile Regiment RA, 15th/19th Hussars and 1st Battalion the Green Howards.

Gloria Hunniford, presenter of 'Ulster Calling', with soldiers of the 7th Royal Horse Artillery, with her co-presenter Sean Rafferty on the right   (*Crown Copyright/MoD*)

Asters (Richard Astbury) interviewing one of his many fans during an outside broadcast of his popular mid-morning programme   (*Neue Revue*)

The reaction to this programme by the wives in Germany was staggering and in a few years the idea would be copied by BFBS TV with Pam Rhodes.

John Russell recruited Richard Astbury from BFBS Cyprus and within a short time he had taken over as the breakfast show presenter. Richard was keen to impress his new boss with his all-round skills, so while a disc was running in the studio, he dashed to the telex room to pick up the latest German news. He checked the pronunciation, did a rough timing and at exactly five minutes to eight began to read the news bulletin. Unfortunately, the Telex machine was old and given to dropping the occasional letter. Instead of 'At least 150 Germans were killed on the autobahn over the holiday weekend', he saw and read 'At l-ast 150 Germans, etc.' The meeting with his new boss was short and to the point!

Several months later he was told to take over the morning show. In the years that followed, he built up a fantastic following. The programme was very controversial, especially when he started using 'live' telephone calls, the vast majority coming from the wives of soldiers who were in Northern Ireland. His conversations with them were full of double meanings and risqué allusions, but avoided rudeness. The interviews were either funny or acutely embarrassing. The listeners' reaction was amazing and 'Asters', as he had become known, and his programme had the highest audience figures of all the BFBS Germany programmes.

Although the wives could request any record from the library, they seemed to go for 'Don't Stick Stickers on My Paper Knickers' or the Frankie Howerd, June Whitfield version of 'Up je t'aime'. Not everyone was in agreement, several officers' wives protested about the programme, but the overall effect on morale was good. Richard Astbury accepted that his programme was not to everyone's taste: 'It was a time of great anxiety for the wives whose husbands were away in Northern Ireland, and anyhow sex makes life more interesting!' When he opened his first fête at Soest, Richard was staggered by the number of people who wanted to meet him and either get his autograph or just talk. It was discovered that his presence at a fête could put an extra 4,000 on the gate!

In his desire to bring new ideas into the schedule, John Russell set up a new Sunday night programme called 'The After Ten People'. It was a sort of 'South Bank Show' on radio, with a variety of stars from the theatre, arts and music appearing on the show. Although such stars as Cliff Richard, Ray Charles, Lena Horne and Eartha Kitt took part in his programme, the guest who really stood out was Steve Biko. After the programme, Biko wrote in 'The After Ten People's' book: 'Differences grow on trees, but if we can ever expect whites to understand blacks, I think the British people will be the first to start such co-operation.' However, time was running out for John. Following a disagreement over a matter of principle with the head office in London, he was posted to BFBS Cyprus. He left a station that had started to throw off most of its old BFN image and was becoming a radio station of the 1970s.

After a short spell as a freelance with BFBS Berlin, Peter McDonagh arrived in Cologne in 1972. He felt the station was still split into two groups – an older element, who were not interested in trying anything that might disturb their way of life, and a group of youngsters who were desperate to see the station brought up to date. The problem was that for long periods of the day BFBS Germany was not actually broadcasting, but relaying the BBC. As audience research later indicated, these relays, professional in content though they were, had no actual relevance to the audience's requirements.

The BFBS drivers' rest room became a hotbed of intrigue. Here the youngsters gathered to discuss what was happening back home in the 'real' world of radio. As Nick Bailey recalls: 'We were the angry young people who wanted to change everything. We felt the station, by trying to be all things to all people, was failing to make progress.' Nick, supported by Sarah Kennedy, took their ideas for change to the management, who decided to call their bluff. 'Who is going to produce these new programmes?' Nick agreed to take it on and supported by Liz Shaw assumed responsibility for broadcasting from 6.25 p.m.

In 1973 BFBS appointed six trainees for their worldwide service, left to right: Sarah Kennedy, Patrick Lunt, Nick Bailey, Richard Gwynn, Richard Clegg, Nicol Raymond. All except Richard Clegg were to serve in Germany on either BFBS radio or television

(*Crown Copyright/MoD*)

until midnight. The new '6.25 Show' incorporated 'The Archers', 'Sportsdesk' and the main news bulletins with as many 'live' interviews as they could obtain. The second part of the programme became one of the most popular on BFBS Germany. Created by Nick, it was called 'Radio Roulette' and was based on the top fifty records with the audience calling in and selecting a number between 1 and 50. Alongside the numbers, as well as the record, there would be a prize, a booby prize or a star prize (that could be anything from a washing machine to a holiday for two) and *the forfeit*! The booby prize could be a bottle of Rhine water or a lock of Richard Astbury's hair but it was the forfeits that made the show. One of the most popular was to get a young soldier to impersonate a senior officer returning home from a mess party. 'Radio Roulette' even had a forfeit of the month competition judged by a panel rather like goal of the month on BBC TV's 'Match of the Day'. Although the '6.25 Show' had the same rating as the very popular breakfast show, the arrival of Format 77 meant the demise of the programme – it did not even get to its first birthday.

Another of the rest-room rebels, Peter McDonagh, ever the inventive broadcaster, decided to send up the rather staid 'German for Beginners'. Using one of the network control room engineers, Dieter Gripp, as the teacher, he launched 'English for Beginners'. After twenty episodes, the programme was dropped following complaints from the British Council. Dieter is still recalled today by both English and German listeners as the 'English-speaking Dieter Gripp'. In 1975 Peter left on a posting to BFBS Malta, but returned two years later with news of the idea that would revolutionize Forces Broadcasting in Germany.

Format 77 had been created in Malta and if used in Germany would give the station a brand new sound. The veterans were unimpressed, but when Bob Pierson, one of the architects of Format 77, arrived from Malta to take over as senior programme director, disagreement turned to hostility. As Peter recalled: 'It was almost a mutiny and after a short time, Bob Pierson left Cologne, but his idea remained and sequence programming had come to stay.' Before Format 77 began 30 per cent of BFBS's audience claimed that its pop music was too noisy, while another 30 per cent argued that it was not loud enough. Once the system was up and running the vast majority of BFBS Germany's target audience (aged under 30) began to identify with it. Colin Rugg, later to become Regional Director of Broadcasting in Germany, found that some of the senior military officers were not too impressed with the new sound. 'They were an audience who approved of listening in theory as opposed to listening in practice. For us Format 77 was vital, live and more irreverent. It brought a dramatic response to the station with an increase in mail and invitations to visit service units. However, there were still those who wanted a return to our carefully crafted programmes of the past.'

The arrival of television in 1975 had had an impact on BFBS Germany's radio audience. Some of the Cologne presenters did not believe that their listeners had deserted them and only changed their minds in later years when they began to watch BFBS TV themselves. After the move to Werl had virtually doubled the TV audience, the programme planners in Cologne decided to concentrate their resources on the period from 6 a.m. to 6 p.m. Colin Rugg often wondered what might have happened to Format 77 if the growth of television had gone according to plan: 'It might have come too late to have the desired effect on the sound and style of BFBS Germany.'

A new programme was making an impact in BFBS Germany. Introduced from BFBS London by Tommy Vance, it followed the musical formula of Format 77 and added to it interviews with some of the world's top personalities. In an interview with Joshua Nkomo about democracy in Africa and one man one vote,

Tommy ended by saying: 'Won't it be marvellous when everyone in Africa has the chance to vote?' Nkomo's reply was fascinating: 'Don't be so damned silly, never give an African a choice!' Another of his guests was Gore Vidal, one of the world's greatest writers. At the end of a fascinating interview Tommy asked him: 'What do you consider to be the most important thing that America has given to the world?' Vidal's answer was short and to the point: 'Kleenex.'

In the 1970s many servicemen from Germany were on emergency tours of Northern Ireland and the wives were naturally worried. Letters were not the answer and as the MoD had never been particularly generous when it came to telephones, BFBS was to prove a great morale booster. From the military point of view, the radio service was important to the many young wives who had never been abroad before, could not speak German and whose husbands were serving in Ulster. Colonel John Mayo, the former Head of Public Relations in BAOR, was a great supporter of BFBS: 'We used BFBS extensively because we knew we could pass on information to the families immediately. It is fair to say that not everyone was totally supportive of BFBS and a few senior officers felt that its news broadcasts should be censored and if there were adverse comments about BAOR or RAF Germany, these items should be excluded. This was of course nonsense but if the officers persisted, I would refer them to the Commander-in-Chief, who was a keen supporter of what BFBS was trying to achieve.'

John's wife Jacqueline was one of the finest exponents of keeping the families in touch. She started out by writing for the housing commandant's journal, then the editor of *Soldier* saw these articles and asked her to write a page for the families in his magazine. After she had been writing for *Soldier* for two years, Ian Woolf suggested that she should become a regular contributor for BFBS. As her broadcasting increased, so did the response. Service wives realized they had a voice and someone who would fight their corner without compromising them. Soon Jacqueline, or Anne Armstrong as she was known to thousands of service families, began to have meetings with the Adjutant-General. She was able to brief him about problems that may not have come up through the normal chain of command. Her critics once described her as 'a misguided missile, or a peptic ulcer in the belly of the Ministry of Defence'.

Perhaps the highlight of Jacqueline's broadcasting career was her interview with Margaret Thatcher for the 1979 Christmas programme. Jacqueline knew if she applied officially there was no way the MoD would sanction the interview. So she wrote a letter, popped it through the letterbox at Number 10, and got her interview. When she arrived she was taken by Margaret Thatcher into her private apartments, whereupon the PM said: 'Just look at this room, typical – furnished by men – with every single radiator covered by heavy curtains.' Then looking at a bulky file in front of her, the PM said: 'The MoD were so frightened of your coming to see me that they have sent me all these briefs.' With that, Margaret Thatcher pushed them to one side and said: 'What shall we talk about?' Jacqueline ended the interview by saying: 'Prime Minister, this is going out at Christmas time, do you have a favourite carol?' To which the PM replied: 'Yes I have,' and promptly recited it.

Although a limited form of audience research was under way, there were times when BFBS received programme suggestions from the 'top brass'. In a letter to Pat Pachebat, Gen Sir Harry Tuzo, C–in–C BAOR, suggested that BFBS should relay the 'Today' programme from Radio 4 instead of their own local programme. Pat replied: 'After consideration, I do not believe your suggestion to be right for the majority of our audience, and furthermore it would deny us an outlet for all types of local information, at a critical listening period.' He waited for the C–in–C's reply, knowing that the C–in–C RAF Germany was also keen on Radio 4. As Pat recalls: 'I had a charming reply from the general saying he quite understood that this idea of his would not be in the best interests of most of his soldiers, and he accepted my decision.'

In the late 1970s the Charter for the British Forces Broadcasting Service Germany was amended. Its main objective was to assist in maintaining the morale of the Forces in the Federal Republic of Germany, including West Berlin, and elements in Holland and Belgium by providing them with a radio and television service of entertainment, information and education, and a link with home. With regard to the programme content, the Charter recommended that locally produced programmes should concentrate on reflecting service life, at the same time endeavouring to bring to the attention of the service community matters of interest relating to Germany's culture and history, and relevant domestic and social matters. It was important that the station should make its listeners feel that it belonged to them by involving them as closely as possible in its programmes and fostering meetings both formal and informal between staff and audience.

There were occasions when BFBS felt they had to lead the way rather than wait until the military asked them to do something, and in 1977, after lengthy engineering and programme discussions, it was decided to provide all night broadcasting by means of recorded programmes on a sequential tape machine system. There were many night and shift workers, plus Op Banner wives who spent sleepless nights worrying about their husbands away in Northern Ireland. So, without asking, BFBS Germany quietly went ahead and did it. Pat Pachebat had been assured by his engineering staff that the running costs were really little more than a handful of electric light bulbs. 'I quoted this at the next Advisory Meeting when challenged by the financial representative. It was a bit of a "whopper", but we got past the committee and were actually congratulated on showing the initiative.' However, there were a few teething problems. Liz Shaw arrived one morning to present the breakfast show. Normally, she would switch everything on and then wake up the duty engineers. On this particular morning, the studio was up and running and Ludwig Marx, the duty engineer, was staring dolefully into his coffee. It appeared that during the night a thunderstorm had set off the overnight system and it had gone through six hours of programmes and announcements, including the close-down announcement, in just under fifty-five minutes!

Liz enjoyed presenting the breakfast show, but after a while became paranoid about over-sleeping. She reached a stage where she had three alarm clocks set, just in case. One dark winter's morning she awoke with a start and looked at the clock. It was a quarter past six and she should have been on the air fifteen minutes ago. This was her worst nightmare: 'I dressed as quickly as possible, threw open the bedroom door and rushed downstairs. As I was trying to open the front door, a sleepy voice from the landing above said, "For God's sake Liz, what are you doing?", I looked up and saw my housemate, Sarah Kennedy, standing there with a bewildered expression on her face. "Not now – I haven't time to talk, Sarah, I'm late," while fumbling furiously with the lock. "But Liz," said Sarah, "it's only half past three!" All of a sudden I felt very tired. I'd misread the clock, but, to make matters worse, I would have to do this all over again in two hours' time!'

Sarah, who had joined BFBS Cologne from BFBS Singapore, was another early morning presenter, who shared the task with one of Germany's great characters – Andrew Pastouna. He had a great wit, a neat turn of phrase and kept his colleagues in fits of laughter with stories usually against himself. On one occasion he was living in an officers' mess in Bielefeld where he was frequently chastised by the regimental padre for his somewhat 'camp' ways. One morning the padre sat opposite Andrew at breakfast and said: 'Oh Andrew, I was thinking about you so much when I went to bed last night.' Quick as a flash Andrew interjected: 'Padre, you should have called me, I'd have come straight over!' The young subalterns almost choked over their fried eggs and bacon. His great passion was buying Rolls-Royces previously used by members of the royal family, renovating them, and reselling them, usually to Americans, and usually at a considerable profit. He often loaned his Rolls to the military when they had a member of the royal family visiting one of their regiments in Germany.

Andrew was a great name-dropper, especially when contacting members of the royal family for the book he wrote about the royal Rolls-Royces. His conversations would be punctuated with: 'As the Queen Mum said to me over tea the other day . . . Prince Michael told me that. . . .' His book, when it was published, was well received by the Rolls-Royce fraternity.

From the very early days of BFN quizzes had been popular with the listeners and over the years the programmes had ranged from the 'Brain of BFG', originally hosted by Vic Andersen and produced by Ian Woolf, to the 'BFN

Frau Doktor Mildred Scheel with Pat Pachebat leaving the studio following her interview with Tommy Vance

(*Crown Copyright/MoD*)

Sports Quiz'. When Alan Clough arrived from BFBS Gibraltar, he found his reputation as a quiz producer had preceded him. He was asked to resurrect 'Brain of BFG', which had fallen into decline after a sad occasion some years before when the quizmaster, being a sensitive soul, burst into tears when a team member queried the score! The new format involved nearly 100 teams each year and Chris Russell, with the help of the Royal Army Education Corps, ran a series of eliminators around Germany. The standard was high and two of the contestants had appeared on 'Mastermind' and one on 'Brain of Britain'. In 1988 the 'Brain of BFG', presented by Charly Lowndes and produced by Alan Clough, won the Bicentennial Pater Award in Australia for the best Original Listener Contest Programme in the International Open category.

There are many versions of the story surrounding the visit to BFBS by the wife of the then West German President, Walter Scheel. Frau Doktor Mildred Scheel had agreed to take part at the last moment in a world-wide Christmas link-up, hosted from London by Tommy Vance. The Scheels lived only 200 yards from the BFBS studio and when BFBS's offer to send a car to collect her was declined, the staff were told she would make her own arrangements. Expecting an official car and possible out–riders, the station car park was cleared of all vehicles. It was then discovered the carpet in the entrance hall of 61 Parkstrasse (the studio building) was rather badly stained and so an engineer was despatched to purchase a bottle of the best carpet cleaner available. Unfortunately, it could not remove all the stains and so members of staff were detailed to stand on the worst areas when she arrived. In the meantime Frau Scheel had decided to walk from her home and went to the BFBS administration building (No.1 Lindenallee) which, for security reasons, was locked. After she had rung the bell several times, a small window was opened by Willi Greesens the German admin. officer. Not realizing who she was, he told her that if she wanted petrol coupons, she would have to go to the studio building in Parkstrasse. When she pointed out she was to be a guest on 'BFBS UK' the penny dropped and, mumbling apologies, Willi let her into the building. In the meantime, the welcoming committee, still in 61 Parkstrasse, was informed of her arrival and proceeded, at great speed, down the corridor that connected the two buildings. Profuse apologies were offered and she was shown into the studio. At this point Tommy Vance introduced his distinguished guest and then asked her if he could call her by her Christian name. She agreed, but the Station Director in Cologne was not too happy about the informality. Frau Doktor Mildred Scheel was quite unperturbed.

In 1976 Dave Raven decided to leave the frenetic world of UK radio and run a night club in Malta. Here he was spotted by Peter McDonagh and tempted back into radio with BFBS Malta. With the impending departure of the Armed Forces from Malta in 1979, Dave realized he needed to think about his future and accepted an offer to work full-time with BFBS Germany. Bob Pierson, Cologne's Senior Programme Director, had worked with Dave in Malta and gave him the midday show. 'My first reaction was awe at the size and disposition of the audience. Instead of Malta, where I had met nearly all 6,000 of them, I now had 100,000 spread over an area the size of England. I obtained a huge map of Northern Germany and with two gross of mapping pins – 144 red and 144 blue – I put a red pin in every forces location across Germany and one blue pin in Cologne. I realized that if I was going to relate to the audience, then I had to know what Detmold was like and where Hohne was in relation to anywhere else, so I planned to visit every BFPO number in my first year. Because the infrastructure wasn't in place, we had a few early disasters. The first time we had no mains leads, the next, no cart machines and the third, no styli for the gram decks. Thankfully, the team of Phil Harding, Jurgen Bock and myself always set out on the Thursday afternoon, arriving at the location in the evening, and set up the kit that night. So there was always time for someone to go back to Cologne to collect any missing items before the show started at 10 a.m. on Friday. Op–Banner was the 'excuse' for the first batch of broadcasts, putting

BAOR's latest recruits Steve Wright, Samantha Fox and Peter McDonagh at the Rhine Army
Summer Show, 1987   (*Crown Copyright/MoD*)

the wives in touch with their husbands in Northern Ireland, but gradually we ended
up going anywhere for any reason. We did shows from NAAFIs with me standing
next to the check-out girls, we went to fêtes, visited the lads at work in truck parks,
firing ranges – in fact anywhere that made good radio.' Before the year was out,
Dave Raven had visited every service area in Germany and the red pins on his map
had all been replaced by blue ones.

Over the years BFBS had its fair share of threatening phone calls and
suspicious letters and parcels but luckily they all came to nothing. The IRA
threat was more worrying, especially to the German staff who, unlike some of
their British colleagues, had not been through the emergencies in places like
Aden, Kenya, Cyprus and Benghazi. A number of security surveys were carried
out on BFBS Cologne but the Military found the measures proposed were
prohibitively expensive and nothing was ever done. Indeed nothing less than a
high steel fence all around the perimeter and armed patrols would have deterred

a terrorist. Pat Pachebat, who had become Station Controller in 1974, recalls that the staff always joked that the terrorists left BFBS alone because they did not want to put our programmes off the air.

However, Pat had a scare early one morning when walking from his house along the Rhine towards the studios. 'It was 5.45 a.m. and suddenly a car with four men drew up beside me and two of them jumped out. I thought "Dear God, so this is how it happens" and really believed my last moment had come. I almost hugged them with relief when they asked me, in broken German, the way to the Polish Embassy!'

BFBS's popularity with its listeners had not diminished. It was highlighted in most unusual circumstances when Tony Davis, the breakfast show presenter, was sent on an OB to Berlin. He was booked to travel on the British military train from Braunschweig to Berlin through the so-called 'Corridor' in East Germany. At one of the official checkpoints the train's duty NCO collected all the passports and took them, accompanied by a posse of East German border guards, to an office where they were checked before the procedure was reversed and the passengers would continue on their journey. For Tony and the rest of the travellers there was a feeling of apprehension and nervousness: 'It was a grey drizzly morning straight out of a John Le Carré novel and after what seemed like an eternity we saw the NCO get back on the train but it did not move away as we had expected. After a few minutes, the NCO appeared at the door of my compartment, 'Mr Davis, I regret to inform you that the East German authorities will not let us move on because they want something from you.' My heart missed a beat, but then he continued: 'They have asked that, as they are great fans of yours and listen to BFBS every morning, would you please give them an autograph and the next time you're on the radio, please give them a mention.' The next morning Tony gave a discreet greeting to 'our East German friends at the checkpoint'.

In 1980 a young inexperienced presenter called Mike Allen wrote himself into the BFBS Germany folklore. Mike had been in Cologne for about four months when he was rostered for the Sunday morning shift which covered the Remembrance Sunday outside broadcast. During the preceding week Padre Alec Smith had briefed him about the service and what would be happening. What happened next is etched forever in Mike Allen's memory. 'The service was coming from the Garrison Church in Münster and my role was to introduce the service and at the end of the programme pre-fade some suitable music to run up to the next news junction. It began well enough. I read my carefully prepared announcement and Ulli, the control room engineer, opened up the fader and in came the dulcet tones of Alec Smith. I listened for a few minutes, then realized I needed to time my religious music fill in case the programme under-ran. I informed the engineer, who had only been with us for one month and whose

Mike Allen with an unusual guest   (*Mike Allen*)

English was a little suspect, that I would be checking on the music so he would have to monitor the service. After a few minutes, Ulli came on the talkback: "We've gone off the air". I flicked my programme output switch – nothing. "Are you sure?" I asked Ulli, at which point, he held up a telephone. "I've got Phil Harding, the OB engineer, on the phone and he says we're off the air." I'd never done an on-air apology before, so I took a deep breath and said, "Well I'm very sorry ladies and gentlemen, we're obviously having a slight technical problem, but rest assured, the engineers are working on it and we should be able to rejoin Padre Smith very shortly." Just as I was congratulating myself on an announcement well done, I heard a trumpet sound the Last Post. I realized what I had done. I had just apologized for the two minutes' silence. With hindsight, the inexperienced Ulli and myself were an audio accident looking for somewhere to happen. I was being correct in monitoring and timing my record, Ulli was being correct in monitoring the output, Phil Harding was being correct by telephoning Ulli and saying: "There's a silence built into this programme, do nothing". Sadly Ulli, in his panic, misinterpreted the message as "We've gone off the air". They say the longest day of the year is in June, but for me in 1980, it was in November!'

The following year Mike and Ulli got their own back with their April Fool. In those days, BFBS ran a listeners' top ten immediately after the 11 o'clock news. Normally the presentation of these records was pretty straightforward with absolutely no negative comment being made about the listeners' choice. Richard Astbury was in his office in Lindenallee and like a good Senior Programme Director was listening to the station output. In between telephone calls, he half heard what he thought was an insult, but dismissed it as impossible. Now he started to listen more carefully, and the rudeness increased with every link to the point where Mike was using bad language. Richard phoned the studio and told Mike very bluntly to 'pack it in'. The next link was even worse: 'How could you choose "Zorba the Greek", it's the biggest load of bloody crap I've ever heard, so I'm taking it off.' By now, Asters was incandescent with rage and stormed across to the studios, pausing only to hear another blast of fresh vitriol from Mike upon the so-called listener. Hurling the studio door open, Richard demanded he stop the insults and he would see him after the show. As he left the studio, he could not understand why the other members of staff were looking puzzled by his outburst. Only then did he go into the control room and hear Mike presenting the listeners' top ten normally. Then he saw a spoof tape going round that had been plugged into the ring-main, just for him. Forgiveness was late that spring!

On 16 March 1981 John Grist, the former BBC American representative, was taken on by the MoD to examine the possibility of a merger involving BFBS and the SKC. Eight months later he submitted his first report to the Vice Chief of Defence Staff, Second Sea Lord and the Adjutant-General: 'When I joined the MoD, I was given a large weight of documentation which had accumulated over several years. What emerged from this reading was that BFBS had done a good job in the last twenty years or so, but for a variety of reasons, it sat uneasily as a small department in the MoD carrying out a function falling outside the mainstream of defence business. If a structure not subject to departmental restraints and ideally with related aims could be found to support it and guarantee that the quality of the broadcasting was sustained, it might be politic to move it from the civil service.' In his assessment of BFBS radio, he wrote: 'It is clear that BFBS radio performs an essential welfare function and that in general it does a first class job with limited resources.' Looking at the development of radio in Germany, he went on: 'One way in Germany to provide more choice and a more specifically local or community content in programmes would be to expand local radio. There are already manned stations in Rheindahlen, Bielefeld and Berlin capable of acting as local radio stations at certain times of the day. More stations could be added. Such stations would provide an important means of communicating with servicemen and families both about community affairs and day-to-day matters – traffic, school buses, clubs and the like – and in times of emergency. For the broadcasters, there would be the satisfaction of a more immediate involvement with their audience.' As with the Knott Report 20 years earlier, one of the first hurdles that had to be overcome was a new corporate title. The suggestions ranged from British Forces Broadcasting, Film and Video Corporation to the Chalfont Grove Corporation, but in the end, John Grist recommended the new organization be called the Services Sound and Vision Corporation.

When news of the merger reached BFBS Germany the staff were vehemently against it for a number of reasons, but they knew that Ian Woolf would be fighting it 'tooth and nail'. Dick Norton was the BFBS Station Director in Cologne: 'I cannot count the number of justifications I had to write for Ian Woolf explaining why a merger would be a bad thing. In the end we lost and became the Radio Division of the SSVC – a nomenclature that I came up with when it was becoming obvious we were on a losing wicket. Against all expectations, the advent of the SSVC I saw as being quite a good thing. From the engineers' point of view, the merger brought a golden opportunity to buy the equipment we had always cherished without having to consult someone at JHQ, so we ended up with pretty much state-of-the-art studios.'

In October 1983 John Bussell took over as SSVC's Director Radio. What he found was 'A highly professional group of broadcasters who had inevitably been somewhat demoralized by the conflicts and uncertainties surrounding the merger.' Part of his brief from John Grist was to draw up a five-year plan for BFBS Radio. His own brief to himself was to provide a positive future for the people in it. John felt that, although the other BFBS stations represented the best in community radio, the biggest station in Cologne was still more like a BBC Regional Headquarters. 'BFBS Germany was the jewel in the crown, but was out of step both with the rest of Forces Broadcasting and with the local and community radio developments in the UK. The so-called local stations in Bielefeld and JHQ Rheindahlen could not provide local output and were producing just a few minutes of network output per day.' History had also overtaken Forces Radio in Germany in the geographical sense. When BFN moved to Cologne there were still many British troops in the area. By 1983 the nearest troops were 80 kilometres away.

Several factors encouraged John Bussell to believe that radical change was possible: some seven years earlier Colin Rugg had with great foresight persuaded the Deutsche Bundespost to apply for low-power FM frequencies at Osnabrück, Bielefeld, Lippstadt, Hohne, Münster and later Rheindahlen. These frequencies had never been activated and Colin warned John that, with local radio developing apace in Germany, there were growing signs that the Bundespost would want the frequencies back if BFBS did not use them quickly. Second,

Colin and his engineering team had developed a unique design for transportable container-based studios which carried their own power, transmitter and mast. These studios were designed in the first instance for the Falklands and Belize, but could be installed in any military location able to provide a simple concrete base.

On the programme side John had strengthened the output in the Falklands by sending major BFBS presenters from Germany and Cyprus on four month detachments. Richard Nankivell from Cologne was one of the most popular presenters to spend time in the South Atlantic. On Richard's return to Germany, John decided to post him to Bielefeld to boost the output and specifically to present a two-hour daily sequence programme from there. This experiment succeeded entirely as a result of Richard's boundless enthusiasm. This was the model for the future local stations!

John's concept was indeed radical! He wanted an interlocking network of five local stations located where BFBS already had low-power frequency. Each station would be able at the flick of a switch either to contribute to the network or to opt out to provide local output. There would be no large headquarters station as such. Each station using container-based studios if necessary would require two presenters and one UK-based engineer.

The scheme required two-way programme and control circuits to and from each station. John's first step was to talk to Colin Rugg who assured him that the plan was technically feasible, but both were aware of the potential obstacles. Cost was inevitably one. The plan would require expensive re-engineering of the programme circuitry, a small increase in programme staff, a slightly larger increase of UK-based engineers, and of course almost all of the German engineering staff would have to be made redundant. Both John and Colin suspected that there could be misgivings at the various headquarters but they had no doubt that the plan would be welcomed at Brigade level. John also had more than a sneaking suspicion that there would be opposition from some of the more traditional broadcasters. 'One presenter told me that broadcasters needed the company of other broadcasters, not of the audience – not a point of view I shared.'

Nevertheless John and Colin pressed ahead and drew up a basic plan to present to John Grist. He accepted it in principle and because John Bussell was about to move on to become Director (Western Europe), asked Colin to develop and cost the plan in more detail.

When Pat Pachebat became Director of Broadcasting he assumed responsibility for radio as well as television and for the implementation of the change in Germany. The final implementation was substantially different from the original plan and not all of the more radical changes were achieved, but John Bussell's aim of getting closer to the audience and of establishing genuine local stations in the Brigade areas were accomplished very effectively indeed.

When Padre Alec Smith was posted to BFBS Cologne as the full-time padre with the responsibility for extending the scope of religious broadcasting, he was following a long line of excellent religious broadcasters from Bob Crossett and Robert Foxcroft, to Stanley Brinkman and Robin Turner. At the time, all Army and RAF chaplains had to record their 'Just a Moment' talks at the studios in Cologne. Some came reluctantly, under orders, and were reminded that in their week 'on air' they would be able to speak to more people than Jesus Christ did in the whole of his earthly life. Alec remembers one chaplain who failed to arrive and as he was working on a week-to-week basis, he had nothing in reserve. 'I phoned his Unit, who confirmed that he had indeed left for Cologne in good time and was travelling in a very fast car. During the afternoon, the telephone rang in the studio. It was the missing chaplain. "And where do you think you've been?" I shouted down the phone; "Sorry, I got lost", he replied. "Well stay where you are and I'll send someone to guide you in. I know how confusing Cologne can be." "That may be difficult", came the reply, "I think I'm looking at a notice that says, Welcome to Frankfurt!"'

The MoD was going through one of those periods of financial stringency, and chaplains were forbidden hotel accommodation and payment for the use of their cars. The next padre due to record was with the Army Air Corps. He rang Alec Smith to tell him he had no intention of leaving home in the middle of the night to catch the only available train to Cologne just for a broadcast. 'He informed me he would be arriving by helicopter and landing it in the BFBS gardens. "You can't do that," I said, "you must take it up with the Cologne/Bonn airport, they must have a Military facility".' The following Wednesday, Alec and his engineer Mick Kiss heard the sound of a helicopter low over the studios. 'That's our padre arriving,' said Mick. 'So we sent a car to collect him.' The hours went by and the car returned without the padre. Telephone calls were made and another car was sent to the airport which returned with a very shaken chaplain, who told his story as he lay on the library carpet with his head in Kay Donnelly's lap being treated for shock. The helicopter was on a 'training flight' and had landed heavily; the pilot had bitten through his lip and was now in hospital and the machine's undercarriage was damaged. Another helicopter was on its way with fitters to assess and possibly repair the damage and all this to save a few gallons of petrol! The chaplain came down again a week later by car, but his scripts were so awful that Alec Smith could not use them.

Charly Lowndes arrived in Cologne as the Senior Programme Director in 1985 and he asked Dick Norton what BFBS did if the Russians invaded, 'Ah, there's a plan.' 'Can I see it?', Charly asked, conscious of its importance. 'Sure', said Dick, 'but we don't keep it here, it's secret and our safe isn't secure.' So they visited another British agency, whose work dictated that they had a secure safe. Charly recalls: 'There was a long cabaret involving the fetching of sealed envelopes from a guarded vault and the signing of each seal as it was cut. Inside the outer envelope was another one, and so on, until eventually we came to a red folder marked 'SECRET – Action to be taken by BFBS in Time Of War'. Inside was a single sheet of paper with the imposing letterhead of the Commanders-in-Chief's Committee, Germany. It contained a single sentence: 'A committee is to be set up to study what action should be taken by BFBS in Time Of War.'

Colin Rugg returned to Cologne as the Regional Director of Broadcasting in 1987. He had a difficult task: 'My agenda, which was not hidden, was to implement the plan which John Bussell and I had formulated and to move the radio service away from Cologne. Several attempts had been made in the seventies and early eighties to do this, but it was always considered too expensive. The problem at the time was that the planners thought in terms of moving from one monolithic structure to another but in a different location. The other part of my agenda was to finish off the effects of Format 77 by taking us back to our roots among the Military. Dick Norton, my predecessor, had played a vital role in raising the profile of BFBS Cologne with the German media by insisting that we were one of Germany's top radio stations. I had to break that link. We were going to Herford and we were going back into a military barracks, back to being the British Forces Broadcasting Service rather than one of West Germany's national radio networks.' The service, if it was to integrate with its audience, would have to return to its audience.

Although Colin had described his posting as the culmination of a dream, he knew that if he succeeded with the move, he would be faced with the prospect of putting many of his loyal German colleagues out of a job, a task which he achieved without too much bitterness.

To get a flavour of what life was like in the small studio complex in BFBS Bielefeld, he spent time with Patrick Eade, who was then the Corps Representative. As Colin recalled: 'I will always remember Patrick telling me that he had no idea what people were talking about when they said we were too remote in Cologne, but when I came to Bielefeld, I realized what it meant to be among our audience and now I felt that I was a Forces broadcaster.' Despite the efforts of Format 77, the staff in Cologne were still out of touch with their audience.

Colin Rugg, Charly Lowndes and Peter McDonagh drew up the plans for the move. In their report published in June 1989 they stated that their first objective was to disband the radio studio complex in Cologne and create a radio network with its centre in Wentworth Barracks, Herford, and with small manned contribution studios in Rheindahlen (JHQ), Bielefeld, Osnabrück, Paderborn and Hohne. They felt this would raise the profile of SSVC broadcasting activities in Germany by the increased regional representation and greater contact with the military audience. They recommended the start date as 1 July 1989, with the move to be completed by 30 September 1990. The plan was endorsed by Pat Pachebat and Alan Protheroe, the new managing director. According to Colin: 'There were many in Cologne who hoped that the new MD could be persuaded to reverse the policy, but he endorsed it wholeheartedly.' As Alan recalls: 'I felt BFBS had not really come to terms with the fact that the war was over. Too many of its staff basked in the past and so I had a few nettles to grasp. When I had a meeting in Cologne and told them what was going to happen, there were many who were opposed to the idea for their life had become too easy. I told them "everyone had to become more involved with the station and especially its audience."'

One of the main benefits of moving back into a military community would be the extra security now available to BFBS. In the late 1980s the IRA campaign against the British Forces in Germany had caused a number of midnight phone calls. The bombings and shootings were announced as soon as details were clear, to minimize the possibility of rumour, and where possible, to minimize the circle of concern. Charly Lowndes, who had taken over as Controller Broadcasting (Western Europe) from Colin Rugg, remembers the time when Monica Dutton, their reporter in Rheindahlen, was caught in her bath when E Officers' Mess was blown up by a car bomb, fortunately without fatalities. 'Pausing only, I have always assumed, to wrap a towel around her, she was quickly on the telephone with a factual eyewitness account of what had happened. Parents of children in the nearby school boarding house were grateful to hear that their children were all safe and accounted for.'

The small British community in Cologne lived in the Volkspark alongside a general who commanded the Joint Service Liaison Organisation. One winter weekend there had been a vague threat against a senior British officer which resulted in a Close Protection team being sent down from Düsseldorf. As the general and his family were in the little church in the Volkspark, the team staked out the car park. Half-way through the first hymn, they came to the door and beckoned to Ian Bishop, the BFBS receptionist, who was a born-again Christian and had the looks of a rock star. 'Is that your car, sir?'. 'No'. 'But we saw you arrive in it.' 'Well, it's my girlfriend's car.' 'Could you explain the package on the front seat?' 'What do you mean?' 'There is a cardboard box on the front seat, sir, with the lid shut and wires leading from it to the dashboard. What's in the box?' 'Oh, that. It's a duck.' At this point, the Close Protection team drew their guns and hid behind a pillar while a puzzled Ian opened his car to show them the duck, which he had found with a broken wing the day before. He was just keeping it warm with an aquarium heater in the cardboard box which was filled with straw.

26 February 1954 to 31 October 1990. Unremarkable dates in themselves but they opened and closed a massive chapter in the history of Forces Broadcasting

in Germany. In 1954 a Brigadier arrived by special train to formally open the new studios. Perhaps an indication of the enhanced stature of BFBS within the military community was that the close-down speech in 1990 was given by a three-star General.

About 150 people gathered in Parkstrasse for a party to mark the last evening. Many were past and present members of the British and German staff. The wall plaque that had for so many years adorned the entrance to Lindenallee was presented to the Lady Mayor of Cologne, who replied with a warm compliment to the city's fourth and smallest radio station. When the chairman made his farewell speech, he talked about the early days in Hamburg and of the great names who had been with us, including Sir Geraint Evans, and looking at his notes he paused and said: 'And that great German conductor Herbert von Car-rye-jan'. The Lady Mayor did not bat an eyelid! The last programme from BFBS Cologne ended with the beautifully moving 'Evening Hymn and Last Post', the melody that had closed the daily transmissions on every Forces Radio station since 1945.

The two rather grand houses which BFBS Cologne occupied from the early 1950s were eventually closed and handed back to the Stadt by Phil Brand and Peter Attrill at a simple handing-over ceremony on 21 March 1991. At the time BFBS's closest neighbour was Tina Turner, who owned the house opposite the Parkstrasse studios. In the summer of 1993 when the developers came to demolish 61 Parkstrasse, prior to the building of a block of flats, they discovered a 500 lb unexploded American bomb buried under the patio. Many of the staff had remarked that BFBS should leave Cologne with a bit of a bang! They almost got their way.

CHAPTER EIGHT

BFN's World of Sport

On the strength of having recorded a fifteen minute test commentary on an Army Cup Match for BFN, I was invited by ITV to audition for their 1966 World Cup commentary team.

Barry Davies

With the war over and time on their hands servicemen in Germany turned their attention to sport. Competitions sprang up all over the occupied zone and in Berlin the 11th Hussars were the first winners of the British Troops Berlin Inter-Unit Rugby Competition for 1945. In an attempt to bring a touch of home to Germany, various top Football League teams came out to play against the Combined Services. The first match covered by BFN was between the Combined Services and a Scottish FA XI, and the commentary was given by Sgt Alan Clarke, who later became the BBC's top sports commentator.

On 20 March 1946 Manchester United, under their new manager Matt Busby, and still playing in the war-time Northern League, arrived in Hamburg to play against the Combined Services, who had in their ranks such exciting footballers as Billy Steel and Leslie Compton. A fortnight later Wolverhampton Wanderers arrived in Germany to be followed by Queen's Park Rangers and Sheffield United. The matches were covered by BFN with Alan Clarke and later Fred Bassett acting as commentators.

Boxing has, over the years, provided BFN/BFBS with many fine outside broadcasts. On Sunday 7 December 1947 in the tramsheds in Hamburg, Cliff Michelmore and Raymond Baxter covered the fight between two giants of the German ring, Walter Neusel and Max Schmeling. Just before the contest began, the promoters demanded an enormous fee from BFN before they would give permission for the fight to be broadcast. As Cliff recalls: 'We pointed out that if they continued with their argument, the Military might stop the contest.' After the fight, Cliff interviewed both boxers: 'The next day one of the Hamburg newspapers wrote, "It was like seeing two old men in bathchairs trying to fight each other just to earn a few marks" – and I felt the paper just about got it right.'

Derek Jones, the well-known presenter of 'Family Favourites' and 'Changing My Tunes', was a big fan of big band music and boxing, but the Whitsun weekend in 1950 placed him in a dilemma. On Sunday 28 May 'Jersey' Joe

Cliff Michelmore interviewing Max Schmeling after his fight with Walter Neusel, Hamburg, 1947
(*Cliff Michelmore*)

Walcott, the number one challenger for the World Heavyweight Title, was fighting the German champion, Hein ten Hoff, at Mannheim. The following day, Duke Ellington was appearing in concert in the Musikhalle. As Derek could not be at both events, he chose the ringside at Mannheim.

Another sport covered by BFN was speedway, which continued to be popular throughout the 1940s and early '50s with the servicemen in Germany. In the early 1950s Derek Jones could often be found commentating from the Hanomag Saints Speedway Club at 12 Heavy Workshops REME. There, 93 British and 45 German employees of the workshops battled it out for the championships on old Norton 500 cc motor bikes. Some of the top names in speedway racing at the time, 'Split' Waterman, Eric Boothroyd and Jimmy Gooch, had come from the Services Speedway clubs in BAOR.

At the time speedway and rallying were of greater interest to the servicemen than motor racing, but on 29 July 1951 Derek Jones and Hedley Chambers did the first 'live' English commentary on the first post-war German Grand Prix. To provide some expertise, they invited Gordon Wilkins, the technical editor of *Autocar*, to join their team. For Derek it was a memorable occasion: 'The

Derek Jones, one of BFN Hamburg's all-rounders who covered Grand Prix meetings and boxing matches in between broadcasts of 'Family Favourites' (*Alexander McKee*)

Nürburgring was a circuit which covered fourteen miles and we had three commentary points equally spaced around the track. However, in those days the top speeds were likely to be around 75–80 m.p.h., so when the cars left the starting grid we didn't expect to see them back for at least ten minutes. Therefore, we were fairly stretched to keep going for the duration of the race.' Alberto Ascari won the race driving a Ferrari and in a supporting 500 cc race a young English driver called Stirling Moss, driving a Kieft, caused a sensation. Stirling's car had drum-brakes at the front end, but at the rear apparently nothing: the secret was a single disc-brake mounted inboard and under the cowling. As Derek remembers: 'A couple of German journalists were fascinated by a car that appeared to have no brakes on the rear wheels. "But how, Herr Moss, do you make the car stop?" Stirling came back with the classic riposte: "Who wants to make it stop, I just want the bloody thing to go!"'

Stirling Moss was to feature in one of the most exciting German Grand Prix ever covered by BFN. In 1957 Alastair McDougall and Alan Bruce were in the grandstand with Gerald Sinstadt and Alan Grace at Breitscheid. With two laps to go Mike Hawthorn and Peter Collins driving Ferraris were being chased all the way by Juan Fangio in a Maserati. Following some breathtaking driving Fangio overtook the two Englishmen to record a sensational victory. Stirling Moss, driving a BRM, could only finish fifth. Earlier that year BFN had covered the 1,000 km race at the Nürburgring and in later years covered the French, Belgian and Dutch Grands Prix as well as the Monte Carlo Rally.

Flt Lt Don East passed his radio audition and although he joined BFN as a member of the Music Department, his interest in sport kept him very busy. When Jean Borotra came to Hamburg in 1950 to play in the West German Tennis Championships, he was invited by Don to come to the Musikhalle for an interview. 'The interview was due at 12 noon and he arrived on the dot but somewhat breathless and apologized for keeping me waiting. I began my interview "Monsieur Borotra, I believe tomorrow is an important day – isn't it your birthday?" He was delighted: "You BBC people are wonderful", not realizing that I was a junior member of the British Forces Network. "Here you are at the age of 52 competing in the Hamburg championships and yet you were one of the four musketeers who won the Davis Cup for France in the thirties. What's the secret of your success?" "Vill power, everything is vill power. Hannibal crossed the Alps by vill power, we practised six hours a day – now the young men want to go out with the girls after one hour."' Seventeen years later Jean Borotra played at Wimbledon in the veterans' competition.

Gerald Sinstadt began his broadcasting career with BFN Austria before moving to Trieste in 1953. It was here that he covered his first major sports event, England's first Under-23 Football International in Bologna. In 1954 he was posted to BFN Cologne. From the start he was keen to establish a sports awareness on BFN, and with the help of Bill Crozier set off to cover an England B game at Gelsenkirchen. At the time BFN had limited broadcasting hours and so there was no chance of 'live' commentary. It was agreed that Gerald would record his commentary and the edited highlights would be broadcast the next day. When the OB van arrived at the stadium, the engineers discovered that the power supply was over half a mile away and so the commentary was recorded on a portable tape machine. Unfortunately, they only had three reels of tape which ran out just before Bedford Jezzard completed his hat-trick. Later that night, back in the studios in Cologne, they checked their notes and recreated the important goal. Next morning no one was any the wiser.

In the early fifties the standard of Army football in BAOR was very high. Even players of the calibre of Gordon Banks could not be guaranteed a place in his unit's team. So Gerald approached Dennis Scuse, BFN's Station Director, with the idea of setting up a local sports magazine to keep the serviceman and his family in touch with what was happening in BAOR and 2 ATAF: BFN Hamburg's 'Sportsman's

Jock McCandlish (right) with Stirling
Moss at RAF Geilenkirchen
(*Crown Copyright/MoD*)

Diary' was resurrected. At the same time, Gerald set up a programme called 'Late
Night Soccer Special' with two of his stringers, Flt Sgt Jock McCandlish and SAC
Alan Grace monitoring the BBC regional programmes for the background to the
Saturday results. The popularity of this programme could be judged by an article
which appeared in the Heart of Midlothian football programme on 25 January
1958. Craftsman Andrew Downie had written to the magazine: 'You can imagine
how every Jock in West Berlin and the rest of Germany listens to "Late Night
Soccer Special" which Flt Sgt McCandlish co-produces and presents. It is not just
that he keeps us in touch with what's going on back home in Scotland, but he adds
a personal touch as in my case, when he suddenly announced: "Craftsman Downie,
your team won again today."'

Jock McCandlish was always on the lookout for a good story and when he heard
that Stirling Moss was going to be driving in the German Grand Prix, he wrote to
him suggesting that he should visit RAF Geilenkirchen on his way back to the UK.
To his delight Stirling agreed. Jock now had to clear the visit with the Station
Commander. His next concern was how many people would turn up to the

Station Cinema on a Bank Holiday Monday. He need not have worried, on the day it was standing room only. Jock McCandlish was to continue his connection with Forces Broadcasting until he retired from the RAF in the late 1980s.

With little or no cash in the kitty to pay for stringers, Gerald Sinstadt found and coached his own team. Sqn/Ldr Gerry Edenbrow, an old hand from the BFN Hamburg days, Maj Ivor Jones, as elegant with words and as passionate about rugby as Cliff Morgan, and a young Lt Frank Bough. How Frank started in broadcasting is a story in itself. Gerald was about to set off for Münster to cover an Army Cup match when his summarizer, Capt Pat Massey, phoned to say he had lost his voice. Immediately Gerald contacted the Adjutant of the 2nd Royal Tank Regiment, the host unit, to see if he could help. 'Our soccer officer seems to know quite a bit about the game and has played for his university and Pegasus, maybe he could help.' Years later Gerald was to recall that Frank Bough was very good and he became a regular contributor to 'Sportsman's Diary'. However, on the way back from covering the West Germany–Scotland International in Stuttgart, Frank broke the news to Gerald that he had made his last broadcast for BFN as he was being demobbed at the end of the week. BFN had whetted his appetite and he decided he wanted to continue in broadcasting. With the aid of Gerald Sinstadt and Arthur Appleton, another former Forces Broadcasting member, he went on to BBC radio and television fame.

Pat Massey, whose illness had given Frank Bough his chance, first met Gerald Sinstadt in Hanover when BFN was holding auditions for would-be sports reporters. All the hopefuls failed except Pat, who was about to start on a long and illustrious career of covering sport for BFN and BFBS. When England and Scotland qualified for the 1954 World Cup Finals, Gerald suggested to Dennis Scuse that BFN should cover the event. As funds were still low, it was agreed that he could stay in Switzerland until the home teams had been eliminated. As both went out in the initial stages, Gerald saw the rest of the World Cup on German TV in Cologne.

Europe was now Gerald's oyster and as well as covering Grand Prix meetings he commentated on athletics and boxing. In 1957 he reported on the visit of Manchester United's 'Busby Babes' to Berlin and the following year commentated on the European Cup Final between Real Madrid and Inter Milan in Brussels, a game that he later described as one of the finest he had ever seen.

However, in 1958 the talk in the football world was of the World Cup Finals in Sweden and the fact that the four home countries had qualified for the finals for the first time. Again, Gerald put a case to Dennis Scuse that BFN should cover the event. With all the plans firmly in place, Headquarters BAOR announced that as the BBC were going to cover the Finals, BFN's involvement would be a waste of money. Dennis Scuse agreed that Gerald should go but he would have to take leave in Sweden when he was not actually broadcasting for

Gerald Sinstadt, BFN's sports
editor, 1954–9, well known
today for his television
commentaries on football and
rowing

(*Gerald Sinstadt*)

BFN. In order to assist his expenses, Dennis organized an outside broadcast at
RAF Sylt, and so at least some of Gerald's travel and subsistence costs would be
covered by BFN. It was not the first time that a member of Forces Broadcasting
had to pay for the privilege of broadcasting!

Gerald's previous clash with officialdom had been when Wales were due to play
East Germany in Leipzig and it was decided that BFN would cover the game.
Contact was made with the East German Football Association, broadcast lines
were booked to the East German border, and the host country had agreed to pay
for the lines from there to the stadium. At this point the BBC began to take an
interest and asked Gerald if he would cover the match on their behalf. When the
details of the commentary were announced in the *BFN Bulletin*, Dennis Scuse
received a call from the British Embassy in Bonn. 'How is Mr Sinstadt getting to
Leipzig?' 'By car', came the reply. 'No, that can't be done', said the Embassy,
'because it would mean he would end up with an East German stamp in his
passport.' The Embassy insisted that Gerald sent his passport to Bonn, from where

When the Busby Babes visited Berlin in 1957, BFN's reporters were at the game. The full side including Duncan Edwards, Eddie Coleman and Tommy Taylor turned out against the Combined Berlin team

it would be sent to Berlin for the necessary Military visa. This was duly done and Gerald set off to go to Leipzig via Berlin and Checkpoint Charlie. As soon as he arrived in East Germany, he picked up a 'minder' and was told he must report to the police in Leipzig. His 'minder' was very interested in football and so Gerald had very few problems. However, when he came to leave East Germany, he had to book out with the police in Leipzig. The local police chief was very keen to talk about John Charles and before Gerald could stop them, they wished him 'auf wiedersehen' and stamped his passport with the unwanted East German stamp! Several weeks later he was contacted by the East German Football Association and asked if he could fix up facilities for the return match in Cardiff!

The year 1958 will always be remembered by football fans for the Munich air disaster. As soon as the story broke, BFN immediately made contact with the hospital and, with Jimmy Murphy's help, was able to bring the latest news about Manchester United's injured to their many fans in Germany. In August of that year, Gerald and Alan Grace travelled down to Munich to broadcast a commentary on the match between the survivors and a Combined Munich team.

When Gerald left BFN in 1959 to join BBC's Sport Report, he was replaced by Alan Grace as the station's Sports Editor. Soon the Sunday morning programme 'Sportsman's Diary' was joined by an extra edition on a Monday evening. Capt David Lloyd, later to join BBC's Pebble Mill, and Frank Booth, a genial fire officer in Minden, formed the nucleus of the unpaid sports team, with the sports results being read in Cologne by David Hamilton.

While covering a sports meeting in Rheindahlen, Alan was approached by a very smart young officer who introduced himself: 'I'm Second Lieutenant Barry Davies and I've been asked by my CO to get the unit on the air.' This was exactly what Alan wanted to hear. Some years later Barry could still recall that meeting: 'I remember the occasion very well. I had volunteered to be the unofficial sports officer of 113 Company RASC at Mühlheim. I played a bit of soccer and rugby for the unit, but I was never that good. When I heard that BFN needed someone to cover the North Rhine Westphalia Soccer League, I offered my services and was invited to go to Cologne the following Sunday to, as I thought, hand over the various results. Imagine my surprise when I was informed in the mess on the Friday night that BFN had announced that 2nd Lt Barry Davies would be appearing on "Sportsman's Diary" that Sunday. When I arrived in Cologne I was shown into the studio and after a brief practice, I delivered my piece. It must have gone all right because I was invited back the following week. After that I travelled to Cologne every weekend and my role as a sports broadcaster gave me a certain amount of notoriety with the lads in my platoon and the CO was happy.' Barry covered the services football scene for the rest of the season, including reporting on the match between the British Army and the German Army in Gelsenkirchen.

'It was an appalling night and the drive back to Cologne was a nightmare and to make matters worse, the British Army was thrashed.'

When National Service was extended, Barry found himself posted to Berlin where his first impression was looking out of the mess window and seeing the Russian guns trained on the British Sector. While still trying to send sports reports down the line from Berlin, he found most of his time taken up by going into East Berlin, picking up a tail and then trying to lose it!

After his National Service he went back to England. 'Alan Grace gave me an introduction to Gerald Sinstadt, who immediately rejected me as being unsuitable for radio. The following week I was rung up by the BBC Sports Unit and asked if I would like to help out for the princely sum of six guineas per shift. Apparently the change of mind came as a result of my having worked on "Sportsman's Diary".' Shortly after this Gerald was seconded to BFBS London to set up a Sports Unit. Barry applied for a post and a few months later became a freelance broadcaster for 'London Sportsdesk'. It was during this time that he was sent to do an interview with Fred Winter, the famous steeplechase trainer.

Barry Davies, the BFN sports reporter who became BBC TV's top sports commentator
(Crown Copyright/MoD)

At the end of the interview, Fred remarked that a good outside bet for the Grand National would be his horse Anglo, at the time rated at 66–1. Back in the studio Gerald and Alan talked about the tip, but only Barry had the confidence to back it and made £50 for his trouble.

In 1966, based on the strength of having made a fifteen-minute commentary on an Army Cup match involving the Green Howards and the Royal Leicestershire Regt, Barry was invited by ITV for a test commentary on a youth club cup final. Recalling his time in BFN and the old Sinstadt maxim of attention to detail, he covered his lounge floor with photographs of the two teams so that on the day of the commentary, he knew everyone by sight. He passed the audition and the rest is history.

Having started in radio, he was delighted to be invited to commentate on the 1968 Army Cup Final at Aldershot involving the BAOR and the UK champions. During the next few years, he shared the commentary with Brian Moore and Bryon Butler and their summarizers ranged from Alan Mullery to George Cohen to Laurie McMenemey.

When Gerald Sinstadt went freelance Barry was invited to audition for the role of presenter of 'London Sportsdesk'. Again Barry passed and he shared the presentation of the programme for several years with Bryon Butler, Gerald Williams, Cliff Morgan and Nigel Starmer-Smith. 'Our biggest problem was that the programme was recorded on a Tuesday for broadcast in Germany on a Friday night, which meant we could not comment on the mid-week sports events. When we went "live" to Germany in the early eighties, the programme took on a different aspect and remained very popular until the advent of Radio 5's 'Sport on Five' took away our immediacy. It's strange but sometimes when I go to matches for BBC TV's "Grandstand", I'm approached by people who either knew me, or knew of me, in Germany. That visit to BFN Cologne changed my life. I was never God's gift to broadcasting, but I suppose I managed to con a few people.'

By now Pat Massey had graduated from sports reporter to commentator and when BFBS decided to cover the game between Glasgow Rangers and Borussia Dortmund, Pat and Rocky Stone turned up at the ground expecting reasonable facilities for their commentary. 'We were shown a frost-encrusted ladder and told that our commentary position was on the roof. Rocky and I spent a very cold night commentating on a rather boring goal-less draw.'

Post-match interviews were always a problem but when Pat went to see Alf Ramsey for permission to interview England's latest international Alan Ball, he was delighted with the reception: 'Once I get rid of the press, he's all yours.' As Pat recalls, Alf Ramsey could not have been more helpful.

The year 1972 marked another memorable landmark in the history of Forces Broadcasting: BFBS was to cover the 20th Modern Olympiad in Munich. Under

Lt-Col Pat Massey and Flt Lt Rocky Stone commentating on a sports meeting at Rheindahlen
(*Crown Copyright/MoD*)

the leadership of the then Head of Sport, Alan Grace, a small team was selected to plan, prepare and undertake one of the most ambitious tasks ever mounted by the organization. Unlike the BBC and the other major broadcasting concerns, BFBS was required to operate on very limited resources. While the BBC would be spending millions on their coverage of the games, BFBS had a team of six and precious little money. As Ian Woolf remarked: 'It will be a challenge.' Joining Alan Grace was Bryan Hamilton, Senior Sports Producer from BFBS London, former 'Time Out' reporter Don Durbridge, now working for BFBS Gibraltar, John Hedges, the Senior Programme Director of BFBS Cologne, Günter Meyer-Goldenstädt, Cologne's Senior Engineer, in charge of engineering, and a Hong Kong Chinese girl called Yoyo, who acted as secretary cum Girl Friday.

British Leyland had agreed the team should travel to Munich in one of their new Range Rovers. It was a gleaming bright red and was almost unknown on the continent. It drew a great deal of attention which did the team no harm at all when they arrived at the Olympic village. Within a couple of days, everyone knew about the team from BFBS, not so much for their early reporting, but for their transport! A typical day for the team began with a 6.30 a.m. review of the previous evening and overnight results, followed by a lunchtime Olympic newsdesk and an early evening programme of reports, comment, commentary and interviews. The studio was very small, but it was soon filled with many of BFBS's Fleet Street friends, including Ian Wooldridge, Harry Carpenter, Neil Allen and the late J.L. Manning, who were only too pleased to offer their expertise for a few guineas. Among the service personalities who came into that studio was Sgt Jim Fox, who was to win the Modern Pentathlon four years later in Montreal. In Munich his shooting skills let him down and as he remarked to Bryan Hamilton: 'We are not all hawk-eyes in the army.' Lt Mark Phillips was another serviceman who found time to talk to the BFBS team as did the individual gold medallist, Richard Meade. However, some competitors were not so easy to find.

At one early morning planning meeting it was decided that BFBS should go for the American swimmer Mark Spitz, who had already collected five gold medals and stood a very real chance of picking up two more in his final two events. He was not in competition that day and the American team management, seeking to relieve the pressure building up on him, announced that he would not be accessible to the media until his last two events were over. To Don Durbridge this was like showing a red rag to a bull; if an interview could be obtained, it would be a world exclusive. 'In the event, it was surprisingly easy, though I did have some luck. I explained my predicament to an American coach, who took off his tracksuit emblazoned with the Stars and Stripes and the words Michigan State University, leaving him dressed in a vest and boxer shorts. I donned the tracksuit, and put my tape recorder into his Team USA holdall. His stopwatch and official pass went round my neck. With his words: "only fifteen minutes, mind", ringing in my ears, I strolled across towards the entrance to the practice pool and there was Mark Spitz ambling through some practice lengths. When he paused for a breather, I approached him and as casually as possible introduced myself. He was amused by my "fancy dress", but was quick to remind me that he was off-limits. "Anyway, what does BFBS stand for?" I told him it was the British Forces Broadcasting Service, and that did the trick. "If it's for the Military, then it's OK", and promptly added that I should stoop down over him as though I were a coach giving him instructions. This I did and out came a casual relaxed eve-of-the-record interview. As I left, he called out "bye, soldier". I returned to the Range Rover and handed back my co-conspirator's tracksuit with my profuse thanks. "That's OK buddy" he replied, "just mark it down as one for the Anglo-American special relationship". The interview, unedited, was broadcast not only by BFBS and the BBC but later, I discovered, on stations across the United States before the day was out.'

The BBC was amazed by the Durbridge cheek and Paddy Feeney, who was hosting the BBC World Service sports programme, was particularly impressed and took a copy of the recording for his own show. He was not alone in making a daily check with the 'minnows' for the word had gone round the Press Centre that the British Forces Broadcasters were getting some excellent interviews. Another scoop came when Bryan Hamilton recorded an interview with Alan Minter immediately after he had won his bronze medal. Officially Minter should have gone to the after-event press conference, and some of BFBS's media colleagues were a little annoyed about being beaten by the team with the limited resources. When it became obvious that Mary Peters was in with a chance of winning Olympic gold, Bryan decided he wanted the all-important interview. He knew if he stayed in his normal place in the press-box, he would not get anywhere near her until after the official press conference and that would have been too late for the evening programme. So he set about looking for an out-of-bounds route through the bowels of the main stadium. He followed corridors, climbed over building materials and finally found himself by the side of the track, close to the finishing line where Mary would end her final event in the competition – the 200 metres. On the day of the race he retraced his steps, hoping he would not meet any of the security guards, and came out at the right spot. So Bryan sat down with his tape recorder. While the contestants and the spectators waited for the announcement to be made, he walked across the track and stood alongside Mary Peters. As soon as the announcer said 'Gold medal winner and Olympic champion, Mary', out came his tape recorder and the interview was being broadcast in BFBS's news magazine programme before the BBC reporters had returned from the press conference.

Sadly, Munich will always be remembered for the massacre. It was just after five o'clock on the morning of 5 September, when members of a Palestinian terrorist group, Black September, scaled the perimeter fence around the competitors' village and forced their way into the Israeli building. One Israeli athlete was killed instantly, another was mortally wounded and ten others taken hostage. For their safe release the terrorists demanded that 200 Palestinians held in Israeli prisons be allowed to go free and that they, the terrorists, have safe passage out of Germany. The West German Chancellor, Willy Brandt, flew to Munich to take charge of the negotiations.

The Olympic Games were suspended and BFBS had a major story on its hands. Alan Grace, who had just returned from hospital with strict instructions to take it easy, took over the studio production, with Don Durbridge, John Hedges and Bryan Hamilton searching for the background to the massacre. Their first stroke of luck came with a visit from Paddy Feeney, who offered them an interview with the Hong Kong Chef de Mission. He had been in the room immediately above the Israelis and ended his interview with: 'I must go now, there are men with guns.' Bryan talked his way past numerous checkpoints to get into the village and spoke to many of the stunned athletes about their feelings. Comments were sought from many of the international journalists who were present and an official line from the Games' organizers was recorded. Back in Cologne BFBS Germany was on stand-by to go 'live' with the news and at exactly 12 o'clock Don Durbridge put together the full story of the Black Day in Munich, beating the BBC's 'World at One'. The following day, a Memorial Service was held in the main stadium, with the Olympic flame burning and the Olympic flag at half-mast. The Games resumed the following day. Just before the BFBS team packed up, it was visited by Ian Trethowan, Director General of the BBC, who expressed thanks for the many items BFBS had supplied to the corporation, and remarked on the unusual methods employed!

In the late 1960s 'London Sports Desk' had started its own 'Sports Review of the Year', but once BFBS TV began showing BBC TV's 'Sports Personality of the Year', BFBS radio's version was dropped. Ralph Dellor, who had been producing a sports compilation for BFBS TV, suggested that Forces Broadcasting should produce its own Sports Personality of the Year based on the votes from servicemen and women. The first programme was broadcast in 1981 from the LWT studios on the South Bank. Ian Botham had been voted as BFBS's sports personality but because he was on an England tour in India, Alec Bedser, the Chairman of Selectors, agreed to accept the award on his behalf from Prince Michael of Kent.

Before Ian left for India, Ralph decided to interview him after a recording of 'This Is Your Life', because BFBS could not afford the exorbitant cost of a live link on the actual night. Ralph had Ian's answers on tape and by adding a touch of distortion to the quality, gave the impression the interview was 'live'. It began: 'Ian, are you there?' with the reply, 'Yes, Ralph, and a very good evening to everybody.' Its effectiveness could be judged when Desmond Lynham, who was in the audience, met Nigel Starmer-Smith the following day. As Nigel remarked to Ralph: 'Des thought the programme was excellent, but he thought you were very lucky to get your call through to India on time!'

The following year the presentation moved to the Tower of London and Princess Anne agreed to present the award which had been won that year by Daley Thompson who, like Ian Botham the previous year, was unable to attend the ceremony. Steve Cram accepted the award on Daley's behalf and a new feature that year was the appearance of a services sports personality. The first winner was the former world record holder for the marathon, Cpl Steve Jones of the RAF. In later years the programme came from the National Army Museum and featured Steve Davis and Sebastian Coe among the winners.

A new sports programme, 'Services Sportswatch', was started in BFBS Cologne in 1982 by Tom Scanlon. The idea was to condense the weekly reports from the old divisional areas into an informative and entertaining weekly half-hour programme. The biggest problem was to find volunteers who had sporting backgrounds and were keen to try their hands as broadcasters. One of the first to volunteer was Julian Tutt, well-known today on BBC radio and television, but in those days a captain in the Army Air Corps. As Tom discovered, Julian not only had his own tape recorder, but he had his own helicopter, albeit a khaki one, which was very useful for travelling to events on behalf of 'Services Sportswatch'.

A year later another sports programme started on BFBS Germany. Richard Astbury, the Senior Programme Director at BFBS Cologne, decided to replace 'Sport On Two' from BBC Radio 2, as it then was, with the 'Saturday Sports Show'. With SSVC television now able to reach most people in BFG, this meant that on a Saturday afternoon there was non-stop sport on television and non-stop sport on radio, so it was decided to create a programme which would cater for sports lovers but which would offer sufficient alternative entertainment for people not interested in sport.

The original host was Tony Davis and the initial mix of the best of BBC's sports coverage coupled with good music, proved to be a winning formula. Paul Chapman, then one of the BFBS receptionists and his wife Claudia, who were the producers, decided to incorporate not only the news from Liverpool, Manchester United and Arsenal, but also Borussia Dortmund, Borussia Mönchen Gladbach and VFL Bochum.

It did not take long for companies in Germany to offer prizes, with a sporting connection, for the programme. Marlboro started by giving VIP tickets to the various European Formula One Motor Racing Grand Prix, but the winners had to make their own way to the venue. Tony Davis suggested to Marlboro that they should reduce the number of tickets they were giving away but offer instead all-inclusive packages where the winners would get flights and hotel accommodation thrown in for good measure. During the past two years the BFBS winners have gone to the Brazilian Grand Prix in Rio de Janeiro and the Australian Grand Prix in Adelaide.

Soon other prizes became available and the 'Saturday Sports Show' was able to offer as prizes tickets to top soccer matches in England, including internationals, and the FA and Coca-Cola Cup Finals. As the popularity of the programme grew, so did the list of top managers who were interviewed for the programme, among them Howard Wilkinson, Joe Royle, Glen Hoddle, Gerry Francis, Ron Atkinson and Bobby Robson. When the 'Saturday Sports Show' interviewed Bobby Gould, he could not do enough for Forces Broadcasting. His son was with the Forces in Germany at the time and Bobby answered many of the questions by drawing comparisons between the world of professional football and the British Forces. As Paul Chapman explained: 'I always tried to ensure that whoever was doing the interview was given sufficient time to prepare the questions.'

The 1972 Olympic edition of *Listen*

In 1983 an unknown American called Corey Pavin won the German Open Golf Championship and within five minutes of sinking his title-winning putt, he was in the BFBS radio car talking to presenter Richard Nankivell about his life in golf. Other sporting personalities to talk to BFBS were John Parrott, Willie Thorne and Steve Davis from the world of snooker, Jackie Stewart and Nelson Piquet from motor racing and Bjorn Borg and John Lloyd from the world of tennis.

Throughout the 1980s, 'The Saturday Sports Show' produced high ratings in the annual audience research, but in the '90s, with so many listeners in Germany able to receive BBC Radio 5's 'Sport on Five' on BFBS 2, and with SSVC TV's relay of 'Grandstand' still going strong, Paul Chapman decided to change the programme title to 'Saturday Live' and carry a little less sport, although still concentrating on football, and increasing the music, fun and competition elements.

Sports coverage has come a long way since the Hamburg days. The efforts of BFBS Germany in covering all aspects of sport were rewarded in 1988 when Alan Miller's 'The German Sports Programme' took first prize at the Bicentennial Pater Awards organized by the Australasian Academy of Broadcast Arts and Sciences.

CHAPTER NINE

Television – the Realization of a Dream

At one BFN Advisory Committee meeting in October 1959, I proposed the setting up of a television service. I was not surprised that the idea was turned down flat. It was described variously as 'far-fetched', 'expensive' and 'in any case where would we get the frequencies from?'

Ian Woolf, Director of BFBS 1973–83

In 1959 the Army Board considered Ian Woolf's suggestion but rejected it and gave the project Priority 7 on the schedule for improvements to the conditions of service. However, by 1973 the TV project was listed as Priority 2 and it was decided to launch a full study into the feasibility of television for the Forces in Germany. The results were encouraging, so the Army Board endorsed the need for a 'live' TV service, and in April 1974 put its case to the Treasury for funding. Six months later the Treasury gave the go-ahead.

On 15 April 1975 Peter Blaker, the former Under-Secretary of State for Defence for the Army, put down a parliamentary question regarding the progress of the plans for transmitting British television programmes to the British Forces in Germany. The Under-Secretary of State for Defence for the Army, Robert Brown, replied: 'Contracts for the London Control Centre, the interim studio and the transmitting equipment have been placed or are being negotiated. An interim recorded service consisting of a balanced mixture of British programmes should be available to about 17,000 servicemen and their families in the Celle area by Christmas this year and will be gradually extended to cover all troops in West Germany during the following two years.' He went on: 'Everyone will agree that the project is available for the morale of our troops and their wives and families. The service will be a balance of BBC and ITV programmes.'

One back-bencher suggested that as the British troops in Germany were costing the British tax-payer more than £400 million a year, would it not be better to 'transmit' the troops back to Britain unless a suitable offset agreement were concluded with Germany, to which the Under-Secretary replied: 'The question of an offset agreement does not arise from the question, and the "transmission" of troops back to this country does not arise either.'

On the same day the steering group for TV for BFG met and discussed the statement in the House, the arrangements for the selection of programme material and handling audience reaction for this new service. One of the suggestions put forward at this meeting came from the Services Kinema Corporation's representative, who felt that it should be represented in both BFG and the UK when it came to programme planning. It claimed that it had a wealth of knowledge of the Service's taste in visual entertainment, and had very close links with the potential audience. However, the representatives from the BBC, LWT and the IBA emphasized that detailed programme selection should be left to those at working level.

The MoD had decided to give the contract for running television to LWT which, as a small company (only on the air at weekends), found it easy to adapt to BFBS's needs, and the fact that its managing director, Brian Tesler, had served with Forces Broadcasting in Trieste no doubt helped too.

In the middle of September 1975 the printing section of 15 Comp Ord Depot RAOC at Viersen were asked to print a TV Times for the new BFBS Television. It was called *View*, and in the first edition Ian Woolf wrote: '18 September is going to be an historic day for all of us in BFBS. After thirty-two years of radio broadcasting to the British forces all over the world, beginning in Algiers in 1943, we are taking our first step into television. And it is going to be quite a big step, because we shall be on the air for over fifty hours a week – in full colour!

The moment when we begin our first transmission will be the culmination of almost thirteen years of discussions and detailed planning. Why has it taken so long? Because of the complex technical and copyright problems which are involved in providing a service to so many scattered units and families without interfering with West Germany's own television channels.

When we go on the air for the first time and say "This is BFBS television", we hope you will be watching and you will enjoy the programmes we present. Rest assured, however, that none of us will be satisfied until a direct link between London and Germany is completed, which it is hoped will be in two and a half years time. Then we shall be able to bring you not only recorded programmes, but also news, sport and current events "live" as they happen.'

For Ian, it was the end of a long battle. Despite having no Board of Directors to support and help him, he had forced the idea through, overcoming seemingly insuperable barriers – the cash-conscious Treasury, the technical uncertainties and the all-powerful copyright holders. However, as late as 4 August 1975, he wrote: 'The starting date is still not firm. The reasons – the MoD is trying to keep the opening quiet for political reasons, and the various unions and rights holders

John Harrison, the first Controller
of BFBS Television
(Crown Copyright/MoD)

ranging from Equity to the Musicians' Union have still not signed on the dotted line.' He kept up the pressure and, eventually, the problems were resolved.

Now everything was in the hands of John Harrison, a National Service broadcaster with BFN Cologne in the mid-1950s, who had been seconded from the BBC where he was Science Features Organizer to become the Controller of BFBS Television. He soon got a taste of MoD life. On his first morning he was issued with his own small towel and a small bar of soap by BFBS's assistant Admin. Officer. 'But there's soap and towels in the gents already.' 'Yes', replied the Admin. Officer, 'but your grade entitles you to your own.' One week later she returned: 'I've come to collect your towel.' 'It's all right,' said John, 'it doesn't need changing, it's not dirty.' 'It's not that, but because of defence savings, your grade is no longer entitled to it!'

He then discovered that the BFBS headquarters telephone system in King's Buildings stopped working when the switchboard closed at 5 p.m. As John often worked late into the evening, he applied for his own outside line. 'Impossible,' came the BFBS Admin. reply. 'But what happens if a member of the royal family dies suddenly after the switchboard has gone home? I can't telephone Celle to advise them on how they should proceed, so they could continue broadcasting something unsuitable like "Top of the Pops" and, you never know, it might get into the tabloids!' He got the line.

His first task was to add professional expertise to the operation and recruit the nucleus of his management team. It included Colin Ward-Lewis, also on secondment from the BBC, as Head of Presentation, and Richard Barnes from Anglia TV took up the post of Senior Presentation Assistant in London. Peter Holwill was recruited from BFBS radio to take over programme planning. For Peter it was a completely new experience: 'Although I already had some twenty-five years of radio programme planning with BFBS, I quickly found out that TV programme planning was a completely different kettle of fish. I was appointed in January 1975 and had nine months to familiarize myself with TV programming, including copyright, secrecy between BBC and ITV reprogramme scheduling, preparing recording schedules, and checking on the ratio of programmes taken from BBC1 and 2 and from ITV. I had to understand the purchased programme system and ensure that the ratio of different types of programmes met with everyone's approval.'

In early July two listener/viewer groups were assembled in Celle and Verden. They were invited to air their views on the types of programme they would like to see on the new service. The Celle group was strongly in favour of seeing recordings of main sporting events a few days after they had taken place, and wanted the schedules to include children's programmes, documentaries, comedies, including 'Dad's Army', and good television drama. No one at that meeting was in favour of seeing 'Coronation Street'.

Although the servicemen in Verden were unlikely to receive the new service for at least another twelve months, they were looking forward to its arrival and felt that it would fill a large gap in their entertainment. The group was made up of all ranks and wives, and accepted that the programme content would emphasize entertainment, as opposed to more serious programmes. They were extremely interested in programmes for children and especially for Open University students. Their only regret was that the proposed fifty-six hours per week was not going to be enough for those living in the isolated areas. Like their colleagues in Celle, they were not interested in seeing 'Coronation Street'!

In July, John Harrison attended a meeting at Lansdowne House to discuss the transportation of the tapes from the UK to Germany. He pointed out that as each tape was worth £150 and black markets existed in recorded programmes, if any of the BBC or ITV programmes fell into the wrong hands then the position of BFBS would be seriously jeopardized. He also made the point that the television service was of great interest to the British press which would regard 'Army loses television programmes' as a very good story. The Army Postal

Service informed the meeting that its charges to transport the tapes by airmail would be around £25 each, although one-offs of national importance would be treated as emergencies and would be sent free of charge.

In the early days BFBS TV recorded its programmes off transmission at the LWT headquarters. The programmes were then edited to avoid advertisements and any topical references or trailers. The idea was that everything would work on a three-week cycle: record one week, trail the programme the next and transmit in Germany during the third week. At the same time, it was agreed that 'in vision' announcers were required and Hilary Osborn and Stephen Withers, already well known to BFBS radio listeners, were chosen. The choice of these two, rather than experienced announcers, was part of a deliberate policy that BFBS should find and train its own. However, Hilary's domestic situation caused a few ripples in the civil service. She wanted to work part-time, but the post was full-time. As John Harrison recalls: 'When I asked what this meant, I was told it was someone who would be a career civil servant, and who would retire at sixty. I pointed out that a woman announcer might just be past her best by the time she reached sixty, so finally they agreed that Hilary could join us on a part-time basis.'

The three days leading up to the launch of BFBS TV in Celle proved to be fairly traumatic for John Harrison and his staff. On Monday 15 September with only one announcer, Nicol Raymond, in post, plus the station controller, Jim Luxton and the programme organizer, Robert Neil, BFBS Television was trying its hand at operating the new equipment. Although the staff had seen it briefly at the London Weekend Television Centre at Wembley, they found the task of presenting and running the tapes very intimidating, with at least one of the three RCA videotape machines having a mind of its own. The following day John had gone to Viersen to check with the printers about the new BFBS *TV Times*. When he arrived in Cologne, he phoned Celle to see how Tuesday's rehearsal had gone. He was disheartened to hear they had not even started because the videotape machines were still giving trouble and Nicol had had a bad fall, and was in hospital suffering from concussion. By the time John arrived back in Celle, all attempts to rehearse had been abandoned and the senior engineer, Roy Norris, was trying desperately to get the machines to work. He finally succeeded in the early hours of Wednesday morning. With Nicol out of action, Jim Luxton would have to handle the first evening's transmission. The console was very complex with five television sets and 140 knobs, switches and faders to get used to, and the whole operation was housed in a 30-foot trailer, custom built for BFBS by Dell coachbuilders to plans drawn up by London Weekend Television's Engineering and Projects Department.

LWT had put two clocks in the trailer, one in the announcer's cubicle and one in the VT area. When Jim was testing the equipment he found the VT operators were constantly messing up their time cues. After a certain amount of

Jim Luxton, BFBS TV's station manager with Roy Norris, the senior engineer and Ekkerhard, Doris and Maria, the VT operators, Celle, 1975   (*Crown Copyright/MoD*)

annoyance, he realized that the two clocks were several seconds apart. Apparently LWT, in order to keep costs to the required minimum, had installed cheap models. Luckily Roy Norris managed to get a proper system installed just before the official opening of BFBS TV.

Back in London Colin Ward-Lewis and Richard Barnes needed a stopwatch. However, the MoD took such a long time to obtain one that John Harrison, who had far bigger problems to worry about, said: 'Go out and buy one.' They did – but not knowing who stocked them, went to Harrods. The MoD paymasters were not amused!

The full run-through on the Wednesday evening began chaotically. John records what happened next: 'The carefully planned two minutes of music, BFBS symbol and the clock running up to 7 o'clock started late, so when the music stopped and Jim Luxton said "This is BFBS Television, it is 7 o'clock", it was in fact obvious to the viewer that it was already half a minute past. Worse was to follow. When the opening tape eventually started (with the words "it's 7 o'clock . . .") it was even later.

Shortly after this the screen went blank. Meanwhile the videotape machines continued to give trouble. Fortunately London Weekend Television had decided to come to our aid and arrangements were made for two engineers to fly out the next day. They arrived about six hours before transmission was due to begin.'

Thursday 18 September, D-Day for BFBS Television. John Harrison's team was determined to get the opening sequence correct. However, rehearsals were delayed and curtailed by the continued refusal of the machines to work properly. Shortly before 7 p.m., with the machines now serviceable, Jim Luxton sat down at the console with his hastily prepared script, and spot on the second, brought in Hilary Osborn on screen saying: '7 o'clock on 18 September 1975, a historic moment for us in BFBS as we open up our first television service.'

The programmes on that first evening were a pageant of military music called 'Music on Command' staged at Wembley Stadium in aid of the Army Benevolent Fund, followed by 'The Benny Hill Show', 'Miss United Kingdom' and a feature film, *The Virgin and the Gypsy*. When 'Miss United Kingdom' was on air John popped out of the trailer for a breather. He was spotted by a soldier, clutching a can of beer. 'You just come out of that studio?' 'Yes', John admitted. 'There's just one thing I want to say to you.' 'What's that', said John, fearing the worst. 'Bloody good', he said, 'bloody good.' BFBS Television was up and running.

While all eyes that night were focused on Trenchard Barracks, Celle, back in King's Buildings in London Peter Holwill was working until nearly midnight rearranging his schedules for the following week because of the last-minute withdrawal of permission to show films on the new service.

The response from the Military to the new television service was very enthusiastic. Gen Sir Harry Tuzo, Commander-in-Chief British Army of the Rhine, wrote to Jim Luxton: 'Very good reports are coming back about the television service you are providing in Celle. I am very sorry, though, to hear of the various difficulties which have beset you and of the unfortunate accident to your announcer. You are obviously overcoming them with great skill and I need not tell you of the great importance we all attach to what you are doing.' Maj Gen John Stanier, Commander of 1st Division, wrote: 'I know that what you are doing will change the lives of the people in Celle quite enormously and we all look forward to the time when the television network is able to spread right across Rhine Army.'

Having got on the air and attracted considerable interest throughout BAOR, BFBS Cologne naturally felt left out. A suggestion was floated that Celle should be managed from Cologne. John Harrison and Jim Luxton were horrified: 'partly because it would lengthen the chain of command, partly because Cologne could not see the output so was literally in the dark and partly because of our low opinion of its output.' Luckily Ian Woolf had already decided to keep things as they were.

Patrick Lunt, then known as Rick Lunt, had just completed his two-year official training period with BFBS Cologne when he received a telephone call from John Harrison inviting him to spend a couple of months with the new BFBS Television Service in Celle, as an out-of-vision announcer. 'I welcomed the chance for wider experience and a new challenge, and agreed. Going to TV was fine but getting away from it was rather more difficult! As the equipment was new, complicated and as everyone was discovering, somewhat unreliable, once one was competent to "fly solo", John Harrison wasn't going to throw away a valuable asset and start training someone else. I could see his point, but I found the work at the time desperately uncreative and yearned to get back into radio.'

After a year with television, Patrick was finally released and despatched back to BFBS Cologne. He decided to make the 250-mile journey by bicycle. 'All went well for three days; my map reading skills didn't let me down, I was covering about 70 miles a day and stopping at a Gasthof at night. Then disaster struck. I was cycling quite fast downhill on the cobbled streets of Hagen when my front wheel went down a tramline, and locked solid. Flying lessons, and a bumpy landing followed. I picked up the bits of bike that had flown in all directions, dusted myself down, and then realized that my knee didn't work any more. The 'last leg' (no pun intended), had to be completed by taxi, train, taxi and the odd bandage!'

The original BFBS TV team in Germany had been recruited from BFBS Radio. John Crabtree, who arrived in Celle from BFBS Malta, initially found it took time to come to terms with the disciplines of television. After years of the flexible and freewheeling style of BFBS Radio, John now had to think in split seconds. Half a second either way could mean a clipped start to a programme.

In the early days, television continuity often required newcomers to learn the job as they went along. This was particularly interesting for viewers as the mistakes were as good as anything to be seen on 'It'll Be All Right on the Night'. There is a story of one announcer who was being schooled in the art of continuity, and the big moment came for his first announcement at the end of 'Dallas'. Having written his link, he was instructed by his tutor to read it 'over the end credits, when I tap you on the shoulder'. The picture on the screen faded to black, he was tapped on the shoulder and launched into his first television announcement. 'That was the last in the current series of "Dallas". Next week at this time there's comedy with some vintage Benny Hill.' Half-way through the announcement he looked up from his script at the screen and his voice trailed off as he did so. The black screen had, in fact, not signalled the expected end credits; instead it had been faded back up to the infamous scene in which JR lay dying, having just been shot. Of course, the tutor blamed the announcer for getting it wrong!

Sometimes tiredness or boredom could overtake a continuity announcer. Nicol Raymond remembers one such night: '"Match of the Day" was the last programme and I must have been feeling tired because I nodded off. Now that would have been all right had I been at home, but I was the duty out-of-vision announcer and had to close the station down once the programme had ended. I was lucky because I woke up with ten minutes to go, breathed a sigh of relief that I was in time for the end of the show, and comforted myself with the thought that the German videotape operator, Ekkerhard, would have checked with me before the programme ended. To my horror, I discovered that he was asleep as well!'

When John Walton of *Soldier* magazine visited BFBS Television in February 1976, he found that Jim Luxton was taking a realistic approach to the popularity of the service: 'I expect when the honeymoon is over we shall start to get letters asking why didn't we get a particular programme, or why we didn't carry that one. What is happening is that people are staying in more, and in particular when wives have husbands away in Northern Ireland or on exercise, they have something to look forward to each evening.' The local schoolteachers had noticed the effect of 'Cellevision' on their pupils. There had been a run on books from the school library connected with featured television series, and programmes had also shown up in their essays. Another indication of the popularity of the service came when Jim Luxton reported that soldiers from other areas were driving to nearby Schnell Imbiss and sitting in their cars watching 'Match of the Day' on portable TVs.

The Northern Ireland factor, Op Banner, had indeed been the key to the funding for BFBS TV. Units from Germany were serving four-month tours on a fairly regular basis, leaving behind large numbers of wives and children, often in isolated areas. As one general explained to John Harrison: 'Having to pay for television may mean we have two fewer tanks, but there's no point in having equipment if we can't keep the men who operate it.'

Lt-Col Nichols, the station commander of Trenchard Barracks, organized a study into the effect of BFBS Television on the serviceman's way of life. In his report he noted: 'Except for the very small minority, who for a variety of reasons are opposed in principle to television in the home, all married personnel in quarters have television sets installed. The medical authorities have reported a decrease in trivial out-of-hours consultation and fewer distraught young mothers are attending the medical centres. Although Celle has never been a crime-ridden station, it is felt that there is a noteworthy decrease in drunkenness and other related offences. There were no drink and drive cases in Celle over the Christmas and New Year period 1975-76.' The report concluded: 'From the evidence available, BFBS Television in Celle is a success. There has been a significant effect on social life and patterns, but this has been largely beneficial.'

For the time being, live news was excluded from the schedules but current affairs and topical programmes were recorded and flown out to Germany as quickly as possible. The rich mix of BBC and ITV resulted in a programme blend often envied by visitors to Germany.

By now the German media were becoming interested in this new television channel and Jim Luxton became the focal point of their attention. In an article that appeared in a local newspaper, he pointed out that a great deal of work had been carried out by BFBS in resolving financial, technical and copyright problems. 'We present television only for our British soldiers and their families. Our transmitters are directed to the English quarters and the beam is low powered and so is the power of the transmitter. It only covers about 5,000 metres.' However, the German newspaper pointed out that it was now possible for Germans who lived in the areas to receive BFBS TV, providing their sets had been converted. Shops in Celle were specializing in marketing conversion kits for around 50 DM and were quite prepared to erect the necessary aerials. When the newspaper approached those who were watching BFBS TV, it found the German viewers did not realize they were breaking the copyright law.

Nicol Raymond, one of the 'Birthday Time' presenters, with the young viewers' favourite ~ BT 429 (*Crown Copyright/MoD*)

In May 1976 London Weekend Television, which had been contracted by the MoD's Procurement Branch, finished the London Control Centre (LCC) at Wembley. Previously the programmes and continuity links had been recorded at LWT's head office on the South Bank. One of the LCC's objectives would be to feed the new service 'live' across Europe to BAOR. The staff at Wembley were a mix of LWT engineers and BFBS people. It did not take long before the broadcasters began making programmes. However, John Harrison's edict was that there should be no duplication of what was already available. 'We may only have one camera and a tiny studio, but the standards will be as good as the BBC and ITV' (shades of John McMillan in 1945).

The most popular show was 'Birthday Time'. It began modestly enough, just a few minutes a week with birthday greetings being read out by the presenter. A list of children's names was typed on to the caption generator and the list headed by such greetings as 'Happy Birthday', 'Many Happy Returns' or 'Birthday Greetings'. Sometimes the requests included poignant ones, 'From Daddy in Northern Ireland'. Occasionally 'Birthday Time' showed slides of the children who were celebrating their birthdays, and soon the programme was inundated with requests. BFBS TV decided to improve the quality of the slides it was showing and announced it would be outside the Hohne NAAFI on Saturday to take some photographs. On arrival they found a queue of women with small children, all keen to have their picture on television. Although the programme was limited to children between the ages of four and nine, it did not stop some of the young servicemen from trying to get a card past the eagle-eye of the presenter. Many of the more obvious ones were spotted, although a few did get through. The soldiers' favourite trick was to invent a name which, when read aloud, was quite unbroadcastable!

'Birthday Time' had a 'third' presenter – a robot called BT 429 – cleverly named by a young viewer. It had limited movement and just a buzz for a voice, but quickly became a very popular part of the programme. It was quite large and was positioned between the two presenters. As the years went by, it became rather battered and one of its last appearances was on the television stand at the Rhine Army Summer Show. Nicol Raymond, who was the producer, was very worried about the viewers' reaction to a BT 429 which had lost an arm during the journey from the UK, and whose eyeballs the maintenance men had decorated with a red felt pen to give them a realistic bloodshot look. She need not have worried because during the three days of the show it was greeted by children and adults alike with affection, and a member of the St John Ambulance produced a new sling every day to keep its arm in place.

Another programme that went down well with the viewers was the BFBS TV production called 'Take Five'. This took the form of an interview with a

Joanna Lumley, one of the guests on BFBS TV's 'Take Five', with Stephen Withers
(*Crown Copyright/MoD*)

personality who would be appearing shortly on BFBS TV. The first interview involved Frankie Howerd, and Stephen Withers still recalls the moment when the comedian reached across and grabbed his scriptboard and said: 'Oooooooh, I should have known, it's going to be an interrogation.' Others who gave their services free included Ernie Wise, Joanna Lumley, Tom Baker, Donald Sinden, Angela Rippon, Tom O'Connor, Dennis Waterman and Rolf Harris, who painted a new set for the children's 'Birthday Time' while doing his 'Take Five'.

The Military's interest in the new service continued to grow. At a meeting with the MoD, a colonel suggested German lessons for the troops. 'Why don't you cut the present BBC TV German teaching series into five-minute chunks? Most of the chaps just want to know how to order a beer.' When John Harrison approached the Army's Director of PR, Brigadier Martin Farndale, with the suggestion that BFBS TV should be interviewing senior officers he found the brigadier was enthusiastic and so the series 'Command' was born. The first to be approached was Sir Frank King, C-in-C BAOR. He agreed to the interview but his staff felt they should vet the questions in advance. 'We refused on the basis that the interview would be lacking in spontaneity.' John won the day and soon a series of senior officers was making the journey to Wembley to be seen by their troops on television in BAOR.

Following the opening of the Celle transmitter (which served approximately 4,700 viewers), it was originally thought by the Royal Signals that the next four transmitters would be operating before the end of 1975. Unfortunately there were serious delays and the first test transmissions started in Hohne on 3 April, Munsterlager on 29 April, Fallingbostel on 28 May, and Soltau on 1 June. All four became operational on 7 July and BFBS TV's audience had increased to 14,000.

Shortly after this, a pilot survey was undertaken in which 121 people were stopped at the NAAFI shop in Celle and asked for their reactions to the new service. Only one had not seen BFBS TV. The impact of television on the service families in Celle was best summed up when one of the TV staff, shopping in the NAAFI, heard a mother shout at her two small children who

When Dr Who (Tom Baker) went to Germany to promote the new series, he was invited to try something other than a Tardis *(Crown Copyright/MoD)*

were misbehaving: 'If you don't stop mucking about, there'll be no telly for you tonight.' Immediately they were as good as gold!

For the first eight months the programmes were recorded at LWT's headquarters at South Bank, but once the LCC was operating the tapes, now averaging eighty a week, were transported between Wembley and Celle by the Army Postal Service. In an effort to bridge the gap left by the absence of live news, the team at Wembley compiled a special programme called 'Could the Russians Win a War against the West?' This was based on a series of reports that had been shown in the UK on 'News at Ten'. The viewers were also given a chance to see the image of the army being presented by the current recruiting commercials on ITV, when six were presented together with an explanation of the policy behind them in a programme called 'The Professionals'.

Copyright clearance was now the most important aspect of Peter Holwill's life back in London, especially when trying to obtain purchased programmes such as films. Some companies would make a deal over the telephone, others wanted a contract in writing, while some refused point blank. Each film, individual programme and sometimes individual episodes in a series would need clearance. 'There were times when I received a call to say that a certain episode of "Panorama" or a wildlife episode could not be shown because it contained inserts from a foreign-based company which would not grant permission for BFBS to show its material.'

When the network was completed between Celle and Werl, the trailer was moved overnight to Vittoria Barracks in Werl. Although it was capable of being towed, it was decided that since it had been standing for three years, and to protect the delicate equipment, it would be moved on a Crusader tank transporter. This presented some problems, as the trailer was fairly high and on the Crusader it was certainly too high for many of the bridges in Germany, so the RCT and the RMP had to select a route that bypassed low bridges. The move was given a very high profile and planned down to the last detail. At the end of the evening's transmission, the trailer was switched off and loaded on to the transporter. It then set off slowly to the accompaniment of blue flashing lights, etc. Amazingly, the station was on air later that day with Jim Luxton welcoming the latest group of viewers.

Once in Werl, the engineering team discovered they had a real problem in keeping BFBS TV on the air. During the winter months the staff were confronted by the systems either icing up or overheating. The videotape recorders used two-inch width reels of tape that weighed 24 lb and when they were placed on 'fast wind', they needed air brakes to stop them, so each tape recorder had its own air compressor capable of producing 100 p.s.i. To keep the pressure constant, a tank the size of a petrol tank was fitted. As autumn turned to winter the first problem arose – condensation. As the site at Werl was on a hill, it did not take long for the tank to freeze. A frozen tank meant no air, which meant no pressure could be applied to the brakes. The first solution was demonstrated by John Harris and David Young who spent an interesting hour underneath the vehicle in minus temperatures, using their wives' hairdryers to blow warm air on to the frozen pipes. It eventually did the trick, but was very time-consuming. The next solution was to fit a greenhouse warming cable to the underside of the tanks, but as the temperature continued to drop, the cable ceased to be effective. Then the Royal Engineers fitted a skirt around the trailer, with reasonable results until the temperatures plunged again. The only cure lay in the BFBS trailer being housed in a portable helicopter hangar.

The next problem they faced came during the eleven-week ITV strike which affected the BFBS TV recording facilities. As Brian Scott, who was the engineering manager in Werl, recalls: 'In order to keep faith with our viewers, a system had to be devised to record BBC and ITV shows in the UK. It was agreed that some of the London-based staff would tape the programmes at home, using professional broadcast-quality machines.'

For Peter Holwill and his colleagues it was a case of recording extra programmes, often starting at 5 p.m. with 'Blue Peter' and staying on duty until after closedown. Each programme had to be recorded on a separate tape, which often meant a quick change when two selected programmes followed each other. Once that had been done, it was just a case of dealing with the paperwork! In the morning a driver would collect the tapes which were then despatched from Luton airport to Germany. Back in Werl, Brian Scott had to hire suitable equipment from the Germans to play back the tapes. It might have been primitive, but the viewers in BAOR never missed out on the happenings in 'Coronation Street'.

Pam Rhodes had been working as a programme organizer for 'This Week' when she was offered the chance to front a short series of schools programmes. Thames TV invited her to do some daytime continuity. When she was seen by Richard Barnes he suggested she might like to join the BFBS continuity team as an 'in vision' announcer. Shortly after this Pam became involved in 'Birthday Time'. In 1976 John Harrison wondered whether BFBS TV could do something similar to the BFBS Radio Christmas Greetings programme from Northern Ireland. John contacted the chief planner at BBC Belfast and asked if he could borrow a studio. With the promise of full support from the BBC in Northern Ireland, he and Pam set off to record Christmas greetings from the men of 49 Field Regiment and 94 Locating Regiment Royal Artillery, who were doing a tour in Belfast. The trip to Northern Ireland had been in jeopardy until the last minute because the BFBS London Admin. Department was reluctant to issue flight tickets at such short notice. It was only when John used his standard ploy, 'What if the tabloids found

In 1976 BFBS TV went to Northern
Ireland to record a programme with
the soldiers from Germany; the
interviewer was Pam Rhodes
(Wilfred Green)

out the MoD were refusing to let a programme of soldiers' Christmas greetings go
ahead?', that the tickets were made available.

Gloria Hunniford, who had worked on 'Ulster Calling' for BFBS Germany in
the early 1970s, called into the studio to meet Pam. At the time Gloria's
husband, Don Keating, was working as the director for the BFBS TV
recordings. The following year Pam returned to Belfast to record 'Greetings
from Northern Ireland' from the men of the 3rd Royal Regiment of Fusiliers to
their families who were living in Fallingbostel. The programme was also
broadcast on Christmas Day.

On 4 July 1980 the trailer came to rest at Rheindahlen. Like the journey from
Celle to Werl, a route avoiding low bridges had been worked out by the RMP
and the German police, but at the eleventh hour it was realized that one of the
autobahn bridges was too low to allow the trailer and the low loader to proceed
with safety. The German police made last-minute alterations to the route which
took the trailer off the autobahn at an Einfarht (entrance) and diverted it

through a nearby market town from where it would go back on to the autobahn at the next junction. With the Polizei and RMP in attendance, the trailer went through the town leaving a trail of destruction in its wake. No one had worked out that the overhead traffic lights would also be too low for the trailer!

Because the recorded service was originally only expected to last two and a half years, no camera facilities were provided in Germany. However, Ian Woolf was still determined that BFBS TV should have its own production unit in Germany and he persuaded the MoD to purchase an Electronic News Gathering (ENG) camera and had it shipped out as 'spares'. This caused a few problems when the unit arrived in Rheindahlen as the new studios lay directly beneath the offices of the MoD's watchdogs, the defence auditors, so the camera had to be smuggled out when it was needed for a recording. However, after a series of security promotions, including 'Early Bomb Warning', had been made with the camera, it was officially agreed that BFBS could use it.

Although the final move was complete, the television team had to wait until September 1981 before the new studios and control room were completed. After four and a half years of waiting, the families in JHQ were able to see the BFBS Television Service for the first time. As a result of the move the audience had risen to well over 100,000. However, viewers at Wildenrath, Bruggen and Laarbruch would have to wait until the following year before they could see BFBS TV. For John Harrison, his important role of establishing a television service for Germany was coming to an end and he was replaced by a former head of BFBS Germany, Pat Pachebat. During the last few months of his tenure, John had frequent discussions with Ian Woolf about the future of BFBS Germany. Ian favoured co-location in Cologne to make full use of the splendid premises there. John dreaded the idea. 'I agreed that co-location would be sensible but I was unhappy with the thought of TV going to Cologne. Radio had been fine there when the Army and RAF units were still based in and around the city, but once they had moved away, I felt the station had lost touch with its audience. Living in a palatial house in Marienburg with never a soldier or airman in sight was, I was certain, no recipe for good down-to-earth Forces Broadcasting. Boredom, self-satisfaction and self-indulgence seemed all too apparent on the air – I thought. So I was quite happy for TV to stay in Rheindahlen.'

When Pat Pachebat took over from John, BFBS TV had just received its first ENG equipment. Although they had no experience of using either the camera or the associated editing gear, it was decided by Ian that some ENG coverage of 'Exercise Crusader' should be undertaken. The BBC was persuaded to loan Roger Casstles, who was a news producer in the BBC's Birmingham studios, to BFBS, and after a series of discussions with him, Pat decided to co-opt Nicol Raymond and Guy Francis as the reporters and hire in a German cameraman.

With another cameraman and a tape-editor coming from London Weekend Television, plans were made to produce fourteen nightly reports, each of fifteen minutes duration. So in September 1980, BFBS TV went 'off to war' in two hired Range Rovers. Pat recalls: 'I think we were regarded initially by the Military hierarchy with some scepticism because the operation was an entirely new experience for us, but attitudes changed overnight following the impact of the first TV Crusader report.' For the very first time in the history of BFG, families at home were able to see what their menfolk were doing when they went away, as they so often did, on exercise. The coverage of Crusader was so successful that when the director of Army training visited the Australian Staff College a few weeks later, he took copies of the BFBS TV videos with him.

It was decided in 1981 that a team from BFBS TV should go to Northern Ireland to interview servicemen from Germany. So Pat Pachebat, John Harris, Judy Fisher (former BFBS Cyprus) and John Crabtree set off for the province, visiting

In July 1980 John Harrison (centre), who had launched BFBS TV, handed over to Pat Pachebat (left). With them are Peter Holwill, the senior programme organizer, and Pam Dumbrell, the programme secretary   (*Crown Copyright/MoD*)

North Howard Street Mill, Belleek and the Maze prison. John Crabtree, one of the interviewers, remembers the visit well. 'It must have been appalling television; interviewing rows of soldiers, all standing "at ease", all saying the same thing. We had no idea how these sequences should be structured, but the surprising thing was that when the programme was transmitted, warts and all, it received much glowing praise from the audience, particularly the families of those we had interviewed.'

The following year, after seven years of waiting, the services were at last able to see 'live' news broadcasts from the BBC and ITN, and the sports fans could settle down on a Saturday afternoon to watch 'Grandstand'. However, BFBS TV was still only on the air from 12 noon until shortly after midnight, with an afternoon break on weekdays. It was not until 1988 that the afternoon gap was filled.

From Germany's point of view, the junctions in and out of the 'live' links could be extremely hair-raising. At that time, the BBC in particular could be very flexible in its start times, and on several occasions the BFBS announcer was left waiting for the Nine O'Clock News to start while the BBC announcer was trailing programmes which would not be carried by BFBS TV. In 1982 the MoD finally agreed to the establishment of a small ENG team for BFBS TV in Germany, something Ian Woolf had been advocating since the start of its service in 1975. Now BFBS TV could build on its successful coverage of Crusader. Mike Allen was presenting the mid-morning show for BFBS Germany when Pat Pachebat asked him if he fancied setting up a local production unit in Rheindahlen. 'At the time, I had worked on a couple of specials from Northern Ireland in 1981 and '82, and had acted as a reporter on Exercise Crusader earlier in the year, so my experience was limited, but the idea sounded exciting.'

To assist him, Vaughan Savidge was posted in from Gibraltar. Like Mike, he had limited TV experience, which had been mainly in the area of dubbing kung fu films in Hong Kong. The next member of the team was a service dependant – Sue Cavener. She had been brought up in a service environment and knew her way around the military system. At this point it was decided by Jim Luxton, the station manager, to send Mike on an attachment to the Tyne-Tees local magazine programme, 'Look North'. By the time he returned, the local production unit had grown to five and a new services magazine, to be called 'Scene Here', was on the stocks. For the first edition Mike went to interview a female wrestler called Sexy Susie, who was touring Germany as part of a NAAFI entertainments deal, and spent most of his time being thrown around the ring, much to the enjoyment of his colleagues. He can still recall that first programme and the autocue: 'Everything had to be written out by hand on a sheet of plastic, and as John Crabtree had the neatest handwriting, he offered to help out. This system, although primitive, worked and we continued to use it for several months.'

Despite the rather amateurish beginning, the response to 'Scene Here' from the service audience was quite staggering. At long last they had their own programme and everyone wanted to be seen on it. The task of sorting out the possible stories fell to Sue Cavener. In order to give the programme a BAOR flavour, the team began to travel around Germany and into Berlin and covered such stories as the Queen's visit, Battlefield Tours, the joys of gliding, Jim Davidson on tour, a programme about the re-formed RAF Band (following its terrible coach tragedy) and the Berlin Military Train that travels from Braunschweig to Berlin. Vaughan Savidge was carrying a couple of sun-guns (portable lights) up the concrete steps at the Charlottenburg railway station when he tripped and fell. 'My front teeth broke the fall. These were the same front teeth that had already been knocked out and capped when I introduced them to concrete at the age of fourteen.'

Alan Miller was presenting the Saturday afternoon sport and music show for BFBS Cologne when he was approached by Mike Allen with: 'I've had a great idea – wouldn't it be good to have the "voice of sport" as the "face of sport" on "Scene Here"?' Mike went on to elaborate on his plan. During the week a camera crew would film the action and then Alan would stand in the middle of a sports field and supply the narrative. The first programme was recorded on an extremely wet and cold Friday morning with no cue card and a mass of sports results to memorize. 'The first night it went on air, I sat very nervously in front of my TV as I hadn't actually seen the finished product. To my horror, the end of the show came and went and the sports news had been edited from four and a half minutes down to thirty seconds. Apparently the story of a corporal at RAF Bruggen who was breeding gerbils in his married quarter was deemed far more important and so the sports news became a "nice little filler" to end the show.' Thankfully, this was not the norm and very soon services sport came into its own. By now Alan had been allocated studio time and so he could swap his raincoat and the sports field for a suit and a studio chair. He was never very keen on the make-up, but it was nice to be warm!

Mike Allen was joined by Pat Pachebat, Roger Casstles, Nicol Raymond, John Harris and Jim Luxton in 1984 as SSVC TV set out to cover 'Exercise Lionheart'. (The now familiar BFBS Television logo had disappeared following the merger of BFBS and the Services Kinema Corporation in 1983.) Once again, it was decided to go for daily fifteen-minute reports and similar arrangements to Crusader were made for getting each day's video cassette back to the TV unit in Rheindahlen. Sometimes it was touch and go, with frantic calls being received by the helicopters to hurry things up while the editors were putting the final touches to the programme. Occasionally, the team in Rheindahlen had difficulty in locating the helicopters, often resorting to standing on heli-pads or in the fields flashing a torch like the French Resistance

BFBS TV's own 'Three of a Kind', Mike Allen, Judy Fisher and John Crabtree

(*Crown Copyright/MoD*)

looking for British agents. On at least one occasion, a reporter was forced to run across a field clutching the important tape, and then trying to flag down a passing German motorist to get him and the tape back to Rheindahlen.

During the exercise, SSVC TV set out to record a church service in a field. As the padre prepared the altar he made a striking picture, silhouetted against the light at the open end of the tent. He was bending over his padre's Field Communion kit and the cameraman, sensing a dramatic shot as the padre lifted the Cross out of the case, moved in for a close-up; there, lying on the top, was a pack of 200 cigarettes!

As Pat Pachebat recalls: 'It was not all sweetness and light. By the time Lionheart came around, everyone was fully aware of the tremendous impact made by our TV coverage, and we were under constant pressure from units to cover their part in the exercise. On one occasion, no doubt following orders from above, a senior Army officer took me aside and said, "I've cancelled your chopper to cover the RAF Harriers in the field this afternoon. Instead, we think you should go to an Army activity." I was so angry at this blatant interference with our plans that I really hit the roof. "If our chopper for the Harriers is not reinstated immediately, I will personally ring up the RAF C-in-C and tell him that the Army has cancelled our planned coverage of his Harriers, and believe me, you are going to cause the biggest inter-service row this Command has ever seen." There was a moment's pause and when he saw I meant every word, we got our chopper back.'

Having gained a degree of confidence, SSVC's next project was to ask the Commanders in Chief (Army and RAF) to provide, in alternate years, a Christmas message for the British Forces in Germany. John Crabtree remembers an interview with Gen Sir Michael Gow which was recorded at the general's home in front of a roaring fire, surrounded by Christmas cards and with his faithful hound at his feet. Throughout the entire recording he was absentmindedly stroking the dog. 'After having had several takes, we were so in awe of the C-in-C that no-one had the nerve to ask him to stop, and so it was no surprise to hear, following the broadcast, that viewers were puzzled as to why the general was listing to one side and twiddling what appeared to be an old hearth rug.'

During the next two years 'Scene Here' went from strength to strength and its number one presenter tried his hand at free-fall parachuting, white-water rafting, hot-air ballooning, scuba diving, bobsleighing and caving. As Mike recalls: 'I would never have tried these pursuits on my own, but because I had a camera with me, the nerve held.' The most exciting project that 'Scene Here' attempted during Mike's time was a 'special' covering a three-pronged adventure training expedition to South America. The first part was on Lake Titicaca in Bolivia (the highest navigable lake in the world), the second in a caving system in the north of Peru where the expedition, made up of ten soldiers and two officers, tried to discover the world's deepest caves, and the final part was to trek across the Andes in search of the lost city of the Incas, Machu Picchu. With John Dunlop, the cameraman, the 'Scene Here' duo spent a month in South America. The trek to find the Inca city took eight days with a caravan of donkeys carrying the kit, which included portable generators and the petrol required to charge up the batteries, plus all the film equipment, and two horses to carry Mike and John. Slowly, they made their way to 16,500 feet and in the process suffered not only altitude sickness but chronic dysentery. Mike still considers the resulting programme to be his greatest achievement.

Shortly after he returned from Peru, Sue Cavener was killed in a gliding accident. As he recalls: 'She had been the mainstay of "Scene Here" since its inception, and much of its success was due to her meticulous work.'

After two years it was decided that 'Scene Here' should go out on a weekly basis and the staff was increased to ten. The pressure on both Mike and Vaughan to continue the previous high standard was immense and Mike felt it was time to leave the SSVC and return to the United Kingdom. 'In many ways I was lucky to have been in at the start of "Scene Here". Technology had got to a stage where TV production was much more manageable. Single-man crews were becoming the norm and equipment was definitely user friendly. When I look back, I find it amazing that in 1988 our reporters were covering the story, writing it up and then editing it ready for transmission. Many of the young people who started with us went on to do well in the television world in the UK.'

One of the new members of the 'Scene Here' team was Rob Olver, who two years earlier had been a porter with BFBS Cologne. He joined the TV continuity team in Rheindahlen and within a short space of time found himself one of the reporters on the programme. In 1990 a new producer, Tony Cook from ITV, was brought in by Gordon Randall, SSVC's assistant director (television), to give the programme a harder edge to its stories, and this coincided with the start of the Gulf War. Straight away, 'Scene Here' became a 'live' programme with the ability to react to events, while at the same time doing all it could to reassure the families in Germany. The response from its audience was excellent and at one stage it had a reach of 94 per cent, probably the highest for any radio or television programme in Europe.

The Gulf War presented SSVC TV with a number of challenges. The demand for news naturally increased, and with the agreement of the BBC and Sky News, SSVC TV was able to carry breakfast bulletins from both organizations. Once the air war began, the issue of casualty reporting arose. Should there be serious casualties, morale could only be worsened if SSVC attempted to impose a news blackout. Charly Lowndes was Controller, Broadcasting (Western Europe): 'We had no monopoly of news: if SSVC avoided bad news, it would soon circulate, probably with the added distortions of rumour, from viewers to Sky direct via satellite, or from German TV. I was relieved to find no difficulty, or indeed need, in pushing this view with HQ BAOR. Information rooms were set up in the families offices of the units which had gone, and the teletext system was used to provide an extra channel to families. Indeed soon after 7th Armoured Brigade had been mobilized, the teletext system had been used to alert all quartermasters of armoured regiments to the need to assemble all possible stores and spares for the tanks being sent to the Gulf.'

Rob Olver, Mike Collcutt and Ross Cogswell were the first SSVC TV team to visit the Gulf in September 1990. Understandably they were apprehensive about being sent to a war zone and one of them asked Charly if SSVC was able to provide emergency evacuation arrangements similar to those he believed had been provided by ITN in another war zone – namely a group of mercenaries on standby with a helicopter in a neighbouring country. Charly recalls: 'I felt comfortable in replying that I could promise him the direct support of not one helicopter, but three squadrons, and no mercenaries but an armoured brigade of the British Army. For unlike other TV teams, we were family!' When Charly himself went to the Gulf in February 1991 he, Glen Mansell and Steve Vink had

Jon Bennett recording voice dedications, Kuwait, February 1991   (*SSVC*)

the unusual experience of sharing a Tri-Star with several pallets of MILAN anti-tank missiles.

BAOR's involvement in the Gulf War saw SSVC TV place more emphasis on news and current affairs, with output adjusted frequently to incorporate a 'Panorama' or similar programme. At the same time, SSVC TV went to full daytime television in Germany, which has continued ever since.

Like Rob Olver, Steve Britton had been a television continuity announcer but now became involved in the programme making. During the run-up to the Gulf War, most of the early news centred on the Germany-based 7th Armoured Division – the Desert Rats. SSVC TV decided to provide coverage of the RAF's involvement, specifically for its families in Germany. Steve Britton found the support given from on high to be first class. 'Within twenty-four hours of this idea being put to him, Air Vice-Marshal Peter J. Harding, the then Deputy Commander British Forces Germany, had organized everything for us. We were able to produce a twenty-five minute programme which fulfilled a need for the previously neglected families.'

Another officer who was extremely helpful to Steve Britton was Lt-Col Bob Stewart, the CO of the Cheshire Regt: 'We were filming his Battalion's departure from RAF Gutersloh, as they left for Bosnia for Operation "Grapple One". Again, from a families' welfare perspective, we felt a need to get into Bosnia. Despite being very busy, when we approached him, he gave us his total support. We drove to Bosnia from Germany and it soon became apparent that the Cheshires had been receiving virtually all the attention from the media. As we made our way along the main supply route to Vitez, we decided to film all aspects of the British logistics contingent. As a result, the Germany-based families of drivers, engineers, cooks and posties were given their first real glimpse of what their men were doing rather than pictures of "The Teeth Army". Not everyone in the British Forces in Bosnia was driving a tank or flying a Tornado. For the families of the support element, the Forces Television Service was sometimes their only link with the men in Bosnia.'

A programme that caused a difference of opinion between the Army and SSVC was called 'Harry's Game', which was very critical of army interrogation methods in Northern Ireland. The senior officers in BAOR thought it was unfair and tried to pressurize the SSVC into not broadcasting the programme. As Pat Pachebat recalls: 'It could be seen by every soldier in the United Kingdom, so the objection seemed pointless and smacked of near-censorship. We even offered to fly the producer of the programme to Germany to take part in a phone-in and answer any points which came from the military. However, this was vetoed by the security people on the grounds that some of the soldiers calling in might give away information to the IRA. In the end, SSVC went ahead and broadcast the programme.'

John Rudler-Doyle, a veteran of Independent Television News, was working for Television South West when he saw a vacancy for someone to produce and present a weekly news/current affairs programme in Germany. The organization called the 'SSVC' was unknown to him, but after a board it appeared he had the job. On the eve of his departure for Germany, however, Gordon Randall explained they had given the job of production to Tony Cook. 'Instead', he explained, 'your role will be to direct half-hour documentary style films aimed at the British servicemen and their families. We will call them "Specials".' Although somewhat taken aback, John was destined to have the best job in SSVC TV. He was to witness and film at first hand some of the momentous changes in post-war Europe.

By the autumn of 1990 the reunification of Germany was about to become a reality. John recalls: 'The situation was the perfect material for a documentary, but where best to capture the historic and exciting moment? I felt everyone would be going to Berlin for the big day, but I wanted to film somewhere else, and then one night it came to me and I scribbled a name on my bedside notepad – Colditz.'

When John arrived nothing appeared to have been done to the place since 1945. What little paint there had been was peeling off, roofs needing repair had been left to collapse, there were no hotels and only one fairly basic café. Something else caught his eye. As John recalls: 'The obsession in Western

Germany to obliterate all things associated with the Nazi period was not repeated in Colditz. A local bridge built in 1938 was still referred to by its original name – the Adolf Hitler Bridge.' The programme was called 'Colditz Revisited'.

Once the Wall had come down and the cold war was over, the armies of both sides could start to go home. John Rudler-Doyle wanted to film in a Russian Army camp before the Red Army left East Germany. Normally such a request would have been rejected, but through a contact called Anatoli Smirnov, the deputy head of the Novisti Russian News Agency in Cologne, John was able to get permission to film at a Red Army base near Perleberg, a small town about 200 kilometres from Berlin. There was only one problem: the SSVC TV team would have to wait until it received a formal invitation from the base commander, and that took five months to arrive. It did not take John long to spot the reason for the delay: 'When we finally drove through the gates, it became obvious. They had taken that long to clean up the place. Everywhere and everything was glistening. There was new paintwork on every piece of equipment and the giant murals, a popular art form throughout the Soviet Union, had been repainted. Our welcome was fantastic, we had a guard of honour and 'Russian officers lining up to greet us with the traditional bear–hug and the triple kiss on the cheek. It appeared our hosts were determined we would be impressed, and we were. "You can film what you like", they told me, "we have no secrets here." Even Anatoli smiled at that remark.'

The success of the 'specials' meant that to keep up the standard John had to look farther afield and in 1992 he produced a film called 'Convoy to Smolensk'. BFG had collected thousands of marks to buy supplies and the Berlin Garrison arranged for their shipment to Smolensk in time for Christmas.

Twenty-three British Army lorries, painted blue for the trip, plus a fuel tanker and a Russian breakdown vehicle, made the journey through Poland and on to Russia. After three days on the road the team arrived in Smolensk – a city of extremes. As Mike Colcutt, the senior cameraman, recalls: 'We were met by a pall of brown fumes rising from the drainage system, which was ignored by the local people queueing for the last couple of loaves at what appeared to be a corner shop. On the hill above the river stood the city's magnificent cathedral complex. We were welcomed by the Metropolitan – which is what they call the bishop – and invited in for a banquet. Inside the cathedral there were priceless icons and a hundred or so bearded 'Rasputins' and a few token ladies dressed in traditional costume. On the table in front of us were whole carp and various kinds of shellfish and heavy Russian wine. It looked like an altar of food. After the banquet we visited the orphanages. The standard of accommodation was appalling. Several of the children, victims of the Chernobyl fiasco, looked as if they wouldn't last much longer, but I will always remember the expressions on

When Nicholas Soames, Armed Forces Minister, visited Bosnia he was interviewed for 'Scene Here' by Petrie Hosken

(*Crown Copyright/MoD*)

their faces as they got their Christmas teddy bears. The rest of the visit went smoothly but we heard that, in all probability, after we had gone, a fleet of closed vans would visit the hospitals and orphanages to re-assign the spoils.'

It was a very difficult and heartbreaking job for the volunteers to select suitable orphanages. The SSVC TV team filmed hundreds of children in their appalling squalor and in the end two orphanages, one at Baia Mare and the other in the mountains of Transylvania at Simleul Silvaniei, were chosen.

The same recruitment drive that saw Tony Cook and John Rudler-Doyle join SSVC TV brought in Petrie Hosken. She started in the Continuity Department but one morning strolled into Tony Cook's office, put her feet on his desk and declared: 'If you ever need a presenter for "Scene Here", I'm your man.' Tony was somewhat taken aback, but impressed by her nerve. Within a few weeks he decided that 'Scene Here' lacked what he called 'the tart factor' and placed her alongside him in front of the 'Scene Here' cameras. Petrie can still recall her first programme: 'As the programme countdown was happening, I turned to Tony

and said, "I hate this, what am I doing here?"' Petrie went on to become the
longest-standing presenter of 'Scene Here', and later, in Chalfont, co-hosted the
programme with Richard Astbury.

In November 1991 the system input point for TV moved from Rheindahlen
to the SSVC headquarters in Chalfont. Two years later, the TV service was
enhanced by night-time broadcasting from the Open University headquarters at
Milton Keynes. At the same time, the effects of drawdown were being felt by
the SSVC and, as part of their savings, the Rheindahlen production unit was
transferred to Herford and John Rudler-Doyle left to become a freelance
producer in the UK. 'Scene Here', for so long the flagship of Forces TV in
Germany, was also affected by the cutbacks. The production of the programme
was taken over by the television team in Chalfont and beamed by satellite to the
rest of the world twice a week.

Satellite broadcasting, which had been used for the first time during the Gulf
War to relay programmes to the servicemen on 'Operation Granby', took SSVC
Television into a new and more sophisticated era of broadcasting. In 1975 taped
programmes were flown from London to Germany to be transmitted locally.
Twenty years later, service families can watch 'Noel's House Party' at the same
time as it's being transmitted on BBC 1. Highly topical documentaries and
discussion programmes are regularly shown live or within hours of the UK
transmission.

Germany remains the SSVC's main audience. From offices in Herford and
Rheindahlen, reporters and cameramen keep viewers in touch with all aspects of
Forces life – from the trauma of resettlement to the fun of fund-raising. When
units are detached overseas, the SSVC's television teams pay flying visits to record
how they are settling in to their new environment, and at the same time provide
a vital welfare role by recording messages for their families back in Germany.

Rob Olver is one of several reporters covering stories in Bosnia for 'Scene
Here'. 'I try to find stories that are different, especially those showing just how
much the British Army is doing to rebuild some of the shattered communities:
The Royal Highland Fusiliers building a kindergarten for Croat and Muslim
children, physical training instructors teaching the youngsters how to box. But
the story I shall remember most of all concerns a little boy we met just outside
Gorni Vakuf. He approached us carrying a home-made gun which, we were to
discover, fired nails. He looked at us, pointed the gun and pulled the trigger.
Luckily we were not injured. Terry Graham, our cameraman, kept on filming
and we got some amazing shots. The little boy then smiled, waved and walked
away as if nothing out of the ordinary had happened.

Another Bosnia veteran was Petrie Hosken. On her first assignment she
covered the handover from the Cheshire Regt to the Prince of Wales Own

Regt of Yorkshire in central Bosnia, and in the next two years, she was to visit this troubled area on eight occasions. 'I saw so many changes and had so many experiences, not all good, but I felt strongly that SSVC was right to be there. I remember on one occasion when I was being taken out of Sarajevo by Dutch troops to Kiseljack with some British medics. (I found out they were off to an orphanage in a very explosive area and I decided we should go with them and so we hitched a lift.) Trying to cross the Serbian front line, our armoured vehicle was stopped. In the subsequent search, a heavily armed Serbian soldier asked to see my UN pass which, of course, I didn't have. Lt-Col John Skipworth, the Senior Medical Officer, was about to say I was Press when I gave him a look to say DON'T, because the Serbs hated the press. The soldier then accused the UN of trying to smuggle a female spy out of the city and demanded I be handed over to him. The conversations became increasingly hostile and were very frightening. Thankfully I was not handed over and the threat of Warriors being sent from Vitez saw us on our way. Within hours, I had a UN pass!'

Petrie left the SSVC in Chalfont to return to Germany as a radio-cum-TV

Petrie Hosken with Russ Cogswell and Mark Hearn after Petrie had become the first civilian woman to fly in a Tornado
(*Crown Copyright/MoD*)

reporter and to present a weekly two-hour radio show for the Germany-based troops serving in the Balkans. Her place on the reporting team went to Katie Roy, a former secretary in the Television Department, with Caroline Young, formerly a radio producer with BFBS London co-presenting 'Scene Here' with Richard Astbury.

'Scene Here' attempted to find something of interest for everyone in every edition, and the policy appeared to be working. In an audience research carried out in spring 1994, viewers' comments ranged from: 'Informative' to 'Useful and irreplaceable'. One wife added: 'I watched the programme a lot when my husband was in Bosnia.'

According to Steve Mylles, SSVC TV's controller of programmes, 'More than 80 per cent of the British Forces in Germany registered themselves satisfied or very well satisfied with our programme schedules and the friendly presentation masterminded by Richard Barnes and Bob Jones. This is quite a tribute to the small team at SSVC responsible for getting the best of the four UK TV channels into one service exclusively for the Forces. However, there are still some servicemen in Germany who cannot receive the satellite service but have access to a taped compilation prepared in Chalfont by David Kenworthy which amounts to twenty four hours of weekly entertainment on video.'

In 1981 BFBS TV had attempted to bring the royal wedding to the viewers in Germany with mixed results. In 1995 Richard Astbury, one of the main presenters of 'Scene Here', was informed that Buckingham Palace had approached the SSVC because the Palace Press Office felt that Princess Margaret, the SSVC's patron, should make a media contribution to VE-Day. SSVC had three weeks in which to prepare. The recording was made at Kensington Palace on Thursday 30 March. Princess Margaret recalled for the cameras the friendly rivalry between the two princesses during the war years and how she wanted to enlist just as her elder sister had done. Her love and admiration for her parents as war leaders was also plain to see. The programme was broadcast by SSVC TV in Germany, on BBC 1, and subsequently rebroadcast in Australia, New Zealand and Scandinavia with news organizations in Germany and America also transmitting excerpts in their VE-Day bulletins.

Following the success of this programme, the SSVC was approached to record a similar programme with the Duke of Edinburgh. This was recorded in Buckingham Palace and covered his memories in the Navy during the Second World War. Again the programme was broadcast by SSVC TV in Germany and BBC 1 on VJ-Day.

As president of the National Maritime Museum, Prince Philip's love of the sea runs deep but he confided that his first preference might have been to the Royal Air Force had not his family – particularly Lord Louis Mountbatten –

When it was decided that the Duke of Edinburgh would give an interview for VJ-Day, the SSVC were invited to make the programme and Richard Astbury was the interviewer   (*SSVC*)

pressurized him into becoming a Naval cadet. It was a decision that probably saved his life, as he himself freely admitted, though his Naval career certainly put him in the front line, particularly at the battles of Crete and Cape Matapan where he earned a Mention in Despatches.

After rubbing shoulders with royalty, Richard Astbury returned to his normal role of running the Combined Services Entertainment Department in Chalfont, the home of the SSVC.

CHAPTER TEN

Blue Berets and Flak Jackets

War is not normal, but the radio is a reminder of normality. It is also, unlike television, very private. You can listen on your own, perhaps on a Walkman, and hear a message or a joke which is your own. These moments of privacy are rare.

Charly Lowndes, Al Jubayl 1991

When BFN Hamburg began broadcasting in 1945 its audience was desperate for news from home. Although the station was on the air for seventeen hours a day, it could only provide six daily ten-minute news bulletins, all relayed from the BBC Light Programme, with occasional local input coming from the 1st, 8th, or 30th Corps newsletters plus a Royal Navy news. News from the RAF did not appear until 1946 and British newspapers in the early post-war days were almost unobtainable in Germany.

Fifty years on, the BFBS listeners are more demanding. They are now bombarded with news and information from a huge variety of sources. Programmes ranging from BFBS Radio, SSVC TV and BBC are on satellite, and the British papers arrive in Germany on the day of publication. In Germany at least BFBS has competition. Drawdown reduced BFBS's audience by half.

The period 1992 to 1995 was a time of great change. Roger Hudson, as Editor, News and Information, had been responsible for setting up Germany's news system and hiring reporters in the regional studios. He was the first to implement the bi-medial concept of radio and television reporting, but with Options for Change and the resultant drawdown of Forces after the Gulf War, he moved to the then broadcasting headquarters in Rheindahlen as Station Manager, to oversee the inevitable effects that drawdown and rapid technological advances had on BFBS.

The relocation of the television transmission point back to the UK, the use of bi-medial reporters, the increasing use of sophisticated computer technology, and the centralization of radio and TV reporting in Herford, meant that on the way there were a number of casualties. When Roger arrived in Rheindahlen, there were 52 staff there. When he departed for London in 1995 there were only 12. 'It was a miserable time', he said, 'The German employees were the main difficulty, particularly after often long and loyal service.' The German labour laws were very strict and at the time the Works Council very active, and on two occasions Roger nearly found himself in court over procedural matters. By the time he left though, BFBS in Germany was in good shape, ready to face the new era brought about by 'Options'.

Although the total number of staff working for the new BFBS Germany network was less than half the number employed at BFBS Cologne in the 1970s, the audience reaction to this network concept was enthusiastic.

Alan Phillips, BFBS Germany's head of news and information, thinks there is a very good reason for BFBS remaining the Forces' favourite broadcaster. 'It is the local access that we give our audience and our unique ability to reflect what's going on in the military community. Today we produce up to thirty radio

BFBS Germany was broadcasting live from the beach at Arromanches on 6 June 1994. The OB truck christened 'GLADYS 2' was the only vehicle allowed on the beach. From their privileged commentary point Alan Grace and Patrick Eade described the moving scenes when the British veterans paraded for the Queen   (*Soldier* magazine)

and six television stories per week. The aim is to keep the military audience in touch with things that affect them as people. Our reporters have been trained in both radio and television techniques, so the research they do on any story can be used by the reporter for both media. Although the SSVC Television Local Production Unit moved to Herford in 1994, one crew remained in Rheindahlen to cover stories in its area. The co-ordination of all the news coverage was in the hands of the news and information office, which also looks after the interest of the five BFBS local stations.

Sometimes the military's idea of what makes news is not the same as ours. Their view (although it is changing) of what is worth covering often seems confined to parades or the presentation of large cheques to charities. Sometimes stories warrant coverage that the Command would rather BFBS left alone. However, this mentality is changing: more and more senior officers understand that they lose credibility with their increasingly sophisticated soldiery by pretending something isn't a problem when it clearly is. The great majority of the Forces recognize the value in having your local reporter to do something to get the lads on the radio or the television.'

By now a new door had been pushed firmly open by Lt Gen Jeremy McKenzie, the last commander of 1st British Corps, and one of the architects of the Allied Rapid Reaction Corps which symbolized the new political and military thrust of the NATO Allies. Its role was flexible, its composition multinational and its deployment could be anywhere in the NATO countries or beyond. This was the context for re-examining how BFBS Radio could support this new kind of commitment in Europe. Instead of a barracks-based, static deterrent force in northern Germany, BFBS might be needed at very short notice to supply news, entertainment and music to troops in cramped temporary accommodation during exercises or on operations in alien surroundings. Often they would be working long hours with minimal recreation and welfare facilities.

This was exactly what Charly Lowndes found when he went to the Gulf in 1991. He knew that the troops of 4th and 7th Armoured Brigades and their Logistic Support had been working flat out before they left Germany in the autumn of 1990, but the shooting war on the ground did not start until February of the following year. The servicemen's appetite for news was understandably acute: their lives were affected by events and decisions in New York, Washington, Moscow and Baghdad. The link with home was needed to keep morale high as tension mounted before the inevitable battle. It was during this phase that BFBS provided its most valuable service. Once the war broke out there was little opportunity to offer a proper news service to those involved and anyway their opportunities to listen were limited.

Once the war was over the desire for news grew and once again BFBS had a vital role to play.

When Marc Tyley became general manager of BFBS Germany in 1995, he quickly became aware of the many changes faced by Forces Broadcasting: 'We had to deal with defence cuts, redundancies, budget cuts, long unaccompanied tours in Bosnia and an almost overwhelming sense of uncertainty as to the future of BFG. As a result we deal more with the real issues of the day than ever before, giving the Command and the audience as a whole a chance to air their views on their radio station. We cover all the major issues, resettlement, health care, government reports that impact on the services and political issues. We act as a conduit for a great many people as they try to find out just what is going on and how it will affect them.'

Marc Tyley is determined that BFBS Germany has to remain at the very heart of its audience and not become peripheral and as such a dispensable commodity. 'Our role in keeping the Forces in Bosnia in touch with their families is a key one. The programme "Calling the Balkans", broadcast every Sunday between 12 and 2 p.m., receives more mail than "Family Favourites" did in the seventies. Even with telephones widely available throughout Croatia and parts of Bosnia, a dedication on a Sunday lunchtime is just as much a part of Forces life today as it ever was and has not lost any of its magic. This is BFBS at its very best, bringing families closer together and broadcasting a programme with presenters who know the audience and know the problems. Many of the presenters have visited the Balkans and know the places they are mentioning every week.'

BFBS started broadcasting to the Balkans in 1992, following the deployment of small medical teams to Croatia in the first manifestation of UNPROFOR. The wisdom of opting for a satellite distribution system came into its own as they were able to provide TV and radio into previously unplanned areas at short notice. The next phase was the arrival of the Cheshires in Bosnia, and the subsequent expansion from one Battalion Group to a Brigade, over successive Op Grapples. By November 1995 BFBS had 18 radio and TV transmitters operating in Croatia and Bosnia. The radio programming was a mix of BFBS London and BFBS Germany made possible by the sophisticated telecommunications links using digital audio which Peter Ginn and others had devised to link London and Herford.

Caroline Young was one of the BFBS reporters who went to Bosnia in December 1994. During her visit she met the men of the Royal Engineers from Hameln and the Royal Highland Fusiliers from Fallingbostel at Vitez. 'On Christmas Eve the church atop the hill behind Vitez was ablaze with candles – all the way up the hill the Stations of the Cross were marked out in flaming torches. As midnight struck the locals celebrated in their favourite fashion – hundreds of rounds flying into a star-cluttered night sky – tracer sharply visible against the

Cathy Pearson, one of the SSVC engineers, installing the uplink in Bosnia for broadcasts back to
Germany via London   (*Charly Lowndes*)

snowy backdrop.' Caroline's other memories of that visit include hearing the UN
soldiers teaching the local children to sing 'We ain't gonna study war no more', and
coming under a snowball ambush at Burgonjo where the local children could not
understand why the girl in the blue flak jacket was under attack from every side.

Then in December 1995 UNPROFOR was wound up, and NATO took over
with the Implementation Force, IFOR. This involved the arrival of HQ 3 DIV,
renamed HQ COMBRITFOR (Forward) and MULTINATIONAL DIVISION
SOUTH WEST, under the command of General Mike Jackson, a former member
of the SSVC board, known to his HQ as the Prince of Darkness and described by
The Times as the 'fiercest looking general in the British Army'. The two British
Infantry Battalions, the Light Dragoons, with artillery and logistical support, moved
north and west towards Banja Luka and Prjador and immediately went out of range
of BFBS and SSVC TV. This meant that tired soldiers could not catch up with the
news, follow the soccer results or listen to something other than cassettes.

Charly Lowndes, who visited Bosnia at Christmas, recalled: 'It was deeply
moving to be told how much BFBS meant to the soldiers who were coping
with their new role and a Bosnian winter. It was nice to be appreciated, but
frustrating when that appreciation took the form of "We miss BFBS like mad.
When will we get BFBS back again?"'

Shortly after the end of the Second World War BFN was launched from the magnificent splendour of the Musikhalle in Hamburg; nine years later it moved into a custom-built radio station in the millionaires' part of Cologne. In 1990 BFBS's new home was located in a former Wehrmacht barracks in Herford, the one-time base of a Panzer support group. The cellars below the BFBS studios are virtually unchanged from those days. The original brickwork survives, as do the original bombproof cellar doors. One of the first priorities was to remove an old kitchen and convert it into Studio One, a task that was completed by Peter Attrill's engineers in nine months. It was their thirteenth studio installation in five years. When Peter checked out the Hohne cinema as

Caroline Young in Bosnia recording messages for her Christmas programme, December 1994

(*Charly Lowndes*)

a site for the Hohne studio, he came across some Second World War German cinema tickets and some beer and cigarette coupons all neatly stacked in bundles in the loft.

The new studios, like the Musikhalle in Hamburg and Parkstrasse in Cologne, were reputed to be haunted, and various members of staff reported strange and inexplicable happenings around the former record library. Simon Guettier was on duty early one morning when he heard the library door handle clicking open and shut. At first he thought little of it until he realized he was alone in the building. Other members of staff heard the sound of a portable step-aid used for reaching the highest shelves being moved on its castors. One of the programme operation assistants, Wendy Cleeton, claimed to have seen a shadowy figure walking the corridor and disappearing into the library. When she went to challenge the stranger she found both the corridor and the library empty and the building securely locked!

BFBS Germany has always been popular with the German audience, although some, as they have grown older, find the latest pop music hard to understand. Ilse Griffiths first heard BFN in August 1945 and later when she was employed in 714 Headquarters Military Government Drawing Office, she was able to hear BFN in a British environment. 'One day our sergeant walked into the office with this "People's" radio set, all bakelite with a fretwork wooden swastika in the centre, plugged it in and we were away. Soon the office was singing "You Are My Sunshine" and "Don't Fence Me In".' Ilse married a Welshman in 1947 and they stayed on in Germany. BFN became her constant companion. 'It was my source of news and entertainment from Alastair McDougall's "For You at Home", to "The Archers", "Mrs Dale's Diary" to Asters' rather naughty housewives' programme. When we went on holiday to Cyprus, Malta or the Costa del Sol, we always tuned in to the local BFBS station.'

BFBS Germany fascinated the younger listeners and Jutta Meier and Oliver Zoellner wrote their thesis on Forces Broadcasting. BFBS's German listeners have always been great supporters of the Wireless For The Blind (WFTB) Appeal which began in the late 1940s and still continues. In 1994 listeners wishing to contribute were able to use their credit cards for the first time. In recent years a lucky listener has won a luxury car having bought a raffle ticket for the WFTB Appeal. Perhaps one of the most unusual items ever offered was donated by the Scotch whisky firm Springbank Distillers who admitted that they had made a mistake and matured one of their malts in casks designed for sherry maturation. The resultant whisky smelt and tasted like the fine malt it was – unfortunately it was bright green in colour! However, within two hours a thousand bottles had been sold for the WFTB, and the New Year was seen in by families all over Germany toasting themselves with green whisky.

Lt Gen Sir Michael Rose, Commander of UNPROFOR in Bosnia-Herzegovina, talking to
Charly Lowndes for the programme 'Sitrep'   (*Charly Lowndes*)

What does the future hold for BFBS? According to Marc Tyley: 'There may
be a time when BFBS Germany becomes BFBS Europe. Whenever the Forces
are operating abroad, either on exercise or active duty, BFBS will be there living
up to its long-running slogan "Keeping You in Touch". Wherever the reporters
go they can always be assured of a warm welcome. As a young soldier said to
Dave Boyle, the BFBS breakfast show presenter at Al Jubayl during the Gulf
War: "Blimey, if *you*'re here, it can't be that bad!"'

The Haunted House

On Sunday 25 June 1995 BFN/BFBS celebrated fifty years of Forces Broadcasting in Germany with a concert in the Musikhalle. Taking part were the NDR Big Band and the Royal Tank Regiment Cambrai Band. The compères were Robin Boyle, Chris Howland, Sarah Kennedy and Richard Astbury. During the interval the First Mayor of the Free and Hanseatic City of Hamburg, Dr Henning Voscherau, unveiled a plaque to commemorate the association between Forces Broadcasting and the Musikhalle.

Among the guests who returned to Hamburg was Nan Boyle, who as L/Cpl Nan Pomeroy had joined BFN in 1946. For her it was a kind of homecoming.

And, half a century after those heady Hamburg days, we came back – some by ferry, some by plane, and yet others, by road. For those who had not been fortunate enough to be in at the start, it was perhaps a 'jolly' (although we would have called it a 'swan' in the 1940s), somewhat akin to a coach trip to see a stately home. For a privileged few, it was in the nature of a pilgrimage – overladen with sadness at the gaps in our ranks for various reasons – above all, with memories of those who had not 'grown old as we who are left grow old'.

On the coach trip around the city, there was a spontaneous spatter of applause as the Musikhalle came into view, but we were not to go inside until the Sunday. In the meantime, there were our colleagues and friends to meet again. There was much surreptitious glancing at lapel labels, and a moment of mental adding of lost hair and subtracting of rounded figures and wrinkles before recognition dawned, followed by hearty greetings, and the inevitable 'do you remembers?' Then the laughter began again – the laughter that always seemed to be part of the essence of BFN, springing from the relief that, by some miracle, we had come through a world war, and there was no longer any necessity for us to kill or be killed by our fellow men. In addition, by some miracle, we had suddenly been presented with a fascinating gift – the opportunity to supply entertainment through the radio. Most of us had little or no experience of how to do this, and no doubt, some of our mistakes (or 'cock-ups'!) would have scandalized the professionals, but I like to think that we would have been forgiven for these for the sake of our sheer enthusiasm for the job.

Sunday came at last, and, once more, we were inside the Musikhalle – through the main entrance too, for the side doors that we always used were

The Class of '48 – Gordon Savage, Tim Gudgin, Keith Fordyce and Ted Greenfield recall memories of BFN Hamburg at the reunion in June 1995   (*Gordon Savage*)

firmly locked. Because of this, our first sight of the concert hall was on the ground floor, not the familiar balcony level that we used to scurry across on the way from Presentation or Music Department to Variety Department, and the all-important canteen. This last venue was the most important place in the building for us – not because of the tea (which usually consisted of hot water poured on top of a mixture of sugar, dried milk and tea, and was only drinkable if one gave up the attempt to equate it with any previous example of our national beverage) but because it was in the canteen that we floated ideas for new programmes, held script conferences, and kept up with the station gossip.

All the 'offices' we knew so well have now regained their original functions of cloakrooms (in the strict sense of the word), peopled only by attendants hovering over notices which proclaim that they will guard patrons' coats and hats for 1.80DM. 'Continuity', once always so full and busy, has become two rather small, empty rooms, and 'Studio B' (where we once held weekly dances, and uniform boots pounded the parquet floor to the rhythm of the quickstep) now boasts a stage, a small balcony, and opulent permanent seating for well-behaved audiences to listen to classical music.

But it was not the changes which held us spellbound and brought unexpected lumps to the throat. It was the fact that so much was the same. The Musikhalle is haunted still with friendly ghosts. Not only with the memories of those who have passed on from this life – although one would not be surprised to catch a glimpse of Hedley, or Maggie, or Geraint, or half-a-dozen others, but also with the ghosts of our own youth. Stand quietly in the upper corridors as I did, and you will catch an echo of those times. The ornate and stately Musikhalle may have returned to its former splendour but, deep in its fabric, there will always linger the spirit of the enthusiasm, laughter, and sheer joy of living that was all part of the magic of being a part of the British Forces Network in Hamburg.

The Musikhalle, where the story began   (*Philip Towell*)

Index